GWASG CARREG GWALCH

D1826296

A Semester in Zion

Meic Stephens spent the Fall Semester of 1991 as Visiting Professor in the English Department at Brigham Young University in Provo, Utah, a State which the Mormons claim is their Promised Land. This journal is a day-to-day account of his time in the USA, during which he visited the Nevada desert, Las Vegas, Salt Lake City, the Grand Canyon and San Francisco. An agnostic, he was highly critical of the doctrines of the Church of Latter-day Saints but found much to admire in the Mormon character.

This book is also, in part, a memoir in which the author recalls people and places from his boyhood in Pontypridd, his undergraduate days at Aberystwyth, his years as a Plaid Cymru activist in Merthyr Tydfil, his friendship with Harri Webb, Glyn Jones, Leslie Norris and other Welsh writers, and in part a commonplace book in which he jotted down observations, anecdotes and quotations that came to mind while he was living a long way from home.

One of the book's main themes is his thirty-year search for his paternal grandparents in Radnorshire and the Border counties – his father was an illegitimate child – a quest which was brought to a conclusion in 2002 by means of DNA tests.

The interleaving of journal, memoir and commonplace book makes this a rich, humorous, warmly personal and often revealing document that will appeal to a wide variety of readers with an interest in Wales, its literature and politics, and in a Welsh patriot who has played a distinguished role in his country's cultural life.

Meic Stephens was Literature Director of the Welsh Arts Council from 1967 to 1990. He taught at the University of Glamorgan from 1994 until his retirement in 2003, latterly as Professor of Welsh Writing in English, and is now Professor Emeritus. In 2000 the University of Wales awarded him an honorary MA and the senior degree of DLitt. Among his many publications are *The New Companion to the Literature of Wales* (University of Wales Press, 1998) and *The Literary Pilgrim in Wales* (Carreg Gwalch, 2000). He is also editor of the Corgi Series, selections from the work of Welsh Writers in English (Carreg Gwalch).

A Semester in Zion

a journal with memoirs

Meic Stephens

ISBN: 0-86381-849-8

Cover design: Anthony Evans

Published with the financial support
of the Welsh Books Council.

First published in 2003 by
Gwasg Carreg Gwalch, 12 Iard yr Orsaf, Llanrwst,
Wales LL26 0EH
℡ 01492 642031   ▤ 01492 641502
✆ books@carreg-gwalch.co.uk   website: www.carreg-gwalch.co.uk

'Camerado, this is no book, who touches this touches a man.'

Walt Whitman

Author's note

However tempting it may be to preface this book with a disarming note in an attempt to anticipate the reader's perception of its shortcomings, I am content to let it begin on page one and take its own chances. After all, the diary as a literary form has a long and illustrious history and should need no apologia or explication, least of all from those who are vain or self-indulgent enough to publish their journals.

The diary is, moreover, a form that exists in as many varieties as there are diarists, from Pepys and Byron to Kilvert and Gide, from Mansfield and Woolf to Kenneth Williams and Alan Bennett, so that there seems little point in trying to say, at the outset, what sort of diary the reader will find here. Diaries, like holiday snapshots, if they are to give any pleasure at all, should speak for themselves and the least said about them by the fond diarist the better.

Even so, there are a few facts that will prepare the reader for what follows, and they can be quickly given. This journal was written between 26 August and 12 December 1991, when I was Visiting Professor in the English Department at Brigham Young University in Provo, Utah. It is, however, rather more than a day-to-day record of my life on campus during the Fall Semester of that year. For reasons that will soon become evident, I had a lot of free time on my hands in Provo and, left largely to myself in a staunchly Mormon community, had to fill it as best I could.

Shortly after my arrival, I found that one way of keeping myself amused was to drive in all directions, often for days at a time, into the desert and wild places of Utah and the six contiguous States; I also went on a trip to Las Vegas and spent Thanksgiving in Cupertino, California. Another was to write, besides a diary, a sort of commonplace book into which I could jot whatever observations, memories and anecdotes came to mind. They often did so not in any chronological order, but in a patchwork of disparate and sometimes incongruous entries that seemed not only to reflect something of my unfamiliar surroundings but also to say a little about my life back home in Wales. Thus began, in draft, a memoir which I had not had the time, or inclination, to contemplate up to then. Life, it seems to me, is largely episodic and it is only the most vivid episodes, good or bad, that one remembers with any clarity, and so I decided to write about mine in an episodic way. If there are any aspects of my life which are not treated here, I can only half-promise to write about them in some other context.

To my Mormon hosts I offer something like an apology for not appreciating their Zion as they would probably have wished. At best agnostic, I have difficulty even with the Christian orthodoxies and found what they believe about Moroni, Kolob, Joseph Smith and the hill Cumorah, and such bizarre practices as the baptism of the dead, pretty hard to take. It is not enough, it seems to me and as the Mormon missionaries argue, simply to believe what one has been brought up to believe, and if 'the glory of God is intelligence', as the motto of Brigham Young University has it, it is incumbent upon us all to question the doctrines and practices of the Church of Latter-day Saints, particularly when it is intolerant of dissent and hostile towards other churches. Nevertheless, I found much to admire in individual Mormons, including several of my students and colleagues, and I hope I have made that clear enough, though I don't expect ever to be invited back to Provo.

This published text, which like most diaries was not intended at the time of writing to see the light of day, differs from the original only in a few small ways. I have given it better shape by getting rid of repetition, clarifying a number of references, tidying up the necessarily hurried style, dispensing with about 25,000 words (I found it easy to murder my darlings, especially when they threatened to become darkly introspective) and turning those passages first written in Welsh into passable English. Although I have deleted a number of unflattering comments about people who are still in the land of the living, I have resisted the temptation to add anything with the benefit of hindsight, preferring to let the entries stand, however inadequately, as a record of my daily round, my thoughts and opinions during those four months in 1991 when I was a long way from home. Reading them over at proof stage twelve years later, I have been struck by how light-hearted, even frivolous, some of them now seem, but to say more than that here would be to attempt to disarm criticism, and so I shall desist.

The reader curious to know the outcome of my long search for my father's father, which was left unresolved in the autumn of 1991 but which I resumed on my return to Wales, may like to know that during the summer of 2002 I approached the son of the man whom a Glascwm woman had said was suspected of fathering Annie Sophia Lloyd's illegitimate child and, with his kind permission and by means of a DNA test, I learnt that his father was also my father's father. I have nevertheless decided not to name him here in order to protect the sensibilities of his family, who know nothing of the child. The story of Annie Sophia Lloyd and my father's illegitimacy is the subject of my *pryddest Gwreiddiau* with which I came close to winning the Crown at the National Eisteddfod in 2003; the poem was published in the magazine *Barddas* (Autumn, 2003).

I am grateful to the friends who have given me permission to refer to the letters they wrote me while I was in Utah and, in particular, to Don Dale-Jones, M. Wynn Thomas, Sam Adams and Leslie Norris, who read the work in draft form and commented on it. I have not always accepted their advice and responsibility for what is here recorded must, of course, be mine.

Two passages have been inserted which first appeared, prior to my going to America, in the magazine *Planet* under the titles 'In John Jones's Country' (82, August/September 1990) and 'The Garth Newydd Years' (83, October/November 1990). Another, which I wrote largely in Utah, was later published in *Planet* as 'A Small House in Meadow Street' (105, June/July 1994). Also included here are notes which I used in my *Planet* column, 'One Man and his Wales' (86-91, April/May 1991-February/March 1992), some of which were written in Provo. I am grateful to the magazine's editor, John Barnie, for permission to reprint this material.

Meic Stephens
Whitchurch, Cardiff
October, 2003

Monday, 26 August, 2001

The plane touched down in Salt Lake City at 8.30pm. By my own clock it was 3.30 the following morning. I'd left Cardiff at 7am, so the journey had taken more than twenty hours, a full day and almost half a night, during which I hadn't been able to sleep much. I am, at best, a white-knuckle air-passenger. I spent part of the time watching a film starring Michael Caine, and although I declined an ear-piece that would have provided the soundtrack, I was more or less able to follow the plot, so passed an hour or so in that way. It was like watching tv with the sound turned down and making up the dialogue, something I often find myself doing at home; not many people know that.

This wasn't the first time I'd flown across the Atlantic – I visited Montreal and Quebec in the 1970s – and I don't feel as if I'm now much further from home than I was in Moscow, Leningrad, Tbilisi, Svaneti, Novgorod, Pskov, Sukhumi, Ordzhonikidze, Kiev, Baku, Talinn, Tashkent or Samarkand a few years ago. Perhaps the immigration officer at Atlanta helped create that impression. Why had I visited the USSR so many times over the last twenty years? Was I or had I ever been a member of a Communist Party? Did I have any guns or illegal substances or subversive literature concealed about my person or in my luggage? What was my purpose in visiting the United States of America? And then, with a plastic grin, and before I could begin to think how I might answer any of these questions, Have a nice day!

I'd have preferred the cold, withering stare of the Soviet official with a hammer and sickle in his grey fur cap, his lingering gaze at my lupine bumps as he checked my passport and visa photos against the mug-shots of wanted criminals under the counter of his bullet-proof kiosk, the wordless nod as he stamped my papers and, at last, as if against his better judgement, let me into his country. At least he took his job seriously and made me feel I was entering another time-zone, another political system, another world.

At the airport in Salt Lake City, where there were no formalities of any kind, I was met by Leslie Norris and his wife, Kitty, who drove me to their home in Orem, about an hour away up the Wasatch Valley and the town next to Provo, my ultimate destination. I went straight to bed and fell asleep the moment my head hit the pillow.

'I amna' fou sae muckle as tired – deid dune.'

Tuesday, 27 August

I awoke this morning about lunch-time and, drawing back the curtains at my window, was astonished to see high craggy mountains, extensive fir-woods and a clear blue sky over all.

The Norrises' red-brick house is large, modern, comfortable and tastefully furnished, with light wooden floors and John Elwyns on the white walls, and there's a long garden and lawn at both front and back. They have a dog called Gwenno, a standard poodle that's about as tall as a Labrador. She has a black, unclipped coat and the most expressive eyes I've ever seen in a pooch. We took to each other immediately and soon she was lying against my feet, waiting for me to take her out to play with a ball in the garden. Leslie and Kitty are inordinately fond of Gwenno, and I can see why.

The afternoon was spent with cold drinks on the patio. Later in the evening, as it began to grow cool, Leslie and I took Gwenno for a walk by the river Provo, renewing our old friendship. We first met in 1965 when Ruth and I were living in Merthyr, Leslie's hometown, and I'd just started *Poetry Wales*. He called at our house in Courtland Terrace in Twynyrodyn early one Saturday morning when I was still abed after a late night correcting proofs, and left me a sheaf of poems that I later published as a Triskel Press booklet under the title *The Loud Winter*, now a collector's item.

I like Leslie and we get on well, going over the news from Wales. He's badly out of touch with the literary scene back home, and feels it acutely, I think, though he pretends to be detached from the personalities and issues involved. Among the names that cropped up in our conversation this evening were those of two younger poets of whom he has a low opinion, and that of R.S. Thomas, whom he claims to address as Ron.

I told him about my visit, several years ago, to the church at Manafon in Montgomeryshire where Thomas once held the living. Making my way round the graves, I came across an old man who was cutting the grass and scraping moss from the tombstones. On hearing him refer to the Reverend Thomas, I ventured to ask what sort of sermon the vicar used to deliver. 'Ah,' said the old man with a deep sigh, 'he did pitch the hay too high in the cratch for the likes of we.'

Wednesday, 28 August

Most of today was spent with Leslie in Provo on formalities: registering for social security, opening a bank account, being allocated an office on campus, finding an apartment (I mean flat), and so on. Everything seems to belong to the Church of Jesus Christ of Latter-day Saints, just as everything in the Soviet Union belongs to the State and is run by the Party.

When Cocteau's Orpheus walked through his reflection in the mirror and went down into the Underworld looking for his Eurydice, he had to pass along a purgartorial corridor in which grey-faced functionaries were stamping the papers of the newly damned.

Thursday, 29 August

Today I moved into Wymount Terrace, up the hill from BYU (as Brigham Young University is generally known) and with a splendid view across the Wasatch Valley, and mountains in the distance that must be the Rockies. The flat, functional rather than comfortable, is, like Caesar's Gaul, in three parts: it has a bedroom, a sitting area and a kitchen; there's a fridge, plenty of shelves and cupboards, a carpet, and a balcony looking down onto a grassy quad that's ringed with pine trees.

The first thing I did after unpacking was put up some poster-poems to brighten the bare walls. Kitty has provided pots and pans for the kitchen and I've rented furniture from the accommodation office on the other side of the quad. I've also bought twenty dollars' worth of groceries in a brown bag but it's too warm to eat much.

I think I shall manage here, for the duration. I haven't had to cook for myself since I was a bachelor in Merthyr, but I've always been able to cope. My specialities are beans or spaghetti on toast, a boiled egg and rice pudding, and I'm a dab hand at anything that involves the dextrous use of a tin-opener.

My neighbours in Wymount Terrace are mostly married students and their children. There are lots of kids and their noise as they run around the quad is somehow reassuring that family life goes on here much as elsewhere. This evening there was a game of American football on tv and most of Wymount's residents gathered to watch it on a large screen erected in the open air, eating hot dogs the while; the game is a mystery to me and likely to remain so.

One of the *locataires* on my floor is a Chinese girl named Cathy whose American husband is a student here; they have a little boy called Charles. When I met her in the stairwell today she was much taken with the way I speak English and said she hoped we could meet regularly so that Charles might learn 'the British way'. I warned her I have a Welsh accent but I don't think she knew what I meant.

Just before I turned in for the night I had a phone-call from home, the first time I've spoken to Ruth since arriving here, and then one from the mother of Tiffany H. Joab, who was in Oregon, I think she said. Tiffany was the previous occupant of the flat: I know because her card was still pinned on the door when I arrived and there's mail (I mean post) for her, some of it weeks old. Mrs Joab wanted to know where her daughter was and seemed unable to accept that she no longer lives here. I think she suspected I had Tiffany tied up in a cupboard, or worse. 'Who are you and whadya doin' there?' she kept asking, 'and how come she ain't called her Mom?' By the end of our conversation Mrs Joab, despite her surname, seemed to be losing patience, for there was nothing I could do to put her mind at rest, poor dab.

Good question, though: who am I and what am I doing here?

I remember our house in Meadow Street when I was a boy in all its unremarkable detail. After all, the first eighteen years of my life were spent there and a man doesn't easily forget the house where he was born and grew up. I find that, wherever else I've lived, and until I had a home of my own, it's there all my most vivid and lasting memories have their source and that, as I grow older, it's there my thoughts return, especially in those moments just before sleep, to a time and place that left an indelible mark on me.

Our house was small but clean, snug and comfortable. It had a living-room, which we called the kitchen, a kitchen we called the back, and a lounge or parlour we called the room. There were three bedrooms: my parents slept at the front, my grandparents at the rear, and my younger brother, Lloyd, and I shared the boxroom, which had just enough space for a narrow bed, a wardrobe and a chair.

The kitchen had a black-leaded grate with brass rail, fender and candlesticks, and always a kettle steaming on the hob. Here we ate, played, talked and listened to the wireless, in front of a coal fire that was never allowed to go out, not even in summer, because before the advent of gas and electricity it was our only source of heating and we used it for cooking and for drying clothes. On the floor there were rag mats, which we made with pegs and sacking in the long winter evenings, in patterns and colours that I like to think amounted to a folk-art. The best china was stacked in a glass-fronted wall-cupboard and there was a sideboard for cutlery and whatever else that didn't have a place of its own. On the walls there was a stuffed squirrel, a kingfisher and three cases of mounted moths and butterflies which had come from my grandfather's home in Pentonville; his father, James Symes, whom I never knew, had been a taxidermist. My mother tells me she burned the lot the other day because their colours had faded and mites had got into the cases.

Just off the gas-lit passage was the room, which was kept for visitors, in which there was a small sofa and two armchairs, a sideboard and an iron grate. The window looked directly onto the street. It had no view except of the houses on the other side of the street, built like ours in the local Pennant stone with red and yellow brick trimmings. Under the stairs was the cwtch, an unlit, slightly musty space which my grandfather, always one for the fancy word, insisted on calling the lazaretto, a sort of glory-hole where lumber was stored. It was there, during the war, when German bombers came droning up the Valley, we would huddle for nights on end. The wailing of sirens on film or tv still gives me the willies.

At the back of the house there was a scullery and pantry, with a cold-water tap, bosh and flagstone floor, where the family's provisions and cooking utensils were kept – a cool, spotless, sweet-smelling place. Outside, in the yard, were a whitewashed lavatory we called the dubs, a strip of ashen earth, some dog-daisies, a bit of privet hedge, a loganberry bush that seemed to flourish on tea-leaves, a wooden shed where my father kept his bike and my grandfather his tools, a clothes-line and mangle for wash-day (always a Monday), and a tall tin bath which, on Friday nights, would be brought into the back and filled with water heated in bowls over the kitchen fire. The back door, which opened onto a grit lane running behind the eighty-odd houses for the length of Meadow Street, had a rather elegant blue and white enamel plate with the number 50 on it, though it was never used by tradesmen or neighbours, who always called at the front door.

A child isn't usually aware of his home and family until he reaches the age of nine or ten, or so I've heard. I think I can recall the moment when I first became aware of mine. It must have been a winter's evening in 1947, when I would have been nine, because it had been snowing for weeks in one of the worst blizzards in living memory. The fire in our kitchen burned bright in the grate, the wireless was on, my grandparents were sitting on either side of the hearth, my mother knitting in her chair, my father busy with his Union papers, and my brother, then aged four, playing on the mat, when I happened to look up and saw them as I'd never seen them before, each an individual absorbed in what he or she was doing and yet part of a tableau to which I, too, despite my fleeting sense of detachment, inextricably belonged. The picture remains vivid in my memory because that night, before going up the cold stairs to bed with our hot-water-bottles, Lloyd and I were given, as a special treat, a plate of porridge with a large dollop of condensed milk in it.

Our house was just across the eponymous field and the GWR line from Forest House, the old home of Francis Crawshay, the local ironmaster, that's now part of what I'm still not used to calling the Polytechnic of Wales; my mother, like most local people, still calls it the Mining School. One of our favourite pastimes as boys was to sneak across the line and aim our catapults at the windows of Forest House, for the sheer delight of hearing the sound of smashing glass. To be able to cross the line unobserved, or at least unchallenged, by the man in the signal-box was a rite of passage that I went through at an early age. Trains passed up and down every few minutes – passenger trains, goods-waggons and engines pulling trucks that were filled with coal on the down run and empty or carrying pit-props on the up. We could tell they were coming by pressing our ears to the track and listening for the vibration. The coal and people of the Rhondda, Cynon and Taff Valleys passed our house several times a day, for which reason I always had the impression that Trefforest was on a main thoroughfare and not without importance in the industrial life of East Glamorgan, which was indeed the case.

At the far end of the meadow, adjacent to the tinworks, lay the Bute woods, a long embankment which had been built to carry trains across the river from Cilhaul to Dynea and thence down the valley to Cardiff, although it was derelict by the time I was growing up. The Bute, named after the Marquess who owned a lot of land hereabouts, was where we played as children. It had a stream, with trout in it, and was a great place for mushrooms, nuts, blackberries and wild strawberries; it was there I saw my first kingfisher, my first red admiral, and my first fox.

Our next-door neighbours were Tom and Blodwen Jones, whose daughters, Mairwen and Gwyneth, were older than me. Tom had been a collier but for as long as I knew him he'd been at home because he suffered from 'the dust'; he joined Plaid Cymru at about the same time as I did, in the late 1950s. Blodwen, from Rhiwsaeson in the Vale of Glamorgan, was Welsh-speaking. We couldn't have had better neighbours. On my twenty-first birthday they gave me a copy of the *Collected Poems* of W.B. Yeats, which I still have.

We belonged, of course, to the working class. There *was* only one class in Trefforest, except for a few families, mostly shopkeepers and tradespeople, who lived up on Llantwit Road in what we thought were posh houses because they had bay-windows. But we weren't poor, at least not by local standards, and there was nothing rough or lumpen about us. Both my father and my grandfather were skilled men with steady jobs in the electricity industry and, even during the long summer of 1926, when just about everything in the Valley shut down, they had never been unemployed.

Nor had they ever served in the armed forces, perhaps because both were in reserve occupations, though they would have been of age in 1914 and 1939. During the second world war my father was in the Home Guard and was issued with a wooden rifle which he let me carry on my shoulder up and down the back lane. My grandfather, as an air-raid warden, used to go out at night wearing a tin helmet and carrying a whistle to make sure people had observed the blackout by putting up blinds and drawing their curtains. For that reason there was a telephone in our passage on which he received his orders for the night and reported any incidents in the vicinity of Meadow Street; ours was the only house in the street with a 'phone and it gave us a certain status.

My father worked for forty-eight years, starting as a tea-boy at the age of fourteen, in the power-station at Upper Boat, a few miles down the Valley, and my grandfather was a cableman with the Pontypridd Urban District Council. Each brought home a decent wage, so neither my grandmother nor my mother ever had to go out to work, as many local women did, though they were kept busy enough at home – cooking, washing, mending, and generally making ends meet. There was always enough to eat and we kept a good table, even when food was rationed during and after the war. It was a point of honour with my parents always to pay their way and never to fall into debt; if we couldn't afford something we did without – Hire Purchase was anathema to them. I never had to go to school hungry or put pieces of cardboard in my shoes, like some boys I knew. We were always well clothed and well shod, though I can remember having the seat of my trousers patched and my jersey regularly darned.

We were, in short, a tidy family, and we boys weren't allowed to forget it. Our neighbours, too, were ordinary (in the Raymond Williams sense): hard-working, law-abiding, warm-hearted, and long-suffering. I've never tended to view the working class through rose-tinted spectacles, as some middle-class left-wingers do, because I'm only too familiar with their shortcomings, but whatever tastes or interests I may have since acquired, and however roomy our house in Whitchurch may now be, it's among such people I still feel most at home.

When I first left home to go to University at Aberystwyth in 1956, my parents, grandparents and many of our neighbours in Meadow Street, Raymond Terrace and Long Row came out into the field to see me off, waving tea-towels and dusters until the train pulled out of sight. That, too, was a rite of passage: the Grammar School boy, the first in his family to receive secondary education, was being ceremonially severed from his working-class roots and the expectation was that he'd never return.

It's strange how images of home and childhood have kept coming into my head since I arrived here. Perhaps it's a way the mind has of ticking over in unfamiliar surroundings. I'm not in the least perturbed by it and shall note down whatever occurs to me, though I don't suppose it will be in anything like chronological order. No matter. This journal (or whatever it turns out to be) will serve as a means of keeping myself company, of talking to myself, of amusing myself even, in what seems to be a pretty austere place – and there's nothing wrong in that. It might even help me answer Mrs Joab's question: who am I and what am I doing here?

It's still one of my keenest pleasures of a cold winter's night, if Ruth doesn't object too much, to go to bed without taking off my shirt, as I used to do all those years ago.

'Nous n'irons plus aux bois, les lauriers sont coupés.'

Friday, 30 August
When I woke up this morning, at about seven, there was a humming-bird feeding on the sticky cones of the pine tree just outside my window. Its tiny wings beat so fast that it seemed to be suspended in the air on nothing more than a beam of shimmering light.

I am something of what Americans call a twitcher, an amateur ornithologist, an interest I've had since I was a boy. Although Trefforest was an industrial village, the hills on either side were marvellous places for seeing birds that are now quite rare, such as the curlew, bittern, peewit, corncrake, ousel and dipper. I even used to collect their eggs, which I learned to prick and blow, and kept them in a wooden box padded with cotton wool and neatly labelled; I knew how to identify birds by their song or cry, and even knew their Latin names. We had our own names for some birds – 'twink' for a chaffinch, for instance, and we called nestlings 'yuckers', a word found in Shakespeare. I spent whole days roaming the Bute embankment, the Berthlwyd woods and the high moorland on Mynydd Meio, and was never happier.

Today was spent getting acquainted with the campus. As I walked from Wymount Terrace down the hill towards BYU, a distance of about a mile, I was overtaken by a girl on a bicycle, a blue-eyed blonde with long brown legs peeping from under her flowery dress. As she sped past me, she was singing at the top of her voice, 'Oh, what a bootiful mornin'!', and I called out, 'That's a lovely song!', to which she snapped, 'You bet!', and then rode on downhill at gathering speed. It set me up for the day – no, the week.

The campus extends over about a thousand acres of the valley floor. Some of the buildings were built between 1884 and 1912, but most are modern and date from the 1950s when Ernest L. Wilkinson was President of the Church. The Latter-day Saints, alas, are led by very old men: none of their Presidents to date was born in the 20th century. The present one is Ezra Taft Benson and he too is in his nineties. The Church is governed in accordance with 'revelations' on the part of a gerontocracy.

Every building at BYU is different from the next and all are separated by landscaped gardens and flower-beds, which makes for a very attractive campus. I was able to locate the Jesse Knight Building, where the English Department is housed, the Harold B. Lee Library, the Bookstore with a section known as the Twilight Zone selling chocolate, the cafeteria known as the Cougareat (it has a stuffed cougar in a glass case just inside the main entrance), and various other buildings, all named after eminent, that is to say wealthy Mormons.

The University has about 27,000 full-time students, almost all Mormons, and they come from every State and more than seventy countries, but there are very few blacks or Hispanics as far as I can make out. It also has a campus in Hawaii. All the staff here are Mormon, except for Leslie and me. This morning the place was swarming with Freshmen – first-year students, the men in grey trousers, shirts and ties, the women in summer dresses and some in white socks, dutifully trooping after guides on 'orientation walks'. The Dress Code, to which Leslie has alerted me, is strictly observed here: they looked so squeaky clean, so healthy and altogether wholesome. There's none of the 'distressed look' so common on campuses in the Yookay. The lawns are manicured and lush, and there's sculpture here and there among the shrubbery, including a very fine life-size bronze of an Ute Indian. No litter and no graffiti. The University's motto is: 'The glory of God is intelligence'. You bet.

It's very hot, in the 90s, and I've caught the sun on my face and arms for the first time this summer. I sat for a while this afternoon near an eucalyptus tree to watch a brass band practise its marching drill with the help of flags and drum majorettes. When one of them came over and asked me to suggest a tune, I said, 'Shenandoah', and they duly played it, *con brio*. I'm very fond of brass bands, especially when the instrumentalists are young, pretty and chirrupy.

At the English Department, where I have an office with my name on the door, I was given a list of the students who will be in my two classes, twice a week. I shall be teaching for four hours on Tuesdays and four on Thursdays, and the rest of the time is my own. Then I had my photo taken for the faculty noticeboard and was introduced to some of my new colleagues, one of whom, William Shakespeare, reckons he's a descendant of the playwright's brother, John.

My official title is Visiting Professor and I am here for the Fall Semester. Of course, all lecturers in America are professors, but it seems I really am a Professor, with the salary and timetable to go with it.

I had an hour this afternoon with Ron Dennis, Professor of Welsh and Portuguese, who told me immediately that he's related to Captain Dan Jones, the Flintshire man who was a pioneer Mormon. Ron spoke to me about the early Mormons in Welsh, which he's learned tolerably well and specifically to read the literature, but I noticed, as soon as the talk turned to other subjects, he switched to English. Is there any other academic in the world who's Professor of Welsh and Portuguese? Still, I can't help thinking it works to the advantage of Welsh: between them, Welsh and Portuguese have some 180 million speakers.

Then there's John Sterling Harris, in the office next to mine, a tall, handsome man, a native of Tooele, Utah, who gets about on crutches after coming down in an aeroplane that he built for himself; I think of him as Icarus. He drives a large Buick, specially adapted since he can't work the controls with his feet, and in this jalopy he took me and Leslie to lunch. John, who teaches American literature and technical writing, is a former weapons instructor in the US Army. He's very friendly towards me, perhaps because I'm a good listener to the tales of derring-do with which he regales me. He's of Welsh descent but shows no interest whatsoever in the fact I'm from Wales.

One of John's duties as a Mormon 'in good standing' is to baptise the dead of the Hungarian nation, which he does in the Temple every Wednesday morning, so that they might have the chance of entering the Mormon Heaven. The Saints justify this bizarre practice by something in Corinthians. The ceremony, as far as I can gather, consists of walking into a pool of water while holding the name and dates of a person on a plastic card, though John won't give me any further details. *Omertà*.

I was taken aback by this disclosure, but John seems to accept it as his life's work and without question, so I didn't press him. When I asked, not altogether jocularly, whether he hopes to finish the task before he dies – there are, after all, quite a few billion dead Magyars – he pointed out that his father and grandfather did it before him and he has sons and they will have sons who will carry on the task after him.

I called on Leslie in his office, which is just down the corridor. He says he has severe difficulties with the Mormon faith but that the *Book of Mormon*, on which it's based, is 'a good read' full of exciting events and colourful characters, a bit like *Gone with the Wind* or *How Green Was My Valley*, I suppose, only more so. As for the Mormon people, among whom he's lived now for some twenty years, Leslie admires them enormously. The University has been extraordinarily kind to him, providing him not only with a post at BYU, where he is Humanities Professor of Creative Writing, but also showering him with all kinds of academic honours.

Mrs Joab rang again tonight and we had another little chat about Tiffany. I promised that if ever I come across her daughter, I shall ask her to call her Mom immediately. But I hope I shan't. The girl is probably living in Hawaii with hibiscus in her hair and a garland round her neck – and I wish her well.

My father rode to work on a bicycle, whatever the weather, and it was his boast he'd never lost a shift owing to ill health. His was a dirty, monotonous, dangerous job and he used to come home sometimes so tired that he'd fall asleep in front of the fire before he could wash or have a meal. He ended his working life as a foreman in charge of one of the four huge turbines that generated electricity for the valleys of East Glamorgan. When he retired in 1972, the works superintendent called him up to his office about a quarter of an hour before he was due to clock off on his last shift and told him he could go home early. I don't think he would have wanted any fuss, but there was no farewell ceremony, no official acknowledgement of his long service. I was so dismayed that, shortly before the power-station was demolished a few years later, I commissioned Sue Shields to make a drawing of the works and she produced a very nice, detailed picture of it, with its four tall chimneys and its cooling-towers that looked like giant milk-churns. But my father didn't want it: he'd seen enough of the old place, he said, though he still went there once a week to chat with his former workmates and collect their Union dues. The picture hangs today above my desk at home.

During the Angry Summer of 1926, when the power-station was shut down for lack of coal, my father, then a lad of sixteen, was put to work knocking the lagging off steam-pipes, as a way of keeping him employed. When he died at the age of 74 in 1984 the post-mortem showed he had, among other things, the effects of asbestos on his lungs. He'd been fighting to win compensation from the Electricity Board for several years prior to his death, and the letter offering some paltry sum arrived on the day of his funeral.

I've been trying to write a poem in memory of my father but find I can't.

Our house was indistinguishable from the others in the terrace except it was somewhat smaller, having been built in a gwli between the older houses on either side. The kitchen was about fifteen feet by fifteen – the size of my study at home – and there we lived, all six of us, cheerfully enough. According to the original indenture leasing the land for a term of 99 years, in which the lessors, Francis, Tudor and De Barri Crawshay, the ironmaster's sons, are described as 'gentlemen' with addresses in the Home Counties: 'All that piece or parcel of land on which the said messuage or dwelling-house stands measures thereat some two hundred and five square yards or thereabouts'. I'd never thought it so small until I saw it described in such formal language. Yet the Crawshays, always a canny lot, made provision for contingencies that my grandparents, the house's first occupants, could hardly have imagined: the lessors' rights to any minerals subsequently discovered under the earth of number 50, without compensation, and prohibition of the premises' use by tanners, soap-makers, farriers, knackers, blacksmiths, inn-keepers or wine-merchants. All my grandparents wanted from the deal was to live quietly in the house and call it home, and that's what they did for the rest of their lives.

Among the things I recall from my boyhood with a certain relish is the food we ate. My favourites were pigs' trotters, tripe and onions, chitterling, black pudding, giblet stew, winkles, cockles, faggots, rissoles, polony, brawn and sweetbread, carrot-cake, junket, arrow-root, baked apple, pikelets, tapioca and semolina. Even during the years when rationing was in force, we always ate well, perhaps because my grandfather knew a man who worked in the abattoir in Pontypridd. Every Friday afternoon on my way home from school, I used to go to his house on the Broadway to collect meat, discreetly wrapped in newspapers. I recall seeing a coconut, a banana and a pomegranate for the first time in the late 1940s.

If ever someone founds a Society for the Revival of Traditional British Grub, I'll join – as long as it hasn't got the word 'Royal' in the title.

Echddoe, ddoe, heddiw, yfory, trannoeth, trennydd.

Saturday, 31 August

Everyone I meet in shops and offices on campus asks me where I come from. Most seem to have heard of Wales, perhaps because there were Welsh people among the first converts to the Church and they left their mark on Mormon culture. Today, I told a girl in the bank that I came from Pontypridd. When she asked where that was, I informed her, for a bit of fun, it was between Tonypandy and Merthyr Tydfil and not far from Llanfihangel Genau'r-glyn. It provoked peals of laughter and the comment that the names struck her as 'typically English'; I let it pass and she hoped I'd have a nice day.

It's now about eight in the evening and the temperature's in the 80s. On the slope of the mountain behind Wymount Terrace, brilliantly lit up by the setting sun and visible from my balcony, is a large white letter Y (the University is popularly known as the Y), about 300 feet tall, the stones of which Freshmen have to paint at the beginning of each Fall Semester.

Soon the Jiminy Crickets will strike up their chorus – it's like the chattering of a huge machine that can't be switched off.

I spent an hour this afternoon writing, for *The New Welsh Review*, a piece about a book on the theory of nationalism by David L. Adamson, whom I don't know. It's very good on Gramsci, whose work I used to discuss with Gwyn A. Williams.

Then Leslie came to take me to his home, where we had a light supper of fruit, cheese, one of Kitty's delicious custard puddings with nutmeg sprinkled on the top, and some good coffee – a rare treat in these parts, I was given to understand, because coffee is one of the beverages banned by the Saints.

Afterwards we sat and talked about the Norrises' life in Utah and their *hiraeth* for Wales. They say they intend coming home at Christmas next year and buying a house near the Hay or in the Vale of Glamorgan, but I think it will be many a long year before they return. One of the things that keeps them in Utah is Gwenno. Leslie couldn't bear to put her in a container for the flight across the Atlantic: many dogs die during the journey and, even if they survive, they have then to be put in quarantine for six months.

On the day I was born, it was very hot and the window of the front bedroom was down to the half, as mine is this evening, and my mother's labour cries could be heard up and down Meadow Street. That evening the house was full of neighbours drinking the barrel of cider that my grandfather had been keeping for the occasion. I was named Michael because my grandmother was a fan of the actor, Michael Wilding, who was born on the same day as me. It was a great piece of good fortune I wasn't called Haile Selassie, who was also born on 23 July.

Sunday, 1 September

I've kept a diary, on and off, for about thirty years, albeit never at any length, and I've fallen easily into the habit of writing in this book every day and carrying it about with me wherever I go so that I can jot things down as they occur to me, on the hoof, as it were, and at odd moments. I also write up the day's events each evening or whenever I have an opportunity of doing so, as now. In this I am doubtless influenced by Francis Kilvert, whose Diary has given me so much pleasure over the years.

Today Leslie and I drove up the Valley to Sundance, the arts centre owned by the actor, Robert Redford, who owns 5,000 acres of land hereabouts. We had a splendid lunch in the restaurant – sausage, bacon, eggs, fish and gâteau – as much as we could eat for about $8 each. Redford, who's married to a Mormon, is sometimes to be seen strolling around the place and Leslie has met him several times. If we'd bumped into him today I intended asking him whether Butch Cassidy and the Sundance Kid really did kill Llwyd ab Iwan, the son of Michael D. Jones, while on the run in Patagonia in 1909, but the opportunity didn't arise.

On the way back we stopped several times to look out over Provo, Orem and Utah Lake, which has fresh water. There are very high peaks on either side of the Wasatch Valley, some of which are said to have no name, though I'd like to know what the Utes call them. We also saw an eagle soaring effortlessly high above us and herds of moose moving resolutely through the woods.

Leslie tells me I'm probably the last foreign writer who will be appointed by BYU as Visiting Professor in the English Department. Most of the staff want young American writers, preferably Mormons, so that students will be attracted to the Department.

In 1955, the leasehold having been relinquished by the Crawshays, my parents bought 50 Meadow Street on a mortgage for the awesome price of £500; up to then they had rented it for a few shillings a week. During my last year at school, in 1956, they replaced the old fireplace in the kitchen with a modern tiled one, and a carpet was put down for the first time. The wall-cupboard was removed to make room for a tv set and the ancient wireless, with 'those faraway places with strange-sounding names' marked on its bakelite dial, disappeared from its time-honoured place by the window. The scullery was extended to make a bathroom and indoor toilet and a hot-water system was installed. Over the next few years, whenever I came home from Aberystwyth for the holidays, I noticed the whole house was undergoing a piecemeal transformation: it was completely redecorated and partly refurbished, and there seemed to be gadgets everywhere – a gas-fire, a hoover, a spin-dryer – that made the house even warmer, cleaner, brighter and more comfortable than I'd remembered it. Chrome, perspex, formica, artex, polyvinyl and dralon were beginning to work their revolution in the taste and domestic interiors of the working class.

In the streets of Provo nothing happens, very, very slowly, if indeed at all.

Monday, 2 September

A pretty idle day, Labor Day. After ringing home in the afternoon, I strolled down to campus in the great heat and discovered the Wilkinson Student Center, the equivalent of our Students' Union, a seven-storey building with a post office, a few shops, a bowling-alley and a games room. But no coffee-shop or bar and nowhere to buy a decent newspaper: caffeine, alcohol, tobacco and news are stimulants prohibited by the Saints. Of these the ones I miss most, I'm bound to say, are the good old *Western Mail* every morning and the six o'clock news on the BBC. I've never smoked and it's good to see the disgusting habit doesn't exist here – at least not in public. Tony Curtis, a furious anti-nicotine man, would approve, though I have the feeling he wouldn't last a week here without blowing a fuse for other reasons.

Tonight I started to read *The Book of Mormon*. The Saints regard this book, together with more than a hundred 'revelations' known as the Doctrine and Covenants, as the Word of God. The text is said to have been discovered by Joseph Smith (1805-44), who in 1823 had a vision in which two personages, whom he took to be God and Jesus, appeared before him in a shaft of light. When the young roughneck asked which of the various religious sects then in America was right, he was told they were all wrong and that their creeds were 'an abomination' in God's sight.

Some years later, when Smith was 22, he had another vision in which an angel named Moroni directed him to 'the hill Cumorah'. There he found a number of thin golden plates inscribed in a language which only the semi-literate Smith, divinely inspired and with the help of two stones, known in Exodus as the Urim and the Thummim, could decipher; he later said the plates, guarded by a salamander, had been written in 'Reformed Egyptian'. All this is supposed to have happened at Palmyra, near Lake Ontario, in what was then New York State, in 1827, a place and time of great religious ferment when several crackpot creeds were spawned. Smith translated the plates into English and a number of his neighbours testified to his having done so, after which, conveniently, they were taken back into the keeping of Moroni. The text was published as *The Book of Mormon* in 1830. Moroni also instructed him that, all others churches being based on falsehood, Smith was to become leader of the new Church, which was fair enough, I suppose, since he'd written its Book.

Joseph Smith and Oliver Cowdery were given the Melchizedek Priesthood by Saints Peter, James and John, who appeared before them, and this invested in them the authority to organize the new Church; the twelve Apostles who govern the Church today are their successors.

The Saints believe that, a few hundred years after Christ's death, His original teachings were corrupted and lost, and that *The Book of Mormon* (sub-titled *Another Testament of Jesus Christ*), all 588 pages of it, restores His message. There are many points of similarity between the texts of the two books, but the basic history recounted in the *Book of Mormon* is unique. It tells in a complex narrative how, in 600 BC, a small band of Hebrews, in flight before the Babylonian invasion, travel by caravan to the Indian Ocean, construct a boat and set out across the sea to a promised land on the west coast of the Americas. There, during the centuries before Christ, they establish a great civilization that has many temples and cities, until conflict divides them into two warring factions – the fair-skinned, virtuous Nephites and the dark-skinned, conniving Lamanites. After the Resurrection, Christ appears to the people of America and teaches His Gospel among them – the Second Coming.

For two hundred years after Christ's reappearance the tribes unite and live in harmony and prosperity. But when human nature reasserts itself, schism and conflict, sin and disharmony reappear, and they again split into two opposing groups until, in about AD 421, one group destroys the other. The leader of the Nephites, Mormon, is killed in the final triumph of the wicked Lamanites who are eventually absorbed by other groups from Europe and Asia, becoming the ancestors of the Indians of North, Central and South America. Moroni, the last prophet of the Nephites, saves the golden plates on which the history of his people is written and buries them in 'the hill Cumorah', where they are to remain preserved until brought forth as a witness to the divinity of Christ 'in the latter days'. It was this text that Joseph Smith was said to have discovered in 1827. The complete absence of any archaeological or paleographical evidence for this baloney does not deter the Saints in the slightest.

Is this, I wonder, part of the appeal for Mormons – to have had Jesus on their own soil, their very own All American Boy? When I point out that there's no evidence whatsoever for Christ's appearance in America, I'm assured that he also appeared in Britain, but that 'the documentation' has not yet been discovered. There's no arguing against such nonsense; it is the vicious poison of closed minds.

It comes as no surprise to learn that the early Mormons incurred the wrath of their neighbours who were as hostile to their theology as they were to their practice of polygamy or 'plural marriage'. Joseph Smith and Brigham Young were said to have had more than fifty wives each – all at the same time. The early Mormons were forced to move from the east coast of America but, as they made their way ever westward through Missouri, Ohio and Illinois, they were persecuted wherever they tried to settle. When Smith was killed by an angry mob at Carthage in Illinois, thus providing the Church with its first martyr, Young was appointed his successor.

The Mormons continued westward, hauling their possessions in handcarts over some of the most difficult terrain in the American West. Many children were born and old people died during the trek. When, on 24 July 1847, they reached the Valley of the Great Salt Lake, sparsely inhabited by Indians and unsuitable for cultivation because it was largely desert, Young is reputed to have announced, 'This is the place', and so Salt Lake City was founded where it stands today. Later the same year, 1,637 Mormons migrated to the Valley of the Great Salt Lake and over the next twenty years another 60,000 joined them. The Mormons' first task was to irrigate and cultivate the desert. Utah at this time was not part of the United States.

The Mormons believe Zion will be built on the American continent and that, after the Third Coming, Christ will have the seat of his power in Utah. They say they are determined to establish the moral, social and political conditions necessary for the reappearance of Christ in America. So I'm spending a Semester in Zion.

Whatever one thinks of the Mormons' religious beliefs, the story of their trek westwards is a stirring one, historically validated, and it reminds me of the Welsh settlement of Patagonia: the Welsh settled in the Chubut Valley because nobody else wanted it and they too made the desert bloom. I found a good account of all this in *The Mormon Experience* (1979) by Leonard J. Arrington and Davis Bitton, Mormons both but not uncritical of the Church in its earliest phases.

Joseph Smith, clearly a man of great vitality and personal magnetism, has been viewed by historians as both a monstrous charlatan and a demi-god. It's clear, too, he was a compulsive philanderer and a bully-boy. Anti-Mormon writers, particularly Smith's unsympathetic biographer, Fawn McKay Brodie, have tended to depict him as a fabricator and the Latter-day Saints as dupes who were exploited by sinister leaders. It's clear that many, particularly ill-educated and poor people, were converted not so much by the tenets of faith as by their own emotional and psychological need for certainty, authority, and order. Above all, Mormonism seemed to hold out hope for a fresh start in a new continent and provided dispossessed people with a sense of belonging and direction. Their descendants are all around me as I write this in the library of BYU.

As a boy I attended Libanus, the Baptist chapel in Trefforest; the name is the Welsh for Lebanon, though I didn't know it at the time. What I remember most is the bickering that went on there over such matters as which hymns were to be sung at the annual *gymanfa ganu*. On the high wall above the big seat (that's what we called it, not the deacons' pew) were painted, somewhat incongruously, the words *Cerwch eich gilydd*. The minister, the silver-haired Mr Washington Owen, looked to me like Lloyd George: he always wore a Come-to-Jesus collar and had a son named Peredur, who once caused consternation when, in full view of the congregation, he hit me over the head with a Bible for something I'd said in his class. The highlight of my time as a boy at Libanus came when, at the age of about ten, I sang 'Oh, for the wings of a dove' in a chapel concert and was given a shilling by Mrs Ferris, the organist, with the admonition not to spend it all at once.

The sermons and hymn-singing at Libanus were in Welsh, which most of the congregation didn't speak. Yet I distinctly recall seeing some of the older people with copies of a Welsh newspaper, almost certainly *Seren Gomer*, which were delivered every week. Ever since, I've always found great difficulty in sitting through a service in Welsh without suffering again the tedium I felt as a child in Libanus. That's partly why I never go to Capel Crwys these days, despite my great admiration and affection for the minister, Cynwil Williams, whom I've known since our undergraduate days. I'm perfectly happy that Ruth goes to chapel and our children attended Sunday School; I even pay an annual subscription. It's just that I don't feel the need to attend the services and there's no point pretending in these matters.

Libanus wasn't all tedious. We used to go to Barry Island twice a year and to Creigiau to pick primroses for the Easter Treat, and there were regular parades through the streets, with banners and gazookas and drums, all of which I found great fun. There were also tea-parties and games in the vestry, at which I baulked because I was a very shy boy.

I was christened but only nearly baptized. During the rehearsal, with the floor of the big seat taken up to reveal the large marble basin into which the water was to be poured, something went wrong with the pipes and they juddered to a stop as the vestry filled up with steam. By the time the system was repaired, a few months later, I was no longer going to chapel, because my mother, to my huge relief, had made it clear I didn't have to go if I didn't want to. I suppose we were living through the twilight of the Baptist cause, of chapel religion even, in Trefforest.

There are about six million Mormons, most of them in the United States. They don't have their own language or racial characteristics but it's possible to speak of a Mormon people if not a Mormon nation. Like the Jews, whom they will soon outnumber in America, they are a religion that has become a people. They make up about 65 per cent of the population of Utah and there are a lot of them in Wyoming and Nevada, too. Every Congressman from Utah is a Mormon and virtually all elected representatives, from Governor down, are Saints. The State's legislature and judiciary, the school boards, city councils, municipal agencies and town halls are all dominated by them. The comparison with the Soviet Union, where the Party has a finger in every pie, seems to me a close one.

The Church is estimated to be worth $30 billion and its annual income is about $6 billion. Saints who want to be 'in good standing' are required to tithe: they contribute about 15 per cent of their income to the Church and are expected to put in many hours of voluntary work as well.

Mark Twain once referred to *The Book of Mormon* as 'chloroform in print'.

Tuesday, 3 September

I took my first classes today. The students are pleasant, extremely polite, attentive and highly articulate, though almost none have any experience of writing. When I asked whether they knew any poems by heart, few did, but one recited 'Pied Beauty', though he didn't know who wrote it, which was my cue to tell them about Gerard Manley Hopkins and his interest in Welsh prosody, by way of introducing myself. They were mightily impressed when I recited the whole of 'The Windhover' from memory: 'I caught this morning morning's minion, kingdom of daylight's dauphin, dapple-dawn-drawn falcon . . . ' all the way to its alliterative climax and not a word out of place – as far as they could tell.

As they'd never heard of Seamus Heaney either, I gave them copies of a few of his poems, including 'Digging', and we had an intelligent discussion of it. Many of these young people are from rural areas and they seemed to understand the farming background to some of Heaney's early poems, which was a good start, though I think they thought he's a Welshman too. They liked, in particluar, the idea of digging with a pen and lowering a bucket into a well 'to set the darkness ringing'.

In an attempt to explain the differences between the Welsh and Irish, rather than go into *Pasg/Casca* and all that, I gave them the old chestnut about the Welsh being the Irish who couldn't swim, but even that fell flat with them. Some have been on Mormon missions to various places in the Yookay but they're not used to hearing about non-American writers and have almost no idea of European history.

I drew a map of the British Isles on the blackboard in an attempt to explain where Wales, Ireland and Scotland are. It put me in mind of my trip to see Dürrenmatt in Neuchâtel in 1974. When I invited him to come to Wales to receive the International Writer's Prize he sprang to his feet excitedly and, drawing down a wall- map of the Yookay, said he'd always wanted to visit Wales, especially such places as Cambridge, Ely and Norwich.

The two hours of my classes today flashed by and I made only one serious mistake. I asked the class to make sure that next week they have a notebook, writing paper, a ruler, a dictionary, a pencil and a rubber – this last caused some tittering.

When I think back to the kind of thing I was writing in the 1950s, I mustn't be too hard on the attempts now being made by my students. One of the poems I wrote as a sixth-former started something like this:

> Rose from my morning to ribbon
> The whistle-wet wood,
> That uncertain dawning was good and golden,
> To wander underwater in a bewilderment of crows
> On the gorse-prowed hills of Wales.

I'm glad I can't remember any more of it; a woeful case of the DTs.

There's a Missionary Training Centre in Provo, not far from Wymount Terrace, and I often see groups of well-groomed young men in black suits and white shirts coming and going. They receive only two or three weeks' basic training at the MTC and are expected to rely on 'the Holy Spirit' when on their mission.

All Mormon males between the ages of 19 and 22 belong to the Aaronic Priesthood and have to do two years' missionary work abroad, full-time and at their own expense; married couples also work abroad, though I've never seen a female missionary in the Yookay. They are always young men, in pairs, going from door to door. We had a visit last year. I asked them about their life as missionaries. They said they get up at six and their day begins with reading the *Book of Mormon* and prayer. The day ends at nine and they are in bed by ten. In fact, they are never out of each other's sight except when in the bath or toilet, and perhaps not even then. This is how the Church spreads its message around the world and makes about a million converts every four or five years. The conversion rate must be a very small percentage of the number of house-calls made but there are so many thousands of missionaries out at any one time they must make some headway, because the Church is said to be the most rapidly expanding in the world.

The Mormons in the Yookay go back to about 1837 when the first missionaries arrived in Liverpool. Converts were baptized in the Ribble at Preston in the same year. A Perpetual Emigration Fund was started which enabled converts to leave for America; once settled, they were expected to repay the loan and the money was then used to finance the next wave of emigrants.

There are lots of squirrels in the Wymount quad and sometimes they make a racket as if quarrelling among themselves. I'm reminded of the notice Gwyn Thomas put up in his garden at Peterstone-super-Ely: 'Squirrels, please wear daps'.

I was once told the word 'daps' is from 'Dunlop all purpose shoes'. H'mm.

The most vivid memory I have of Gwyn Thomas is the night he and his wife Lyn came to our house because some Russian visitors had asked to meet the author of *All Things Betray Thee*, which is admired in the Soviet Union. The Russians seemed to know the novel in great detail and plied him with questions which pleased him mightily. Their names were Giorgi Gulia, Sergei Narovchatov and Maxim Tank (a pseudonym), all members of the Writers' Union and therefore eligible to be let out of the USSR. I had met them by chance in the foyer of the Park Hotel and offered to show them around Cardiff. They turned out to be important members of the Party and Writers' Union and, shortly afterwards, I received my first invitation to visit the USSR.

The night they came to dinner, around midnight, Heledd was woken by the talk and laughter and came downstairs in her *coban*. She and Gwyn immediately started chatting, Heledd in her elementary English since she was only four or five at the time. 'What's that?' the child enquired, pointing to the glass of beer Gwyn was drinking. 'Pop,' he replied, with that lopsided grin of his. 'Do you like pop?' she asked. 'Yes, very much,' he replied. 'How much?' she asked. 'Too much,' he said, and the tears started bowling down his cheeks. I bundled Heledd up and shortly afterwards the evening came to an end. It took some explaining to our Russian guests.

At the Grammar School, where I went in 1949, I found Welsh History to be exclusively concerned with the luminaries of the Methodist Revival and, at the first opportunity, dropped Welsh in favour of French, as the brighter boys were encouraged to do. Whereas I was taught English and French by excellent teachers whom I recall with gratitude, I found the learning of Welsh a dreadful fatigue. In three years I managed only to count up to twenty and to recite a simple rhyme about '*Siôn a Siân a Siencyn yn mynd i Aberdâr, Siôn i brynu ceiliog a Siân i brynu iâr*'. It was only on St David's Day, at the school eisteddfod, that Welsh was used in the assembly hall and even then, for me, the experience of hearing it wasn't unlike that of singing hymns in chapel. I can't say either school or chapel did much to nurture in me the sense of being Welsh.

The History teacher was a Mr Parry, a native of Blaenau Ffestiniog. One of my classmates, Ginger Roberts, used to pretend he had an auntie living somewhere up in the flinty wastes of the North and used the alleged connexion in a blatant attempt to curry favour with Mr Parry. It was Ginger Roberts who had the job of fetching his paper and a large packet of Craven A from the corner-shop every morning, for which, we were all convinced, he was always allowed to win the recitation prize on St David's Day.

'Now tell me, Roberts, where did you go for your holidays this summer?'

'Blaenau Ffestiniog, Sir.'

'And what did you do there, boy?'

'Saw the quarry, Sir.'

'Yes, and what did you think of it, boy?'

'Very big, Sir.'

'What was, boy?'

'The hole, Sir.'

'Anything else, boy?'

'Yes, Sir.'

'Come along then, out with it.'

'Please, Sir, when are they going to fill it in?'

While Ginger Roberts tried to engage Mr Parry in conversation about the incontrovertible delights of Blaenau Ffestiniog, we would rifle his satchel and scribble on the pink covers of his exercise book a thesaurus of all the words we could think of for 'teacher's pet': creep, skunk, toady, rat, snitch, arse-licker, scab, blackleg, quisling, Judas . . .

I once had my ear clipped by the English master, K.P. Davies, who asked me to name the third figure of speech that goes with pathos and bathos; he wanted synecdoche, litotes or oxymoron, I expect, but I said, 'Aramis, Sir'. Ouch.

Wednesday, 4 September

After taking delivery of a television set this morning, at $70 for four months, I went down to the Department to type up my review on an electric typewriter, and then had a salad in the Cougareat, washed down with a large carton of cranberry juice, all for about $4. Afterwards I spent an hour chatting with John Harris, who's very keen on the Great Outdoors and never tires of giving me tips on how to skin a snake, extract water from cactuses and ride the rapids in a canoe made from a single log. I shall have to remember these things, for they are sure to come in handy here.

One of the darker episodes in Mormon history occurred in 1857 when a waggon-train of non-Mormon settlers heading for California were attacked at a spot known as Mountain Meadows in south-west Utah and 120 were massacred. The killing was blamed on the Paiute Indians but also involved was a Mormon militia led by Brigham Young's adopted son, John D. Lee, who was later executed by firing squad at the site of the massacre.

This evening I walked for about two hours up Rock Canyon, under the jagged peak which, at 7,500 feet, overlooks Wymount Terrace. I saw birds, trees and flowers to which I could give no name. No one else around. I've done so much walking since arriving here I've already lost a few pounds and worn a hole in the leather sole of my Veldschoens, which I had tapped just before setting out from home.

There are fourteen knobs on my tv set but for some unfathomable reason, and despite my most diligent attempts to locate them, I can get only four channels. The most memorable thing I saw this evening was an advertisement for air-bags which apparently save lives when they rapidly inflate on impact caused by car collisions. The advert consists of a number of people, both men and women, of various ages and occupations, coming up close to camera and saying, in a variety of American accents and with obvious relish, 'Ah'm aliyive!' One can't help but be glad.

I haven't yet seen the advert for deodorant which Wynford Vaughan-Thomas once told me was his favourite: 'Remember – it may be December outside but it's always August under your armpits!' *Si non è vero è molto ben trovata.*

My first visit to France was in the summer of 1956, shortly

before I went up to Aberystwyth, when I went to stay at the home of a penfriend in the small village of Gacé in Normandy. Gilbert Legendre and his mother kept a *boulangerie et patisserie* in the village's only street. There wasn't much to do and Gilbert worked all night in the bakery and slept most of the day. So I spent my fortnight walking out of the village, which was on a crossroads, and trying to converse with the baffled country people I met on the way. I think they thought I was a German left over from the war. In those days I was still very self-conscious but made a determined attempt to get over it, beginning in Gacé. On my first evening the Legendres took me to a midnight mass in a nearby convent where I was horrified to discover I had to take part in a procession carrying a huge candle and singing, *'Ave, Ave, Ave Maria'*, in which I joined with something less than gusto.

Thursday, 5 September
The news on tv this evening is that Gorbachev has dissolved the Supreme Council of the Soviet Union. Ten of the fifteen Republics, including Sakhartveli/Georgia, have proclaimed their independence, and Leningrad has reverted to the name St Petersburg. This may be the end of Soviet Communism as meted out by Moscow. I saw it coming in 1989 when, with Wynn Thomas and Michael Parnell, I visited Kiev and Talinn, where there seemed to be a political demonstration at every street-corner.

What will do for the USSR in the end is threefold: the rise of Muslim fundamentalism; the desire for free speech and national liberation; and the people's demand for a better standard of life and all the commodities that go with it. I think this not from anything I've read but from personal observation inside the country.

During that trip Mike and I passed many a happy hour on long train-journeys in singing songs from our boyhood. In my case, I learned hundreds of songs from the music-hall to which my grandfather used to take me in Pontypridd and Cardiff, and from playing old 78 records on the family gramophone. I still know the words to such songs as 'Come into the Garden, Maud', 'The Minstrel Boy', 'Who were you with Last Night?', 'The Man who broke the Bank at Monte Carlo', 'A Nightingale sang in Berkeley

Square', 'If you were the only Girl in the World', 'I'll take you home again, Kathleen', 'The Rose of Tralee', and 'I'll be Seeing you in All the Old Familiar Places'.

The last time I was in Georgia, Ruth and I were staying at the Iveria Hotel in Tbilisi. One morning we were coming down in the lift with a group of British MPs who were part of an official delegation to the Soviet Union. Ruth and I were discussing, in Welsh, what we were going to do that day. As we got out of the lift I heard Roy Hughes, the Labour MP for Newport, a good man but hopelessly monolingual, say to another, 'You know, this Georgian language sounds to me a bit like the Welsh we have back home.'

Molly Coddle, Sally Forth, Peter Out, Luke Warm, Willy Nilly, Tommy Rot, Gerry Mander, Terri Torial, Bobby Soxer, Rick O'Shea, Courtney Fish, Rhea Lidiart, Dai Hatsu, Rhys Lowe, Karen Dash, Offa Kinnell.

Friday, 6 September
Grey skies for the first time since I arrived, and some rain. The clouds are low on the mountains, starting just below the tree-line. Everyone says the rain won't last long: it's gonna be snowin' soon.

I spent the day in my office, marking the assignments handed in by my students. The standard of the poems leaves something to be desired. Why, Oh why do young people write about their Souls and Truth and Beauty and Death and Eternity, and in language that's so archaic and flowery as to beggar belief? If I can help at all it will be to encourage them to write in a contemporary way about concrete things and actual situations and real people, avoiding the Great Abstractions. Some hope.

Just before I set out, Gillian Clarke was kind enough to send me some practical tips on how to get students writing creatively, and I've found them useful. One she calls 'taking a word for a walk' – an idea suggested by Paul Klee, no doubt. I tell my students I can't teach them to write but they can improve their writing skills under my supervision. I can't make poets or short-story writers of them, but I can suggest improvements and pat them on the head when they write something that works. They seem to accept this and I had a very nice but not uncritical note from one of them, a Chinese American named Charlotte Yen, saying how much she enjoys my classes and the approach I take. I must be doing something right.

On one of the poems handed in today, instead of writing my name at the top of the sheet, as required, one student had scribbled a laconic message to his class-mate: 'For this forrin guy, old, crazy but inteligant, who nows his stuff.' What better commendation?

This evening I made a point of watching as much tv as possible, into the small hours. For the most part, the programmes were awful. The news bulletins were interrupted by adverts every few minutes. The best current affairs programme is on CNN in which Larry King, he of the gaudy braces and fawning manner, interviews people who are famous for being famous.

It occurs to me there's no sex or violence on the channels I receive at Wymount. I suspect such programmes and the channels which broadcast them are jammed by the Church. It probably has a Censorship Department which is busy making sure the Saints are protected from such things.

The greatest discovery of the 20th century is that women enjoy sex, too. When I said as much to Glyn Jones the other day, he laughed heartily; he will probably note it in his journal.

One of my daughters, I think it was Heledd, told me just before I left home that the Welsh for 'video nasty' is *achyfideo*.

My first poem to appear in print was one with which I won the Chair at the School Eisteddfod in 1956, when I was in the Upper VIth. It was entitled 'On a Welsh Victory at Arms Park'; I think I still remember it:

> The slagheaps rejoiced and the pit-head grinned.
> The Valley sang
> With its blue-scarred faces beaming.
>
> Even Bethel smiled and her concrete cracked.
> Red berets spewed
> From heaving coaches and platforms.
>
> Trying to work their praises in edgewise,
> Dai-capped women
> Cackled to impatient neighbours.

The new parchedig sang in his bathroom,
Thinking of a sermon
To preach about rugby.

Publicans thought of their harvest that night.
'Fancy, three-nil!'
Laughed the tea-sipping policeman.

'Three-nil!' rang the dust under the Valley
And the cage sang
As Shift Two reached the surface.

The whole valley had been down the valley,
Dust-tongues priestlings
Of a religion not Baptist.

Come to think of it, perhaps it would have been better to let the poem rest in decent obscurity in the pages of *The Pontypriddian*.

Saturday, 7 September

Heavy rain in the night and still raining pouring this morning. I'd intended going to Salt Lake City today but it's too wet. Kyffin Williams would like the cloud-capped mountains here.

I took a bus into Provo, billed as Utah's second largest city with a population of about 90,000, but it turned out to be a great disappointment. It dates from about 1849 when the area was settled by Mormons from Salt Lake City, and was rapidly developed after the coming of the railway in 1873. Some of the architecture is from the late 19th century but most of it is much more recent. There seems to be no centre, only one short street with a few shops, the main shopping centre being the Mall, which is two or three miles away. The place is laid out, like all Mormon towns, on a grid, with wide streets and a profusion of trees, mostly poplars. The houses are set back from the road behind large lawns which seem to need constant watering, for this really is desert country. The larger shops, or stores, are spread out over such a wide area that one needs a car to get round them. I was looking specifically for an electric kettle, because the handle of the one Kitty has lent me gets very hot. There were very few people about and it was all a bit forlorn, like Merthyr early on a Sunday morning, but without the chip-bags, dog-shit and vomit. I walked home through the rain after waiting an hour for a bus that didn't turn up, and was soaked by the time I reached Wymount Terrace.

There are huge neon signs up on the main roads out of Provo which read: 'A New World Order'. I shudder at the thought of what that could mean.

The evening was spent writing answers for an interview which David Lloyd of Le Moyne College in Syracuse, whom I've met, intends publishing as part of a book about the republic of letters in Wales. His father was a Welsh minister and his uncle is Professor Brinley Thomas, who's a neighbour of ours in Whitchurch. My contribution will be mainly about the early years of *Poetry Wales* and the circumstances in which I launched it in 1965.

I chose the name *Poetry Wales* after meeting John Jordan, the editor of *Poetry Ireland*, in McDaid's pub in Dublin. On the same occasion I met Garech de Brun, one of the Guinnesses and founder of Claddagh Records; he was the first man I ever saw wearing his hair in a pony-tail.

On the question of whether Anglo-Welsh writing should be concerned with Wales, its people, history and present condition, I shall reply as I always do: I want a literature national in inspiration and international in appeal. What causes me concern is that, instead of contributing to a national literature of Wales, Welsh writing in English could become provincial, looking to America or England for themes, styles and, worst of all, approval, or so like English literature that its Welsh characteristics are difficult or impossible to recognize or define. I'm aware that some young writers aren't a bit interested in things Welsh (some have no knowledge of Wales outside their own little patches) and writers, being on the whole a selfish lot, show an interest only if they can draw some advantage from it. But they should remember that if it weren't for the nationalist revival in the 1960s, what Fanon calls 'the third phase' of post-colonialism, and the community of interest which has grown since then through the work of the Arts Council, the Books Council, the Academy, the publishers and the literary magazines, they might not have a context in which to write now. Them's my colours, anyhow, and I shall show them in the piece I write for David Lloyd.

'Ki tant ne set ne l'ad prod entendut.'

I remember once asking the Head of English at a comprehensive school in Tredegar whether he'd like to have a visit from a Welsh poet under the Writers on Tour scheme. 'No,' he replied, 'there'd be no point – they're all Labour up here.'

There's not a single reference to a bridge in the Bible. I wonder whether there is in the *Book of Mormon*; the Brooklyn Bridge, perhaps.

Sunday, 8 September

I woke up early to ring Ruth before 7am (at the cheapest rate), but there was no answer; no wonder, it was midnight in Wales – I'd forgotten the difference in times. The rain has stopped and there are blue skies again.

Although it's the Sabbath, there were lots of students on campus and I spent a pleasant hour strolling around outside some of the buildings I haven't visited so far, among them the Franklin S. Harris Fine Arts Center, the Marriott Centre, which is said to have 23,000 seats and is used for concerts, and the Monte L. Bean Life Science Museum.

While sitting on the plinth of a monument to Brigham Young, no less, I was called upon to play Cupid by a young man who'd arranged to meet a girl called Vanessa at this very spot. They'd seen each other only once before, while on a Mormon mission, he explained, and neither was sure what the other looked like. James stood some way off and was hoping to see what would happen when Vanessa found me at the rendez-vous. I agreed to take part in the prank, but told myself that when the girl turned up I would quickly explain what was happening, and ask her to walk off arm-in-arm with me. Unfortunately, she spotted him first, so there was no chance to turn the tables on the smitten young man. The couple then came over and introduced themselves and we had a chat. Vanessa was a good-looker, a Spanish Beauty type, and I joked that, had I not been a happily married man, I'd have been jealous of James. Then, at their request, I took a photo of them and they went on their way. About an hour later I saw them sitting under a tree, obviously having renewed their acquaintance, and they waved as I passed by, calling out, 'Hiya, Mac! How ya doin'?', to which I replied in the vernacular, 'Good. I'm good.'

On my way back up the hill to Wymount Terrace I saw hundreds of people coming home from church, whole families in their Sunday best and carrying what look like large Bibles rather ostentatiously, as one sometimes sees outside Evangelical temples in Wales.

I watched a Mormon religious service on tv this evening. Church services usually last about three hours. There's a Sacramental Meeting which all attend, a Sunday School and a Priesthood Meeting and a Relief Society for the women. On the first Sunday of the month there is Fast Sunday: members are encouraged to abstain from food and drink for two consecutive meals and to give at least the cash equivalent to the Church for the relief of the needy. At these meetings any member who feels so prompted may stand and speak of his or her experience of God and the Scriptures. *Gair o brofiad*. Non-Mormons, or Gentiles, are welcome to attend any of these meetings. There are no ministers or paid clergy of any kind.

. . . yes, it does. I've just refilled this pen and wasn't sure it was going to work because the nib was damaged when it rolled off my desk yesterday. I don't understand why my handwriting has become so shapeless. I used to have a copperplate hand, if a little gothic, though nothing as elegant as Leslie's or Raymond Garlick's. But, as I write this journal, I see it's become a scrawl and, I expect, hard for anyone else to decipher, which may be just as well.

I owe my interest in Anglo-Welsh literature to my grandfather, who bought me a copy of the *Selected Poems* of Idris Davies on my seventeenth birthday in 1955. I still have the book, inscribed in his shaky hand. Reading the poems was an epiphany for me. Whenever I take the book down nowadays it serves as well as any madeleine to remind me of the excitement, almost feverish in its intensity, with which I first read about the places and people I was quick to recognize as my own. Oh, I know how easy it is to fall under the spell of poetry that's full of familiar placenames and homely sentiment and meant to win the reader over to its particular point of view, but I responded to Idris Davies – it wasn't unlike falling in love for the first time – with a candour and delight about which I still don't feel any embarrassment and which I wish, sometimes, it were possible to recapture.

From Idris Davies I moved on to books by other Welsh writers that I found in the Public Library in Pontypridd, and soon I'd read just about everything they had on the Local Authors shelves. In this I was helped by Mairwen Jones, the girl who lived next door to us in Meadow Street: she worked at the library and when she was on duty at the desk she'd let me borrow as many books as I could carry, regardless of how many tickets I had.

It was my grandfather, too, who awoke my interest in local history, taking me for long walks and talking to me about such colourful characters as Mabon and Dr William Price. I remember one walk in particular. It must have been when I was about 13. We went, one summer's evening, through Ton-teg and Efail-isaf and then up the Garth, that whaleback mountain which was the boundary of our known world when I was a boy. There I saw the valleys of Glamorgan winding smokily to the north, the Beacons in the far distance, and below us, Cardiff shimmering in the heat, and beyond, the Channel and the hazy hills of Somerset. I think that must have been the day when a map started to form in my mind that I've carried about with me ever since and at that spot, to which I often return, I never fail to feel the primeval tug, that sense of belonging to a particular place, that I take to be at the heart of patriotism.

When the time comes, as come it will, I should like my ashes to be scattered from the summit of the Garth. I hope it's a fine day so that my family and friends can enjoy the magnificent view. As for the music to be played on that occasion, I think I'd like the second movement from Smétana's *Ma Vlast*. For refreshments, faggots and peas washed down with Vimto.

I suppose my grandfather was 'a character'. A man of Churchillian girth, and always well turned out in his black boots and waistcoat with watch-and-chain, he used to sit on the porch of our house and play his tin whistle for anyone who came up or down Meadow Street. He had a huge repertoire and would play any tune on request. The passers-by would invariably stop and chat to him and thus he learned everything that was going on in the village. After he retired, in about 1945, he was around the house much more than my father, who worked shifts and wasn't always at home in the evenings and at weekends, and so I spent much more time with the older man. Sometimes I used to meet him in town on my way from school and, as we came home on the bus, he'd introduce me to all and sundry. He was in best form when he'd been drinking in the pubs on the Tumble, though I was always a bit embarrassed to sit by him when he'd had a pint or three. Once, meeting him near the public library on Tyfica Road, I had to shake hands with Mr Matabele Davies, none other than the Stipendiary Magistrate of Pontypridd whose very name struck terror in the hearts of more than one generation of schoolboys. Afterwards my grandfather and I went into the market and he bought me a glass of the famous sarsaparilla.

One of my grandfather's favourite tricks, on Election Day, was to dress up in his best suit, silk muffler and bowler hat, with a flower in his lapel, and arrange for a Tory car to pick him up and take him to the polling booth. After a great deal of deliberate delay, he would go and cast his vote for Labour, despite the fact he had nothing but contempt for Pontypridd's long-serving and somnolent MP, Arthur Pearson, to whom he used to refer as Rip van Winkle.

I was once in Westminster Abbey at the same time as a small group escorting Robert Mugabe around the famous mausoleum. At one point he stepped right into my path in a narrow aisle and I had to stand back to let him go by. As he passed, he smiled at me and said, 'I beg your pardon'.

I first became interested in politics when I was in Form VI and studying, as part of my French course, the Fourth Republic's colonial policy. From 1954 to 1962 the war was raging in Algeria and I was on the side of Ben Bella and the FLN, especially after I'd read about what French paratroopers did to Djamila Boupacha, and after the fall of Dien Bien Phu.

As an undergraduate I was deeply impressed by the Hungarian

uprising against Soviet rule that took place in the November of my first term at Aberystwyth. We collected money for students fleeing the country, some of whom came to study at the College. When my father discovered I'd contributed ten shillings to the fund, he played hell with me, one of the few occasions on which he came near to hitting me. He never laid a finger on us boys but would often raise his voice and that was enough to terrify us. Another time, after I'd been out canvassing for John Howell, the Plaid Cymru candidate in the by-election at Caerffili, on the day before I was to leave for Brittany in 1959, my father snarled at me and went out tamping into the backyard where he stood staring up at the Barry mountain until he'd regained his composure.

Monday, 9 September
I spent the morning on campus, with not very much to do. In the Library, I read *The Times* (about a week old), and then mooched around the Bookstore. A student named Jennifer Rex came to my office to interview me for the BYU paper, *The Daily Universe,* the purview of which isn't as wide as its title suggests because it's mostly about Mormons and their Church, all shown in a highly favourable light.

This evening I had dinner at the home of John and Susan Tanner, a most charming young couple, and their five small children. During the otherwise splendid meal we drank a pink juice that looked rather like the mouth-wash they give you at the dentist's. John teaches in the English Department and his research interest is in the work of John Milton, about whom he's hoping to have a book published by OUP. The Tanners have been to Wales on holiday and visited the National Eisteddfod two years ago. While I was at their house I was shown seven rucksacks, each packed with tinned food and equipment such as torches, pickaxes, ropes and sleeping-bags. Provo, they told me, lies on a geological fault and earthquakes occur from time to time.

Before the meal John said grace, thanking God for my presence and fervently hoping I would be granted heavenly bliss. I found this a little more than somewhat embarrassing but shut my eyes during his prayer because the children were watching me through their fingers.

John explained that the Church expects its members to hold a Family Home Evening at least once a week and, although he didn't say so, I think the Tanners would be holding theirs this evening. Families are encouraged to spend this time in discussion and reading the *Book of Mormon*, and in recreational activities. Sometimes the evening takes the form of a trip to the cinema or a picnic in the woods. I can't help feeling it's a good idea, at least in part.

As soon as I got back to Wymount Terrace I made myself a large cup of Nescafé (from the jar I brought with me), and then another. I'm beginning to enjoy the surreptitious consumption of coffee as an act of rebellion (or perhaps revolt) against the prevailing orthodoxy in these parts.

The first time I was paid for something in print was when the *South Wales Echo* published my story, 'The Hooters', in 1958. It was about a small boy lying awake in bed on New Year's Eve and listening to the sounds of the street outside. My parents were embarrassed because I'd made transparent references to some of our neighbours, such as Mrs Annie Duster who was houseproud. I was paid five guineas. The feeling I had was akin to the experience of D.H. Lawrence when he showed his father a copy of his first novel and told him he'd got a hundred pounds for it. 'Eeh, lad,' said the old man, 'and tha's niver done a day's work in thy life'.

Bob Hope. Brahms and Liszt. Daisy Roots. Gregory Peck. George Raft. Mutt and Jeff. Rosie Lee. Todd Sloane. Vera Lynn.

Tuesday, 10 September
I had another insight into Mormonism today. After my classes a student came to see me in my office. She declined to give me her name but said she was in her Sophomore year. Although brought up as a member of the Church, she's become very unhappy with the way it treats women, particularly its insistence that they start breeding in their early twenties and have as many children as possible. I've noticed many of my colleagues in the English Department have six or seven children and they're still in their early thirties. When I asked my visitor why this was so, she

explained it was the good Mormon woman's duty to provide physical receptacles for the spirit children of God who could then come down to earth from the planet Kolob. I expressed incredulity at this, suggesting a more practical explanation: that it was important for a desert people, as the Mormons were in their first phase, to have as many children as possible so that there would be plenty of people to work the land and rear livestock. The Church's sanction of polygamy could also be explained in this way, I suggested. But she insisted that what she'd told me was true.

Ruth and I have four children. We decided that was enough when I read somewhere that every fifth child born into the world is Chinese.

Our first child, Lowri Angharad, was born two days after the disaster at Aberfan in October 1966. I was working with the *Western Mail* at the time and had gone there to help cover the story. I shall never forget what I saw. They were still digging children out of the slurry and the little bodies were laid out in a chapel awaiting identification. The message that Ruth had gone into labour was brought to me by a fellow reporter. There were no trains or buses up or down the Valley and all the telephone lines were cut. So I hitched a lift with a Gas Board van and reached the maternity hospital just in time to see Lowri being born.

At the battle of the Little Big Horn in Dakota in1876, in which General Custer and his troops were massacred by Sioux and Cheyenne, among those killed was a Welshman named William B. James from Fishguard. His name appears on the monument at the summit of Monument Hill. I'm reading a book by the General's widow, Elizabeth Bacon Custer, called *Boots and Saddles*. I can imagine the BBC Wales news bulletin at the time: 'Massacre at Little Big Horn: Welshman feared dead'.

Sixty zippers were quickly picked from the woven jute bag.

Wednesday, 11 September
I had a letter today from a Howard Price of Crosskeys in Gwent about the Lloyds, the bonesetters. He'd read an article of mine about Silver John, one of my Radnorshire ancestors, who was murdered for the buttons on his coat some time early in the 19th

century. The old man's body was found in the frozen waters of Llyn Heilyn 'in the Year of the Great Frost'. But Mr Price had nothing to tell me that I didn't already know. The mystery about Silver John is not only who killed him but in what year, since there's no official record of the murder, and so he's become a figure in folklore. There's a rhyme which suggests who the killers may have been:

> Silver John is dead and gone,
> So they came home a'singing:
> Radnor boys put out his eyes
> And set the church bells ringing.

The grass where Silver John is buried above the Harley Dingle is said to be always green. I intend seeking it out when I go home. I enjoy walking the bare hills of Elfael and lingering by the mawn pools.

This evening I went for a long walk up through the residential district behind Wymount, past large bungalows set behind lush lawns, with white fences and Old Glory flying from poles. No one around, not even a dog, or children playing. There was a splendid view across Provo and the lake towards the mountains in the west.

My grandfather, Charlie Symes, was a Londoner who came to South Wales in 1904 on a six-month contract to lay electric cables for Cardiff's new trams. He was working in a trench in St Mary Street one morning when it started raining heavily, with thunder and lightning, so he quickly climbed out and took shelter in the Royal Arcade. As the heavens opened, he fell into conversation with a young woman who was on an errand for her mistress, the wife of a Cardiff shipowner named Powell who lived in Cathedral Road. She was Lilian Gray, a native of Rhymney and a policeman's daughter. My grandmother always made out she was a Churchwoman, a deferential habit I think she'd picked up while in service, and when my grandfather ribbed her on this score he always called her Matilda, the name she'd been given in Cathedral Road.

I have a hazy memory of visiting my great-grandmother, *née* Ellen MacDermott, in Cwm, Ebbw Vale, when I was about nine or

Martha Lloyd née Powell (1864-90) of Michaelchurch-on-Arrow, my great-grandmother, Annie's mother.

Herbert Arthur Lloyd, my father, Christmas 1910, at the time of his removal to Heolgerrig, Merthyr Tydfil.

Annie Sophia Lloyd, Priest Weston, 1930s

Annie Sophia Lloyd later Passant (1890-1971), my father's mother

Blaenbedw, Glascwm

The village of Glascwm, Radnorshire

Charlie Symes (1880-1956), a Londoner,
my mother's father

My brother Lloyd and me, 1945

My grandfather and grandmother, Lilian Symes née Gray
(1878-1962), my mother's parents

*Alma Stephens née Symes (1910-94),
my mother, c. 1935*

*Herbert Arthur Lloyd Stephens
(1910-84), my father*

*The power station at Upper Boat where my father
worked for fifty years*

I promised to do my best.
Patrol Leader, 2nd Pontypridd Scouts,
c. 1956.

Ah, the Great Outdoors, 1955.

Prefects, Pontypridd Boys' Grammar School, 1956

At the age of three   *Graduation day, 1961*

*The view from our kitchen window across the meadow to the old Crawshay mansion
now part of the University of Glamorgan.*

Garth Newydd, Merthyr Tydfil, in the snow of 1962/3

An undergraduate at UCW, Aberystwyth

Pont Trefechan, Aberystwyth, February 1963

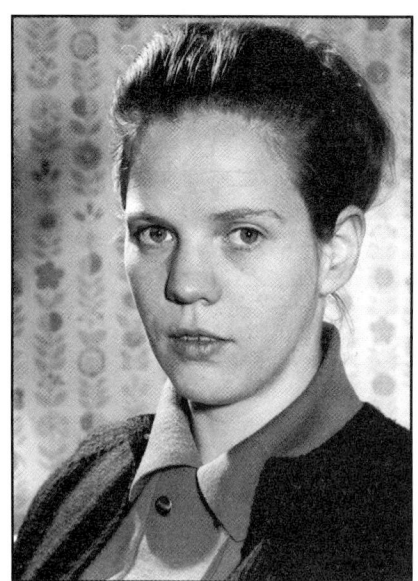

Ruth just after our wedding in 1965

*The Plaid Cymru candidate in
Merthyr Tydfil, 1966*

After Gwynfor's victory at Carmarthen,
July 1966

My friend Harri Webb
(1920-94)

Playing the fool in Museum Place, with Fay Williams and Elan Closs Roberts, c. 1970

Giorgi Gulia and family, Abkhazia, in the 1970s

On the road from Ordzhonikidze to Tbilisi, at the fountain where Pushkin and Tolstoi slaked their thirst, somewhere in the Caucasus, 1974

Dancing in the Caucasus, 1970s

With our children (left to right): Brengain, Huw, Lowri, Heledd

My friend Glyn Jones (1905-95). Photo: Julian Sheppard

My friend Leslie Norris
Photo: John P. Snyder

Visiting Professor
Photo: Ben Hussain

Brigham Young University, Provo, Utah

The road to Wales, Utah   *The dead centre of Wales, Utah*

With Ruth and Huw at Dead Horse Point

Brengain, Grand Canyon, Colorado

Some of my students, BYU, 1991

In San Francisco with Robert and Marilyn Bratman (centre), the poet Laurence Ferlinghetti (in hat), the publisher Nancy Peters (on left); and Colin Edwards and his wife Mary (on right).

Ruth, Blaenbedw, 1990

Blaenbedw, Heol Don, Whitchurch

ten. I have since discovered her father was named Timothy and his parents, Bernard and Julia MacDermott, lived in County Roscommon towards the end of the 18th century, but I don't know where exactly; it's one of the things I intend looking into some day. I hope they were supporters of Wolfe Tone and fought 'to break the connection with England, the never failing source of all our political evils'.

Be that as it may, by the time the sky had cleared, Charlie Symes had arranged to meet Lilian Gray in the same spot on the following Thursday, her half-day off. It was literally *un coup de foudre*. She fell, she once told me, for his jaunty bowler and the red carnation in the lapel of his muddy jacket. Six months later they were married and living in Meadow Street, where my grandfather had found a similar job with the Pontypridd Urban District Council. Their only child, my mother, was born in 1910.

Charlie Symes never went back to London and gradually, over the years, lost contact with his family. I must have relatives living in England, second cousins no doubt, whom I've never met and whose names I don't know. I do, however, have a dim recollection of some English people coming to stay with us in Meadow Street just after the war. What I remember about the visit is that we took them up the Barry Mountain for a picnic and I terrified them by rolling down the hillside and disappearing into the ferns – they thought I'd gone over the edge.

Who was it said the difference between the Welsh and the English is like the difference between Christmas pudding and Christmas cake – they're made of the same ingredients but cooked in a different way?

It was the presence of my English grandfather that served as grit in the oyster as far as my awareness of being Welsh was concerned. There seemed to be a slight incongruity in the way he used the English language. We all spoke with a Welsh accent, of course, and by the time I was born he'd picked up our way of speaking during the thirty years he'd been in Wales. But his register could be quite different from ours and he'd use expressions that weren't in our idiom. One of his favourite exclamations was 'Godfrey and Daniel, blast-furnace manufacturers!' Sometimes he'd use even more vivid phrases –

some rhyming slang, perhaps, or the patter of the music-hall – that seemed to have an exotic charm of its own. And so it was I pricked up my ears to the nuances of the English language, as I came not only to recognize my grandfather's otherness, but also to see the rest of our family, and myself, in a new light. It was a slow, subtle, imperceptible process, part of the complexity of late adolescence, I suppose.

Adam and Eve. Artful Dodger. Ascot Races. Almond Rocks. Aristotle. Apples and Pears.

Thursday, 12 September

I attended a meeting for new faculty at lunch-time today and had a pizza with a young woman who has come to teach at BYU this Semester. She told me she was cut off by her parents after she joined the Church. Like all young members of the faculty, she's on a year's probation and therefore anxious to make a good impression, in the hope of securing 'tenure' of appointment.

A student named Douglas Jole came to my office this afternoon and we talked for a while in Learner's Welsh. He's been on an Ulpan course in Lampeter, *ware teg*.

I remember the occasion when Euros Bowen and I were made Honorary Fellows at Lampeter in 1986. As the citation was read out, Euros kept on interrupting with corrections and improvements on what was being said about him, as we stood on the stage in full view of the congregation.

The reason why I see so few of my students around campus is that they all have part-time jobs, earning money with which to pay for their places at BYU. The only one I've seen more than once is a charming young man named Clint Graviet, who is always ready to chat and from whom I've gathered a good deal about student life on campus.

This evening I saw an excellent documentary about polygamy among the Mormons. It seems that while the Church officially banned the practice as long ago as 1890, in order to be admitted to the Union, there's a fundamentalist church that still practises it. There have been several attempts since 1945 to stamp it out but it persists among those who consider it an essential part of their religious life.

During Joseph Smith's lifetime, the official doctrine of the Church was monogamy. Yet he's reputed to have had at least thirty wives by the mid-1840s, some as young as 14. Urged by his brother, Hyrum, to seek divine guidance concerning 'plural marriage', he had a 'revelation' to the effect that it would not be adultery in God's eyes. Some of the Prophet's inner circle were appalled at this behaviour and told him so. The Governor of Illinois called Smith's conduct 'a very gross outrage' and said he should stand trial. Eventually the two Smiths turned themselves in at a gaol in a non-Mormon town. A mob burst in past the non-resisting guards and shot them both. Smith's death didn't bring an end to polygamy, however. In 1866 Brigham Young, who succeeded him as leader of the Church, declared, 'The only men who become gods, even the sons of God, are those who enter into polygamy.'

In 1890 the Supreme Court sanctioned the confiscation of all Mormon property, a move that was meant to suppress their faith. Shortly afterwards, the President of the Church, Wilford Woodruff, received a 'revelation' that prompted him to declare that plural marriage was no longer officially allowed. Handy things, 'revelations'.

Mormons who condemn the legacy of polygamy speak openly about it as a practice that was part of the pioneers' trials of faith. They speak of a surplus of women in Utah in the early days of the Church, though the Census showed roughly equal numbers of men and women at that time. The kindest conclusion I can draw is that the motivation for 'plural marriage' seems to have been spiritual. Only Mormon men are given the power of salvation and women gain access to the celestial kingdom only through their menfolk. Mormon women were drawn to men who, they believed, could guarantee eternal life. Brigham Young urged women to leave their husbands if they could find a man 'with higher power and authority', and many did.

Even after the Church Manifesto of 1890 officially put an end to 'plural marriage', thousands of fundamentalist Mormons continued to marry multiple wives in secret. Today, the Church says it regards anyone living in polygamy as no longer Mormon.

It's estimated there are between 40,000 and 100,000 such people in Utah, Idaho, Nevada, Arizona and California.

I am the most uxorious of men but I can't help thinking it must be very difficult to be married to more than one woman at a time.

I remember reading somewhere that the poet Islwyn had been engaged to Anne Bowen, but she died before they could be married. Out of his grief he wrote the long poem, '*Y Storm*' – twice. Nevertheless, he subsequently took a wife and lived with her for the rest of his life. But his love for Anne never left him. According to one witness who was with Islwyn as he lay on his death-bed, the poet addressed these last words to his wife: 'Thank you, Martha, for all you've done for me on this earth. You've been very kind. I'm going to Anne now.'

There was a difference between the characters of my grandfather and my father that was to prove crucial as far as I was concerned. My father was a quiet, reflective, cautious man who liked his own company best, having a natural reserve more typical of country people than of the urban proletariat. Whereas he was thrifty, conscientious, well-mannered and teetotal, my grandfather was talkative, gregarious, devil-may-care and fond of his pint. I can't recall ever seeing the two men in conversation, despite their having a trade in common, and I think the coldness between them was caused, at least in part, by my father's disapproval of the older man's bibulous ways.

It wasn't until my grandparents died in the late 1950s that my mother and father were able to spend more time on their own, both at home and in a small car they were at last able to afford. By then the long years they'd spent in the same house as my mother's parents had taken their toll, especially on my father. Ours was a happy home, with lots of love and laughter in it, but the tension between the two men cast a shadow which, even as a boy, I could sense though not understand. Although I don't recall any flaming rows, there was, I think, a smouldering resentment on my father's part that he had to share a home with his in-laws, and in such a small house there was ample opportunity for friction. But there was economic advantage, too, and that was almost certainly why they lived under the same roof, especially after the birth of us boys, for the basic cost of running the home was thus halved and everything else was shared. Even so, my father didn't get on with my grandfather. I sometimes think, whenever I find myself being tugged in opposite directions, that it's my father and my grandfather still failing to see eye to eye in me.

Remember Vigny's wolf:

> *Gémir, pleurer, prier est également lâche:*
> *Fais énergiquement ta longue et lourde tâche*
> *Dans la voie où le Sort a voulu t'appeler,*
> *Puis, après, comme moi, souffre et meurs sans parler.*

Friday, 13 September

Today I took the bus to Salt Lake City for the first time. The route was down the Wasatch Valley, wide with poor soil and grey barren mountains on either side, through Orem, Lehi and American Fork. We passed, on the floor of the Valley, the Geneva Steel Works, an enormous installation not unlike Port Talbot, built during the second world war, with smoke and flames gushing from its chimneys and giving the impression, in such a bleak landscape, of great man-made energy and a certain kind of grandeur. I felt like calling out to my fellow-passengers, just as Emile Verhaeren did when he saw the fires from the smelting works in the lower Swansea Valley: '*Ah, que c'est beau ! Que c'est beau!*' But I didn't.

We also passed the Utah State Penitentiary, which I'd seen all lit up as Leslie and Kitty drove me from the airport on my first night here. The lights were still on but it looked a grim place even in daylight. This is where Garry Gilmore was executed by firing squad for shooting two Mormons in Orem and Provo in 1976. He went to his death willingly, in full awareness of the Mormon doctrine of the Blood Atonement, thus throwing the legal system into chaos, as Norman Mailer has shown in his gripping book, *The Executioner's Song*. After a year of legal wrangling while the prisoner languished on Death Row, Gilmore addressed the firing squad with the words, 'Let's do it!' He was the first person to be executed in Utah after the death penalty was reintroduced in 1976.

Another execution comes to mind: that of Joe Hillstrom, leader of the Wobblies (Industrial Workers of the World), a federation of industrial unions formed in Chicago in 1905. Dedicated to the overthrow of capitalism by direct means, it called general strikes and went in for sabotage. Many members refused to fight in the first world war, which they saw as a struggle between capitalists. Joe Hillstrom was shot on a trumped-up charge of committing a murder in Salt Lake City.

> I dreamt I saw Joe Hill last night, alive as you and me,
> Says I, But Joe you're ten years dead,
> I never died, says he, I never died, says he.
>
> From Santiago up to Maine, in every mine and mill,
> Where workers strike and organize,
> It's there you'll find Joe Hill, it's there you'll find Joe Hill.

Salt Lake City is indeed a city compared with Provo, but not all that extensive. It has some good shops, many office blocks and a few tall buildings which don't quite qualify as skyscrapers. I began the day about 11am with a guided tour of Temple Square which included the showing of two short films. Within the walls stands the huge Temple of the Latter-day Saints, which is not open to Gentiles, that is to say non-Mormons; it has gardens and fountains at the front and a golden statue of Moroni, son of Mormon, stands twelve feet high in the compound. The tour guides are young Mormon 'sisters', pretty, very earnest and reeling off their spiel like clockwork. There's no religious hard-sell but visitors are encouraged to request a free copy of *The Book of Mormon*. The tour takes in the Tabernacle with its superb acoustics (you can, of course, hear the proverbial pin drop from anywhere in the vast auditorium) and an organ with more than a thousand pipes.

The modern history of Utah began with the founding of Salt Lake City in 1847. The region was still officially part of Mexico but the United States won it after the Mexican wars. The first Mormon settlers named it the State of Deseret, but this was changed to Territory of Utah (after the Ute Indians) when non-Mormons objected. The name Deseret means 'honeybee' and was taken from the *Book of Mormon*; the official notepaper of BYU is enbossed with a beehive. Brigham Young was elected Governor of Utah and the territory was admitted to the Union in 1896. Today the State has a population of about two and three quarter millions – roughly the same as Wales – of whom three quarters live between Provo in the south and Ogden in the north, including Salt Lake City.

I soon found Sam Weller's Bookshop, where I spent three delightful hours browsing the shelves of the large second-hand sections on the balconies. I bought two books for Huw: one about Native Americans and the other an encyclopaedia of magic. For myself I bought a copy of *archy and mehitabel*, which I've always enjoyed, a very nice limited edition of *A Shropshire Lad*, and a first, signed, American edition of Kipling's *Songs for Youth*, with the author's bookplate and a sheet of his personal writing paper headed 'Bateman's, Burwash, Sussex', dated 27 October 1925, tipped in. All for $12.

I also went to see the Great Salt Lake at close quarters. It is, in fact, an inland sea about eighty miles long and thirty-five wide, and only thirty feet deep at its deepest point, although its surface area and depth are constantly changing. The saline content is about six times that of the ocean, and second only to that of the Dead Sea, so that it has great buoyancy and bitterness. There's a story, apocryphal I'm sure, that when Brigham Young was told of the lake's existence during the Great Trek into Utah, it was said to be a fresh-water lake, whereupon he gave orders to have it salted: the Mormon pioneers were not supposed to enjoy themselves. The Lake is quite near the city but, when the water's low, as it was today, it can hardly be seen from the highway. Beyond the barren salt-flats the dull grey-green water is visible only as a thin line in the far distance. The lake's waters can be choppy and hazardous but this afternoon there were a few boats out, as well as thousands of gulls, though what they were after is hard to say because nothing much lives in the Lake.

For supper I had ravioli out of a tin and then watched an instalment of *Brideshead Revisited* on tv. *Hei leiff.*

I think of the Housman family motto: '*Aquila non captat muscas*', perhaps because the shore of the Lake is plagued with gnats. Housman was once offered an honorary degree by the University of Wales and turned it down. I checked Sam Weller's today in the hope of finding a copy of *A Shropshire Lad* inscribed by Housman 'to Moses Jackson, with love', but no such luck.

Saturday, 14 September

Today I was driven by Brian and Lorna Best, both members of the English Department, to Kamas and Park City, up in the Uinta Mountains to the east of Provo. It snowed hard as the road climbed to about 7,500 feet and it was bitterly cold, even in the car. We stopped to visit several Mormon cemeteries, for no apparent reason except the Bests seemed to draw some pleasure from inspecting the tombstones, a pastime to which I myself am not averse. It was noticeable that none of the graves was marked with a Christian cross.

We reached our destination at Park City, a former mining village which has been developed into a ski-resort and artists' colony. It had quite a few craftshops and art-galleries in its main street. At Texas Red's restaurant we ate huge steaks and then drove home through some particularly spectacular scenery. Fall is about to begin and, higher up, the trees were already turning red, yellow and orange.

In 1949, thanks to the teaching of Don Herbert at Parc Lewis, I passed the 11+ exam in second position out of 120 boys who went on to the Grammar School that year. The top boy was Brian Reed, who left school before his CWB, as O Levels were called in those days, and I haven't seen or heard of him since.

Of all my teachers at the Grammar School, the only one I recall with gratitude, if not with much affection, is Jack Reynolds, the martinet who taught me French. I was thoroughly grounded in the structure of the language and still know the preterite and past subjunctive forms of all the verbs.

I was about fifteen when my mother asked me whether I knew where babies came from. I said I did, though how they got there was still something of a mystery to me and it was never formally explained. My first experience of girls was running after them down backlanes on dark winter nights and being terrified lest I caught up with them. I learnt a lot about the female form from a girl who was given to taking off her clothes for us boys to admire her body in the privacy of the Bute woods, for which privilege we rewarded her with boiled sweets. I don't know what became of her but she had the makings of *une grande horizontale*.

I was asked today whether I'd write a Culturgram on Wales.

This would be for a series of brochures describing the cultural and social situation in countries where the Church sends its missionaries. I said I would, if only to get a copy of the old brochure and see what they know of Wales. The fee is $300. 'No blockhead ever wrote except for money,' said the good doctor.

Some American culinary terms: splash of red, moo juice, belch water, sea dust, java, looseners, shingles with a shimmy, burn the British, axle grease, zeppelins in a fog.

Sunday, 15 September

I had lunch today at the home of Ron Dennis and his wife, Grace-Marie. He told me more about his illustrious ancestor, Captain Dan Jones (1811-61) of Caerfallwch, who was with Joseph Smith when the Prophet was killed by the mob in 1844. Captain Dan had been converted while ferrying a group of Mormons up the Mississippi and became a leading proseletyzer on behalf of the Saints. He brought several cohorts of Mormons from Wales and even founded a Welsh-language newspaper, *Prophwyd y Jubili*, in Merthyr. He sailed from Liverpool in 1849 with about 250 converts and again in 1856 with 700.

It seems that many Welsh widows brought their husbands'clothes with them in expectation of seeing them again in Utah – which is one of the most poignant things I've heard about the Mormons so far.

At lunch, after we'd all gone down on our knees to thank God for this our food, I committed a *faux pas* while trying to amuse my hosts. Around the table sat about a dozen children, some Dennises and others their friends, from the age of about three to eighteen. The teenagers showed polite interest in the fact I was from overseas and asked me all sorts of naïve questions about life in the Yookay – did I live in a castle and had I ever met the Queen, that sort of thing. At one point I told them we drove on the left and, just for fun, informed them that this rule was about to change. As from next January, I said, all lorries (I said trucks) would have to drive on the right, and if the experiment were a success, all cars would have to do the same as from next April. They believed me, of course, until Pop told them I wasn't speaking the truth and changed the subject.

My salary when I started teaching French at Ebbw Vale Grammar School in 1962, my first job, was £1,070. I recall the high spirits in which we used to go down to the Education Authority offices at the end of each month to collect our cheques. At the age of 24, I was the youngest member of staff, all the others being over forty. Of my colleagues I can remember only a few: Olwen and Dewi Samuel, who taught Welsh and Latin and had been editors of the magazine, *Y Crynhoad*; Tom Davies, the Art Master who'd known the painters Cedric Morris, Heinz Köppel and Arthur Giardelli when they worked in the Settlement at Gwernllwyn House in Dowlais during the 1940s; Idwal Davies, the Biology teacher, who used to give me a lift across the mountain in his car every day; Wynne Roberts, the English master, a Rhondda man who'd been at Oxford with Gwyn Thomas; Eddie Jones, a fine historian who later became Head of a Catholic school in Port Talbot; Marsden Evans, the PE master, whose wife, a native of the Outer Hebrides, had died from the effects of Ebbw Vale's polluted atmosphere; and the Headmaster, R.C. Smith, a remote and morose figure who had been brought up near Rhosllannerchrugog, with whom I never exchanged more than a few vatic words, none in Welsh.

The most exotic member of staff was Aleksandr Moncibowic, a Ukrainian who had come to the Yookay after the war and was head of Mathematics at Ebbw Vale. He'd had a most disastrous military career: he'd fought in the Ukrainian Army against the Poles, and lost; in the Polish Army against the Germans, and lost; and in the German Army against the Russians, and lost again. Monty, as we called him, had only a shaky grasp of the nuances of demotic English as it was spoken in Ebbw Vale and often caused hilarity in the staff-room. He used to mix up his idioms and say things like, 'You are a spanner in the grass' and 'One swallow does not make a silver lining'. Once, during a heated debate, someone told him he knew bugger all about politics, at which he grew very indignant. 'Yes,' he retorted, 'I know bugger all, and you know bugger nothing!' When I had a fortnight off in March 1966 to stand as the Plaid Cymru candidate in Merthyr, Monty and the Samuels were the only ones among my colleagues to wish me well.

Milwyn Jenkins, a native of Ynysybwl and, like me, an old boy of Pontypridd Boys' Grammar School, was Head of French but he wouldn't let me teach the sixth form, so I left Ebbw Vale after four years and joined the *Western Mail* in Cardiff.

On my last day at the school I was chatting with some sixth-formers, including Patrick Harrington, now a distinguished barrister, and Robat Powel who won the Chair at the National Eisteddfod in 1985 with a fine *cywydd* on industrial themes, and they told me the nicknames by which the teachers were known. I knew the boys quite well because we used to meet behind the stage during the lunch-hour to play records of Irish rebel songs. I ventured to ask what they called me and they said, 'Noddy, Sir'. When I asked why, I learned that it had been my habit, while on after-school duty, to come into a classroom, clap my hands and say, 'Time to go home!', just like the puppet on the tv show. I'd thought it might be Spike, the name by which I was known among my own school-mates.

> When this long, last term is over,
> Oh, how happy I shall be –
> One more week of minding children
> Then all summer I'll be free.
>
> Only one more full assembly;
> Keep the tears from my eyes
> When, before the school, we utter
> Our ambiguous goodbyes.
>
> Only one more set of marking,
> Only one more cheque to cash,
> One more prowl around the playground,
> One more lunch of spam and mash.
>
> No more proses, verbs or grammar,
> No more chalk dust in my hair,
> No more pipes and stale discussions
> In the staff-room's stifling air.

No more jokes from Ron and Idwal,
No more bawling from the Head,
No more speaking Welsh in corners,
No more servitude. Instead –

On that fine and final morning
All good manners I'll resist
When I tell the Senior Master
Where to put his duty list!

A pupil in Ebbw Vale, when asked the names of the three men who were thrown into the fiery furnace, replied, 'Richard, Thomas and Baldwin, Sir.'

I heard the other day, before coming here, about an English family who recently settled in a Welsh-speaking village in Montgomeryshire where the *Plygain* is still sung on Christmas morning. Each family in the district has its own words and music from a large repertoire which goes back to pre-Reformation times, and they are very beautifully sung in something between a chant and a carol. Last Christmas, when these incomers were called upon to play their part in the service, they sang 'Jingle bells, jingle bells, jingle all the way'. People do not cross national frontiers without bringing a lot of baggage with them – as I'm finding here in Utah.

Monday, 16 September

A letter today from Huw, now ten, asking whether there's a magic shop in Provo; there is, of course, in one of the Malls. He's doing a lot of shows these days and charging £15 a time, mainly at children's parties and old folks' homes. He has even been on tv as a conjuror – twice. So he has some money to spend on tricks. In his letter he tells me it's his ambition to do his magic on radio. He also says he gave a classmate fifty pence to take his place in a folk-dancing group at school. That's my boy!

I had better write down some of the Tom Swifties that John Harris has given me – before I forget them. They are attributed to a writer named Atherton in whose books the characters never say anything but shout excitedly or exclaim enthusiastically or murmur inaudibly. The new craze consists of choosing an adverb which makes a pun on the meaning of what's gone before. Here are some examples: 'But I like sweet pancakes,' he said surreptitiously; 'I'm as hungry as a sled dog,' he said huskily; 'Though I've said it three times wrong, this time I'll get it correct,' he said forthrightly; 'Thanks, Monsieur,' he said mercifully; 'But I like sad fairy tales,' he said grimly; and so on to screaming point.

Just before I came here I was in the post office in Whitchurch, handing in some bilingual form or other, and as I was about to leave the man behind the counter called out, 'Oi, come back, you haven't llofnodied it!'

Tuesday, 17 September

Two students came to see me today, the first of whom, a lad named George Weatherington, wanted to talk about homosexuality. It was the usual story: he wasn't one himself but had several friends who were. He described himself as 'a rebel Mormon' in revolt against the Church because of the pressures it put on members to conform. Church attendance is obligatory for all students and the Mormon culture at BYU he found narrow and suffocating. We discussed the Mormon view of homosexuality, which is anathema to the Saints, and I told him what I could about the law and attitudes in the Yookay. When I asked why he'd chosen to come and see me, he said I had a reputation among students for being 'a Liberal', which means of course I'm not a right-wing Republican, as most Mormons are, and someone whom they found sympathetic.

BYU is a well-known source of recruits for the CIA.

The second student to call on me was Winston Barrows, a pleasant lad I met when he and his fellow-missionary, by chance, called at our home in Cardiff earlier this year. It was the first time I'd received a visit from the Saints and I invited them in to hear what they had to say. It was from them I first heard the preposterous story about the planet Kolob where God and his wife, presumably Mrs God, and their spirit children are said to dwell, and about the Mormon Heaven, where only Mormons 'in good standing' go. Elder Barrows, as the missionaries style themselves, was on a flying visit to Provo and had thought to look me up.

On my way home I saw the hauling down of Old Glory on campus, a ceremony that takes place every evening at sundown, though this was the first time for me to witness it. Everyone stood to attention and with hand on heart, which I had hitherto seen only in films. Very touching.

I think Mormonism may have most appeal in the Yookay among those who want to become Americans, consciously or subconsciously; a lot of people do. We are all Americanized to a lesser or greater extent, in what we eat, what we watch on tv, what we wear, what we sing, what we do in our leisure time, and in the way we speak.

I've always been a bit bothered by the Red Dragon as the national flag of Wales. No one knows where it came from, unless the Romans brought it to Britain. It's very difficult to draw, especially for children, and there are scores of different versions of it. The red is often indistinct against the green background and 'reads' as black. We must be one of the few peoples in the world who aren't sure what our national flag looks like.

The words 'Y ddraig goch ddyry cychwyn' are from a *cywydd* by Deio ab Ieuan Du in which he asks his patron for the loan of a bull. The 'red dragon' refers to the bull's sexual organ, something Madge probably wasn't told in 1953 when she agreed to accept the symbol and motto as part of the royal badge in Wales.

I don't suppose the Welsh will ever be persuaded to abandon the Red Dragon, and I wouldn't want them to. I think it should be kept as one of our national banners, rather like the Plough and the Stars in Ireland. But I wonder whether it might be a good time to introduce a tricolour as well. The colours red, white and green could be kept, of course, but the stripes need not be the same as the French *tricouleur*: there could be a narrow green stripe on the hoist side, then a white strip of the same breadth, and the rest of the flag could be red, in the ratio 1: 1 : 4. I'd prefer, as a heraldic device, the cross of St David, gold on a black background, to the problematic Red Dragon.

Wednesday, 18 September

I rang home today and was shocked to hear Michael Parnell died yesterday while on holiday with Mary in France; he was 57. I am more upset by this news than by the death of anyone in many a year, except for my father's in 1984.

Mike was a fine man and a good friend to me, through thick and thin. I wrote immediately to Mary to express something of my grief and my sympathy for her and the children. I found it more than ordinarily difficult, not because I didn't know him well enough or feel real affection for him, but because we were particularly close and I haven't yet come to terms with his sudden death.

I recall the Cornish burr in his voice, his grin, his dab hand at the word-processor, his passion for collecting books which filled every room in the house and the garage, the heavy black bike on which he rode around Cardiff, his sartorial preference most kindly described as Oxonian rat-catcher, and more than all, his devotion to Mary and their children. When we went to the Soviet Union last year, it was the first time Mike had been away from Mary since their wedding day, and he talked about her incessantly.

I didn't feel like doing much for the rest of the day, so back to Wymount Terrace for the afternoon with a newspaper I've managed to find. On the way up the hill I called at the Dairy and treated myself to a large ice cream. It's not often a dairy appears in a diary. The lad who served me had spent a year as a missionary in Cardiganshire and had a few phrases of Welsh. I ate my double cornet quietly at a table, thinking all the while about Mike Parnell. He was such a great talker and I never tired of him!

Almost all the news in the *Daily Universe* is about Utah. Provo and Orem have recently been named as the places where, in all the US, the quality of life is highest, and on tv this evening I heard that a nationwide survey has pronounced Utah the healthiest State in the Union. How they decide these things isn't clear. It may have something to do with the absence of serious crime and an excellent health service.

I remember John Ormond once telling me he'd known a sub on the *Swansea Evening Post* who was sacked for writing the headline, 'Swansea Man Weds Swansea Woman in Swansea'.

I'm beginning to perceive a smug or 'goody-goody' strain in the Mormon character. They openly admit they are striving for perfection, 'to be like Christ', which takes some getting used to by an old agnostic like me. Certainly they seem happy – it radiates from them – but I can't help feeling there must be a darker side to it all, and that it has to do with the pressure to conform and obey the preposterous teachings of the Church in every detail. The atmosphere on campus is that of a large school whose Headmaster is never seen but widely feared and where the slightest misdemeanour will be reported. I notice, too, in class, whenever a controversial topic comes up, there's one student who always speaks for the others, as if he's been appointed so to do, like a commissar. The feeling I get sometimes is the one I've had in the Soviet Union, where an equally rigid and all-encompassing regime holds sway and woe betide anyone who challenges it. The feeling makes me a bit mosed in the chine.

'Longtemps, je me suis couché de bonne heure . . .'

Thursday, 19 September
This evening I went with Leslie and Kitty to a concert given by the Utah Symphony Orchestra on campus. It was the first time for me to wear a suit since I've been here. I expected *le tout Provo* to be present but didn't see any of the English faculty during the interval. This, I think, was one of the rare occasions when 'high' culture comes to Provo. There are theatres and cinemas and concert halls in Salt Lake City but if they exist here in Provo, I've seen little evidence of them.

'Culture is the steam off the back of a galloping horse.'

People are very proud of the health and medical services in Utah. On the other hand, Utah is said to be the State with the highest consumption of anti-depressants: Prozac prescriptions, for example, are about 60 per cent above the national average. Death rates from cancer and heart disease are lower than in the rest of the country, but diabetes is higher. Utah has been called 'the land of milk and cookies': sugar is the preferred vice.

One of my earliest memories is of the smallpox epidemic in

Pontypridd when I was about ten. Several people died of it, including Dr Hodgkinson, who'd been looking after people afflicted with the disease. Years later, when I first heard of Hodgkinson's Disease, I thought smallpox was meant. The day of his funeral we were all told to stay indoors. The streets were washed with white disinfectant and the ambulance that brought the doctor's body from East Glamorgan Hospital to Glyn-taf Crematorium raced down Llantwit Road with all its lights flashing and its siren wailing. It was preceded and followed by police outriders wearing masks, in a cortege that struck terror in the hearts of all who saw it, including mine.

Friday, 20 September
This morning I went to a BYU library book sale, but was disappointed to find nothing I wanted to buy. While I was rummaging among a pile of magazines, I fell into conversation with a student named Byron Evans whose forebears, he told me proudly, were from Llangyfelach, where he's never been. I told him it was a great place with a thriving culture of its own and the birth-place of many scholars and patriots. He's learning Welsh and bought a run of Owen Edwards's magazine, *Wales,* in the sale.

Later in the day I went looking for Noël Owen, a Welsh-speaker, I'd been told, who taught in the Chemistry Department. As I was invited to sit down in his office I took one glance at him and saw that he looked remarkably like Ifor Owen of Pen-y-bont-fawr in Montgomeryshire, who shared digs with me at the Sun Hotel in North Parade in Aberystwyth during the late 1950s, and whom I haven't seen since. Ifor had been doing research in Zoology and we'd got on well. He was a bit too *duwiol* for the other lads, going to chapel of a Sunday morning with a hymnal under his arm and not wasting his substance in riotous living like the rest of us, but I learned a bit of Welsh from him and he was a gentle, good-natured lad with a ready grin. Noël was indeed the brother of my co-digger and seemed pleased that I knew him.

He told me, in fluent Welsh, that he'd been converted to Mormonism by missionaries who had called at his home in Menai Bridge in the days when he'd been a lecturer at Bangor. He and his wife had embraced the Church and brought their young family to Provo, where he now has a Chair in Chemistry and a splendid new laboratory. His brother, Ifor, has been for many years in Papua-New Guinea where he has an important job as an adviser to the government.

On local tv this evening I noticed that all expletives, even the commonest like 'God!' and 'Damn!', had been deleted with a beep.

I'm glad I eventually learned Welsh shortly after marrying Ruth in 1965. I was a member of Plaid Cymru for about seven years before I knew the language. My motives were primarily personal: I didn't want to bring up children in a linguistically mixed home. Ruth's parents, and her brothers and sister, were all staunchly Welsh-speaking, and gave me every encouragement; in fact, I've never spoken English to any of them. A few years ago Ruth's mother, Nain, told me that when I first started going to their home they all thought I was a nice, quiet lad but soon learned, as I became more fluent, that the reason why I hadn't been saying much was because I hadn't yet mastered the language.

The ability to speak and read Welsh has given me immense satisfaction. When one speaks the language one knows so much more about the history of the country and the ability to read it has opened up for me a literature in which I take great pleasure. I'm also glad we've brought up four children with Welsh as their first language. There are quite a few eminent Welshmen of whom the same cannot be said.

Saturday, 21 September

'Owain went into hiding on St Matthew's Day in Harvest, and thereafter his hiding-place was unknown. Very many say that he died; the seers maintain he did not.' I once paid for these words to be inserted in the *In Memoriam* column of *The Times*.

This morning, the day of Mike Parnell's funeral, I wanted to be alone with my memories of him, so I rose early and walked up Provo Canyon as far as the trail goes, to an altitude of about 7,000 feet. Soon I could see the summit of Mount Timpanogos, at 11,750 feet the Snowdon of these parts. By 10 am it was very hot. I walked for six hours and caught the sun as it came up over the mountains to the east. The Fall is now well under way, the aspens and scrub-oaks on the lower slopes a blaze of crimson, saffron and burgundy. There was a solitary eagle circling above the tree-line, there were elk and beaver in the forest, and I saw butterflies and flowers for which I had no names. I half-expected to meet a Ute or Navajo, for this is wild country, but saw no one. Just as the trail began to grow precipitous and I could go no further I found myself on the brim of an enormous amphitheatre, as deep as it was wide and filled with silver-green pines. In the far distance, shimmering in the heat, I could make out the Wasatch range stretching for hundreds of miles, and beyond lay the deserts of Arizona.

'Deserts of vast eternity'. The image makes me groan.

Overwhelmed by the panoramic view, I decided that this was the spot at which I should like to commemorate my friend. But how? I sat for a while in the sunshine, taking in the splendour of the mountains and remembering Mike and all the happy times we'd had in each other's company, particularly his Heraclitean appetite for talk, literature, and life. Then, with all the force I could muster, I shouted his name into the clear air of the canyon: 'Michael Par-nell!' The sound ricocheted against the red sandstone bluffs for a few seconds and, before the echoes had quite died away, I was on my way back down the trail into the valley of the Great Salt Lake. I shall never see my friend again and now I've said goodbye to him.

This evening, after a snoooze, I went to Salt Lake City with Leslie and Kitty to see a ballet version of *Anna Karenina* put on by Ballet West, a local company. I don't like ballet but sat through this performance dutifully because I'd commented to Leslie about the dearth of cultural events in Provo. The best bit was at the end, when Anna threw herself under the locomotive, which was wheeled slowly onto the stage in a cloud of real steam and with loud clanking.

After the show, we went to the New Yorker, the poshest restaurant in town, as guests of the people who run Ballet West. Two of the ballerinas were there, as well as the conductor and a man who said he was from Swansea. We had an excellent supper, with lots of expensive wine and about eight courses. I had lobster soup and, to finish, apple tart about as good as my mother makes; no faggots, though. One of the ballerinas was a tiny blonde, pretty enough and dizzy with it. At one point during the meal someone used, in the same sentence, the phrase 'and so on, *ad infinitum et ad nauseam*', at which she exclaimed, 'Whadya mean, Adam and Eve in the garden of Eden?' There was a moment of embarrassed silence, broken only when one of our hosts ordered some more wine, and the table talk resumed.

Why is it Parma ham but Parmesan cheese? After all, they both come from Parma. I asked the Italian waiter at the New Yorker this evening, but he couldn't tell me. And is there still a Charterhouse in Parma?

Henri Beyle. Louis Farigole. Michel Eyquem. Alexis Saint-Léger. Isidore Ducasse. Jean-Baptiste Poquelin. Wilhelm Kostrowitzky.

Sunday, 22 September

This afternoon I walked for two or three hours into the mountains behind Wymount, but found I was stiff after yesterday's exertions. I rang home at 5pm for a last-minute chat with Ruth before she sets out to join me. The rest of the day was spent reading a diary of the first world war, *Some Desperate Glory* by Edwin Campion Vaughan.

The war I remember, just about, is the second. I have a faint recollection of Lord Haw-Haw announcing on the wireless that the Luftwaffe was going to bomb Meadow Street, Long Row and Raymond Terrace, though I think it was talk of it, rather than the broadcast itself, that I heard. People used to light fires on Mynydd Meio and the Garth to attract the bombers and several dropped their loads on open country. I certainly recall ration books and the issue of gas-masks. When the enamel numberplate on our back door disappeared one day, my father told me it had gone to make a bullet to kill a German, and I was glad. I remember, too, the street parties at the end of the war against the Japanese and the dancing and singing that went on into the night, though I can't recall hearing anything about Hiroshima or Nagasaki.

I once had a most eloquent but almost wordless exchange with a man in Orzhonikidze, on the northern side of the Caucasus. The name of the town sounds like 'Old Johnny Keatsy' but this was about the poet, Byron. After a reading put on as part of the Pushkin Festival, an old man came up to me in the foyer of the theatre where I'd read some poems in Welsh to an audience of 6,000, and with a beaming face, said, 'Ah, Byron!'. I replied, 'Yes, Byron!', to which he responded with 'Ah, Byron! Byron!'. I felt all I could do was match him, so I said, 'Yes, Byron! Byron!' But this wasn't enough for him. 'Byron! Byron! Byron!' he exclaimed. I was about to give up byroning when, with tears rolling down his cheeks, he suddenly grasped me by the shoulders and gave me the biggest bear-hug I've ever received, and all the while shouting 'Byron! Byron! Byron!' We parted not in silence but half broken-hearted and in tears – at least on his part.

Monday, 23 September

'On the twenty-third day of September there were two bold young boyos who went to the mountains of green Merioneth from the black mining valleys of Gwent.' *Je me cite, alors!* I remember Dai Pritchard and Dai Walters with great affection and intend writing a short story about them one of these days. I shall call it 'The Third Man'.

Today, advised by Vern Thornton, a friend of Leslie's, I rented a car from a firm called Freedom; it's a grey-blue Chevrolet (but without an air-bag) and the price was $1,328 for three months. I tried it out by driving up Provo Canyon to Sundance, where I had an ice cream in the empty restaurant. The trees are now so red the mountains look as if they're ablaze.

Just after 7pm Noël Owen called at Wymount offering to take me up Provo Canyon and I didn't have the heart to tell him I'd just come down from there. Afterwards he took me to meet his wife, Pat, and some of their children, at their home overlooking Provo. Pat, who's from Llanfechain in Montgomeryshire, could remember Margaret, Ruth's sister, who was at Bangor at the same time as she was, and it was nice to hear her speak of my sister-in-law as Margaret Meredith.

Both Pat and Noël are very pleasant people. Katie, one of their daughters, a delightful young woman who'd gone to school in Menai Bridge, could remember a few Welsh songs and sang them prettily, but the younger children had no knowledge of Wales. The parents seemed not to regret the uprooting of their family in the least and to accept that their children would grow up as good Americans – and, more importantly, as good Mormons. When I asked, out of curiosity, what they would do if a friend turned out to be homosexual, they replied they would pray for him and ask him 'to pull himself together and mend his ways'. If their Church were to admit homosexuals, said Pat, it would be an apostate church and they would leave it. Where would they go, I wonder?

'Braint, braint yw cael cymdeithas gyda'r Saint.'

Tuesday, 24 September
Having driven down to the Department today, I was booked by the campus wardens for parking without a permit. I had to go to the administrative offices and plead ignorance of the parking regulations, whereupon they let me off. 'Go, and sin no more,' they said, or words to that effect.

After lunch in the Cougareat, I went to a faculty/student tea-party (except there was no tea) where I shared a table with two of my students, Jack O'Harrell and George Weatherington, both of whom show some promise as poets and were obviously enjoying the chance to talk to me in a social context. Cynthia Hallen, a new member of the English staff, who has moved to a flat under mine, joined us, but otherwise none of my colleagues spoke to me.

BYU has a College Song that begins, 'Rise, all loyal Cougars and hurl your challenge to the foe!' It's awful, but no worse than the old Aber song: 'Rage, ye gales, ye surges, seethe . . . '. One of the pleasures of undergraduate life in my day was gathering in the Old Exam Hall for a singsong lasting about an hour before the weekly debate began. Much of what we sang were Welsh hymns but we also enjoyed bawdy songs like 'O Sir Jasper' and political ones like *'Bandiera Rossa'*.

This afternoon and evening I spent several hours reading the first batch of proofs for the *Oxford Literary Guide to Britain and Ireland*. They were very clean, not a typo to be seen, and the pictures are superb. I've worked hard in preparing this second edition, writing large parts of it myself, and the result is impressive, if I may say so with the better part of pride.

Dan ei faich mae dyn i fod.

I talked to John Harris today about palindromes. The longest one I could offer him was 'A man, a plan, a canal – Panama' and, in Welsh, '*A dyma'r addewid diweddar am y da*'. John capped these with: 'T. Eliot, top bard, notes putrid tang emanating, is sad. I'd assign it a name: Gnat dirt upset on drab pot toilet.'

Tomorrow Ruth and Huw will be here.

Wednesday, 25 September
At Leslie and Kitty's house this afternoon he asked me, out of the blue, who was the most famous person I've ever met. Quick as a flash, I said, 'Eamon de Valera.' Leslie pressed me to say how I'd met him. It was like this. One afternoon in a Dublin bar we happened to see in the telephone directory a number for the President of the Republic. John Davies (Bwlchyllan) immediately rang it and we were astonished to find ourselves being invited to call on De Valera. Only in Ireland, only in Ireland, as Flann O'Brien used to say.

Next day we turned up at the Presidential residence and with only the minimum of formalities ('Would you mind giving us your names, please?') we were asked to wait in an ante-room. A moment later we were ushered into the Grand Old Man's presence in the office where he gave audiences to anyone who wanted to see him. By this time Dev was nearly blind, but still a tall, gaunt impressive figure, with the *fainne* in his lapel signifying his ability to speak Irish – the only decoration he wore. We talked for well over the allotted half-hour, mainly about Wales and the Welsh language, on which the President appeared to be well-informed.

Then, as we were about to take our leave, he leant conspiratorially across his desk and uttered these words to his young Welsh visitors: 'In my position they won't let me talk politics, you know. But I'd just like to say this: I hope that something of what you want for your country will come true during your lifetime, as it has done for my country during mine.' It was a blessing from the hero of Boland's Mill and it has lodged in my memory these thirty years.

Then it was time to drive in the Chevrolet, with Leslie and Kitty, to Salt Lake City, where Ruth and Huw arrived at 8.30pm. We had an excellent supper at the Norrises' and then up to Wymount, where Ruth and Huw fell fast asleep, just as I had on my first night here. It gave me great pleasure to see them again after a month's absence. After they'd gone to bed, I made myself a cup of coffee from the jar Ruth brought with her, mine having run out a few days ago.

'*Auprès de ma blonde, qu'il fait bon, fait bon, fait bon . . .*'

Thursday, 26 September

I left Ruth and Huw abed and went down to campus to teach my morning class, after which I came back to fetch them and we had lunch in the Cougareat. While I taught my afternoon class they strolled around campus and had an ice cream in the Dairy.

In the evening we drove up Provo Canyon to see Bridal Veil Falls, a spectacular two-level cascade that can be viewed from a parking area near the road. It's a bit like Water-break-its-neck in Radnorshire, but then most waterfalls are like one another. Near by there's a restaurant and craft-shop where I saw jackeroles for the first time. My students have told me about them – stuffed rabbits with small antlers sprouting from their heads – and now I realize they've been pulling my leg, for the jackerole is strictly for tourists, rather like the tins of fresh air sold on the summit of Snowdon. I bought a belt-buckle with a moose's head on it, though I don't suppose I shall ever wear it.

Ruth and Huw are still tired after their flight so we all had an early night.

'Strength and honour are her clothing and she will rejoice in time to come.'

Friday, 27 September

When Emile Verhaeren fell under the wheels of a train at Rouen station on 27 September 1916, seventy-five years ago today, his last words as he lay dying on the platform were, '*Je meurs. Ma femme. Ma patrie.*' Not a bad line with which to take one's exit from the world. One day I shall go to Saint-Amand and put flowers on his grave.

We drove up Provo Canyon and then on to Heber City and Park City to see the shops. Lunch at Texas Red's, where there's a flag, the Lone Star, above the bar and a cowboy ambience which Huw liked as much as I did. Then through Midway and back to Wymount by 7pm. A delightful day – we saw eagles, skunk and buffalo, or perhaps bison.

Ruth and I first met during the General Election in Merthyr in 1964 when Ioan Bowen Rees, her sister Margaret's husband, was the Plaid Cymru candidate and I was his agent. We went over the mountain in her small van to pick up his election address from the printer in Pentre and from then on I was smitten. We went out together for the first time in November of the same year, to a reading given by R. S. Thomas and Hugh MacDiarmid in Aberystwyth. Thomas was his usual glum self, and during MacDiarmid's part of the evening, seemed to be put out by the Scot's bravura performance, swinging his leg throughout in what looked like petulance. At one point MacDiarmid ribbed Thomas for including one of his poems in the *Penguin Book of Religious Verse*, pointing out that it was in fact a bawdy poem, but he made no response. After the reading, Thomas left on his own and we all adjourned to the Belle Vue to sit at the feet of MacDiarmid until the wee hours.

The next time I met MacDiarmid was in 1972, when Trevor Royle took me to his home, Brownsbank, by Biggar in Lanarkshire. I was able to tell him I'd married the woman who'd been with me that night seven years before. We talked mostly about Keir Hardie, for whom MacDiarmid had worked on the staff of the *Merthyr Pioneer*, and about T. E. Nicholas, the Marxist poet, whom he admired. Then, on Palm Sunday 1974 I drove him and his wife, Valda, together with Harri Webb, from Lampeter, where we were attending an Academi conference, to Strata Florida, where we paid our respects at the grave of Dafydd ap Gwilym.

It was on that occasion, too, I introduced MacDiarmid to Saunders Lewis, who was about to deliver his lecture on Guto'r Glyn. Each writer showed a polite interest in the other, MacDiarmid in his bantering way and Lewis with his usual patrician hauteur. The Scot says in his book, *The Company I've Kept*, that he had great admiration for Lewis, but the book was published in 1966, so he must have had the hero of Penyberth in mind rather than the writer because almost none of Lewis's major writings were available in English at that time and MacDiarmid, for all his polymathy, doesn't read Welsh.

The best man at our wedding in August 1965 was John Davies (Bwlchyllan), the first Secretary of *Cymdeithas yr Iaith*. Together we arranged for the first Welsh sign to be put up on a post office (at Llanymawddwy) in 1963 and we'd been among a small group, including John Daniel, who'd taken down the offending sign, Trevine, in Pembrokeshire and put up the correct form, Tre-fin, also painted by me. I'm not sure Bwlchyllan was with me on the night I painted 'Cofiwch Tryweryn' on the barn wall near Llanrhystud in Cardiganshire, but he always refers to it as 'an early Stephens' and to me as 'Signwriter to the Free Wales'.

I remember the Election campaign of 1964 because in those days there was a good deal of heckling at political meetings. At one, in Troed-y-rhiw, one of the speakers for the Labour candidate, S. O. Davies, was Elystan Morgan and the Chairman was Jim Griffiths. I'd been a distant admirer of Elystan's – it was he who'd defended 'the boys from Gwent' – and was among those many young people who were appalled when he left Plaid Cymru, of which he'd been Vice-President, less than a year before. When I asked how Elystan Morgan (not yet Labour MP for Cardiganshire and long before he became a peer of the realm) squared the poisonous nonsense that had been spoken about Plaid Cymru with his recent allegiance to that Party, there was a great snarl from the Labourites in the hall. Elystan remained silent in his seat, but Jim Griffiths leapt to his feet and, glaring and pointing at me, roared with all the rhetorical force he could muster, 'Young man, you have demeaned yourself! You don't know your history – the Welshman has an honourable tradition of turning his coat.' This piece of humbug was typical of old Jim and it stiffened the resolve of the young Nationalists present on that occasion.

'Tonight puts on perfection and a woman's name.'

Saturday, 28 September

Today we saw our first game of American football: BYU versus the Air Force, which the Cougars won, 21-7. The stadium holds 66,000 people and we were entertained before the game by a brass band, cheer-leaders and a display of falconry. I wouldn't have been surprised to see a real live cougar on a leash, so lavish was the carnival atmosphere. The spectators did the Mexican Wave and, determined to make it an all-American experience, we stuffed ourselves with pop-corn and hot-dogs. Before the game started the crowd fell silent for a prayer and then sang 'The Star-Spangled Banner', which I found quite moving.

It's important for a proper understanding of the anthem to know that it was written (by Francis Scott Key) in 1814, during the War of American Independence. While the British were bombarding Fort McHenry, the gateway to Baltimore, Key was aboard a British man-o'-war, where he'd been trying to negotiate the exchange of an American prisoner. He scribbled the poem on the back of an envelope (like so many masterpieces), when after a long night of anxious waiting, he saw, 'by the dawn's pearly light', that the Stars and Stripes were still flying over the fort. So the song, like '*La Marseillaise*', was written in response to a specific event, and may have lost something with the passing of time. Myself, I prefer 'America the Beautiful' as a more general expression of patriotism, but of course it's not up to me.

After the game, which lasted a full three hours, we went back to Wymount for tea and then down to the Mall in Provo, where Huw found the magic shop. He talked most authoritatively with the owner of Magimost and is clearly knowledgeable on the subject.

Wales is a strictly neutral country: we don't even interfere in our own affairs.

When I stood for Plaid Cymru in Merthyr at the General Election of March 1966 I was canvassing the Gurnos estate one afternoon when I was asked by a woman in curlers why Wales needed a Parliament of its own. 'To look after its own affairs,' I promptly replied. 'Oh,' she said, 'we don't have affairs up here, love. It's too cold. We do all go down to Ponty for that.'

Later that same day the dialectic continued when an old man told me he'd be voting Labour because he believed in the dictation of the secretariat.

Grizzled skipper. Spanish Festoon. False Apollo. Hungarian glider. Rock grayling. Black satyr. Arran brown. Chapman's ringlet. Southern gatekeeper. Fiery copper. Green hairstreak. False comma.

Sunday, 29 September

Today is my mother's 81st birthday, so we rang her, and she was thrilled. She still lives in the house in Meadow Street, number 50, where both she and I were born. The lymphoma for which she received chemotherapy in 1985 seems to have been held in check but she's a lot frailer these days. She was, until quite recently, a Junoesque figure who still retained something of the blonde good looks she had as a young woman. The treatment seems to have ravaged her body but not her spirit, which remains as indomitable as ever. On Sundays she goes to chapel (though Castle Square, not Libanus, there having been yet another split) and to a variety of meetings during the week and the occasional outing. She spends her day knitting prodigiously and doing her crossword, and the tv is on day and night. Fiercely independent, and insistent that she wants to remain in her own home until the end, when she does go out it's to do her own shopping or to collect her pension, with the help of the mini-buses that ply between Trefforest and Pontypridd, and she even shops for some of her more incapacitated neighbours. She refuses to have a cheque-book and all her business is done with cash that she keeps in a cardboard box under her bed.

I sometimes wish she'd had a job, because she's intelligent and capable, but my grandfather wouldn't let her work and kept her at home, where there was plenty for her to do. She'd done well at school but had to leave when she was fifteen because she was needed at home. In those days, among the working class, it was a point of honour for skilled men not to have wives who went out to work. So her days have been spent doing the myriad household chores on which the well-being of the family depended. With my grandmother's help, she put out the washing, scrubbed the front step and pavement once a week, and cleaned the windows whenever they needed doing, which was often in a village where the air was laden with grit from foundries, trains and factories. She also made and mended our clothes, did the ironing, prepared three meals a day for the six of us, and always washed the dishes after every meal. In my mind's'eye I don't see her sitting down, unless she's sewing or knitting, but always on the go, with sleeves rolled up and in an enormous apron, tackling everything, as she says, with vim and elbow-grease. Now my father's dead, she doesn't go far, except to visit my brother in Warwickshire or to stay with her friend, Hilda Manders, who keeps the Bon March (as it's known) in Aberkenfig. Mamgu's never been out of the Yookay and has only the vaguest idea of where we are now.

My mother is a great repository of oral tradition, with a fund of stories about local people going back several generations to a time before she was born and a rich vocabulary with which to describe them. One of the things she says of people who have offended her with some untoward remark is, 'Put it down to where it comes from', by which I suppose she means, 'You can't expect any better from the likes of them'; it's an effective put-down. Of someone who is weak or ineffective she says, 'He couldn't punch a hole in a wet *Echo*,' and when she hears of some awful event, 'Worse things happen at sea.' For someone who's not very bright she reserves the remark, 'He's as dim as a Toc H lamp'. The greatest compliment she can pay a neighbour is 'She makes a good sponge' or 'Her washing's white as the driven snow'.

This morning we drove up to Sundance for one of its famous lunches, after which we took the téléférique up the mountain and came back on foot. The trees are now at their best, we were informed by a middle-aged couple we met on the way who told us, *sans blague*, their surname was Silvanus. I wonder whether they will mention us in their diary and make fun about our wearing crowns.

After lunch we went south through a town called Price until we found our destination, Wales, a bleak little place in the foothills of the Gunnison Plateau. I'd spotted it on the map and made up my mind to visit it. There was no one about when we arrived but after a bit I found seven old men on a bench, and we got into conversation. Six of the seven had the surnames Evans, Price, Rees,

Williams, Davies and Jones, and they all knew that Wales was in Glamorgan, where their people had come from. We strolled up to the village graveyard, an unkempt place, with rows and rows of tombstones (no crosses) bearing the names of people who'd been born in Merthyr Tydfil, Mountain Ash and Swansea, all of which were said to be in Wales, Glamorgan. Many of the earliest stones had inscriptions in Welsh and a few had *englynion*. I took a photo of one of these graves, as a souvenir. It was inscribed with the names of Nathaniel Edmunds (1827-1916) and his wife, Jane Jones Edmunds (1832-91), both of whom were born in Merthyr Tydfil.

The dead needed no benediction from me but I nevertheless went round the graves, greeting each one by name and reading almost every inscription aloud. It was the least I could do, for I knew that that, unlike them, I would be going back to the old country.

I bought two copies of a booklet giving the history of the area, one of which I shall send to the National Library when I go home. These Welsh people, it turns out, came to Utah as Mormon converts and to this remote place after coal was discovered here in 1854. An Indian had reported that he'd found 'rocks that burn' and the Welsh went after it in drift-mines. Their leaders were two Merthyr men, John E. Rees and John Price. The settlement had first been called Coalbed but almost all the settlers were Welsh, so they decided to change the name to Wales. They had sold the coal to the US Army, growing rich on the proceeds until the seams were exhausted. Today, with about fifty inhabited houses and a population of around 150, Wales grows turkeys and the fields and roadsides are littered with their feathers.

It was now snowing hard and Wales was no place to be stranded, so we made our way back to Provo.

During that same Election campaign at Merthyr in 1966, an old man crossed the street in Dowlais to tell me: 'What you have to remember about the Welsh is that to your face they're all behind you but behind your back they're at your throat.' A woman in the same street told me she'd vote for me if it wasn't for one thing: if I didn't want self-government for Wales. I shall never forget the result: S. O. Davies received 21,737 votes, the Tory (whose name escapes me) 4,082, and I got 3,361 – the highest vote polled by

Plaid Cymru in the town up to then. After it was all over I was given an old Welsh book by Miss Ethel Williams, a veteran member of Plaid Cymru who'd taught History at Cyfarthfa School. In it she'd written the words: *'Anrheg i un a garodd Cymru'*. It was to be several more years before the Blaid, led by Emrys Roberts, would win a majority of seats on the town council.

In the following July Gwynfor Evans won Carmarthen at a by-election. I took part in the campaign and, with Dai Bonner, had the honour of carrying him on my shoulders as part of the celebrations in Llangadog. Gwynfor is a sort of uncle to Ruth: he married Rhiannon Thomas, the sister of Dewi-Prys Thomas and daughter of Dan Thomas, a bank manager who used to be Plaid Cymru's Treasurer. Ruth's mother is a cousin of Rhiannon's and lived at their home in Liverpool when she was a student at the university there in the 1920s.

Jacques-Anatole-François Thibault. Gérard Labrunie. Anna-Elisabeth de Brancovan. François de Montcorbier. Anne-Louise-Germaine Necker. François-Marie Arouet.

Monday, 30 September
We took the bus to Salt Lake City today. Ruth and Huw went on a guided tour of Temple Square while I had a mosey round the bookshops.

Ruth, having been brought up a Calvinistic Methodist, is, like her minister father, ecumenical in her attitude towards other Christian denominations and tolerant of the other world religions such as Islam and Hinduism. But she's not at all taken with Mormonism; she is, in fact, quite antipathetic, seeing it as a blasphemous parody of Christianity, which in many ways it is, whereas I'm just curious as to how intelligent people can be so credulous. Although I have no religious belief myself, or at least none that I'm able to articulate, I'm interested in those who have, and want to know more about what makes people so sure. Sometimes, when I go past a Mormon Temple, I ask myself, What if I'm wrong and they're right? They never ask themselves the question, otherwise they wouldn't be Mormons. But the more I learn about what the Saints believe, the more preposterous their beliefs appear to be. Yet I still have a sneaking regard for the courage and fortitude they've shown during their difficult history. It's significant, I think, that every time the Church applies to join the Christian community, the other American churches decide it's not eligible.

Taid once told me that, one Sunday at Tabernacl just after the war, at the end of the evening service, he spotted a bearded, shabby old man sitting at the back of the chapel. He took him to be a tramp and, as was his custom, went to give him a shilling out of the collection to help him on his way. As he approached, however, he recognized him as Ernest Rhys. So, instead, he invited him back to the manse for supper. Rhys was in Aberystwyth, he explained, to edit the thousandth title in the *Everyman* series for Dent. The book was to have been an anthology of his own choice, but he didn't live to finish it, dying about a year later in 1946.

J. E. Meredith, Ruth's father, was a Moderator of the Presbyterian Church of Wales. A man of literary interests and widely read in Welsh and English, especially poetry, he had a fine reading voice and it was he who played the part of Emrys in the first radio broadcast of Saunders Lewis's verse-play, *Buchedd Garmon*, in 1937. One of the things he gave me before he died in 1981 was a letter from Caradoc Evans apologising for not being present at a service Taid had taken at New Cross, where he was in the habit of turning up occasionally to listen to what the preachers had to say. Caradoc had had an accident and had been rushed to hospital and he wanted Taid to know he hadn't deliberately stayed away from his sermon. Not exactly the action of a man who detested Capel and all it stood for.

Among the Welsh writers with whom Taid was friendly were T. Rowland Hughes, who had shared a room with him at Oxford, and Gwenallt Jones, whose spiritual mentor he was. He once told me that Gwenallt had been attracted back into the *Hen Gorff* after his brief attachment to Anglicanism because, in the first place, he didn't think the Church gave sufficient place in its services to children and, secondly, the Nonconformist hymns were far superior to anything the Anglicans had to offer. The essay by Gwenallt that Taid published in his book *Credaf* is one of the great statements of Christian faith and Socialist belief. The copy of *An*

Acre of Land, inscribed by R.S. Thomas to Gwenallt, which Mrs Gwenallt gave Taid just after the poet died at Christmas 1968 and which he passed on to me, is one of the most cherished things in my rare books cabinet at home.

Trefforest isn't what it was when I was growing up there in the 1940s and 1950s. For a start, it's lost its focal point – the shops around the square at the top of Park Street, which were ripped out to make way for the road that links the A470 at Glyn-taf with the broadway leading into Ponty. There's not even a road-sign for Trefforest, lest lorry-drivers looking for the Trefforest Trading Estate, which is a couple of miles down the Valley, take a wrong turning off the main road, which many do anyway. The village still has a sub post office and some shops between the railway station and what was once the Cecil Cinema (now a snooker hall), but its fabric has taken on the shabby, dilapidated air of a place no one really cares for any more. Only the Taff seems unchanged: it passes through Trefforest at its usual steady lick but, with the pits in the four valleys to the north now all shut down, it has lost its black sheen and there are fish in it again – cormorants come up river to feed on them.

Some of the allotments beyond Meadow Street, down on the river's bank, are unkempt, lacking takers now that the local supermarkets supply the needs of the people so well. The Crawshay obelisk still lurks behind a hedge near the Castle Inn bridge. The white tips – solidified waste from the Crawshay furnaces – are starting to sustain grass again after a hundred and fifty years. In a conventicle at the top end of Long Row the Sally Army rattles out its gospel of Blood and Fire to the accompaniment of tambourine, trumpet and drum.

'The iron tongue of midnight hath struck twelve. Lovers, to bed!'

Tuesday, 1 October

I received a letter from John Pikoulis this morning asking me to write something about Mike Parnell for the next number of *The New Welsh Review*.

The letter also asks whether I'd like to be involved in editing the *Review* and informs me that an advertisement for the editor's job is about to appear in the *Western Mail*. It ends by inviting me to write to him if there's anything I want to say and with the words 'Have I been cryptic enough?'. This is pretty clearly an invitation to apply for the editor's job, but I'm not sure I want to. I made my mark as editor of *Poetry Wales* for eight years – the longest serving of all the magazine's editors so far – and I think perhaps it's now time for some other Beau Geste to go up onto the battlements to be sniped at by the fellahin.

Lunch, a posh nosh, with a group of people with vaguely Welsh connections in the Skyroom restaurant on the top floor of the Wilkinson Center. The Norrises were there, of course, and Ron Dennis, Noël Owen and his wife, and a man called John Hughes who was said to be a winner of the Pulitzer Prize, though no one seems to have heard of him; he's not a Mormon, he told me, but is married to one.

At the end of the meal it was joke time. Called upon to tell 'a typical Welsh joke', Leslie and I both rose to the occasion, though not with alacrity on my part.

He told the one about a pair of Rhondda colliers who, during the General Strike of 1926 (a word here for our American hosts), won a bet on a horse and came into some money. They decided to spend it on a spree in London, staying at an expensive hotel. On their first evening there, they were approached by an unctuous waiter and asked what they wished to order. Dai looked at his butty and, without waiting for his assent, replied, 'Two hot dinners, please.'

I gave them the story about Cynan, the quondam Archdruid, who was once travelling by train up the Taff Valley on a preaching engagement and found himself in a compartment of which the only other occupant was a tidy little woman who, consumed with curiosity as to who this distinguished-looking gentleman might be, had been eyeing him keenly all the way up from Cardiff.

Eventually, as the train steamed through Llanwerinos, her curiosity got the better of her and she ventured to address him.

'Teacher, is it?'

The great man shook his head.

'Solicitor, is it?'

Again he smiled and found the view across the valley admirable.

'Preacher, I expect,' said the woman, hitting the nail on the head.

At this, and putting down his papers, Cynan decided he would have to satisfy her curiosity.

'Madam,' he announced in his grandest manner, 'you may recognize me because I used to be Archdruid of Wales.'

'Jiw, jiw,' she said, full of concern, 'the drink, was it?'

Aware that there was a serious misunderstanding, he tried to clear it up by saying, 'My name, Madam, is the Reverend Albert Evans Jones.' But it showed on the woman's face that this, one of the most illustrious names of the Welsh pulpit, meant nothing to her.

So, anxious by now that she should know who he was, he added, 'In eisteddfodic circles, they call me Cynan.'

There was a moment's pause and then, with a sigh of sympathy, the woman exclaimed, 'Aw, there's buggers some people are!'

During the course of the meal, as a decanter of the pink liquid that passes for a beverage in these parts stopped at the far end of the table, I asked, 'Do you know the Bishop of Norwich?', but no one took a blind bit of notice.

Seeing the waiters going about their work in the restaurant today brought to mind a warm Sunday afternoon Ruth and I once spent at Llanfair Court, near Abergavenny, the home of Colonel Sir William Crawshay and his wife, Elizabeth. He was Chairman of the Arts Council at the time and was always kind to me: I was the only one of the senior staff to dine at 'Lanfare' Court on more than one occasion.

On the afternoon in question, after lunch, the guests were invited to play croquet on the spacious lawn in front of the house. After about an hour of knocking the wooden ball through the hoops, Sir William bawled out, 'John! Tea!', at which a flunkey, in full livery, including velvet coat, buckled shoes and lace at the wrists, emerged from the house with a huge silver tray laden with teapots and basins, slowly, as if to the 'Dead March'. There were five different kinds of tea and three of sugar. We sipped at our fine china cups while John stood to attention in the great heat of the afternoon. Then, at a loud clap from his master, he collected the tea-things and took the tray back into the house, as funereally as he'd come. I'd never seen the like of it and I was the only one to say thank-you to John.

As for Meadow Street, it looks much the same these days as it did in my boyhood. The houses seem as sturdily built as ever, except many now have fancy doors, pvc window-frames, and some gaudy paintwork. This isn't the first sign of gentrification: the street's appearance remains obdurately proletarian. Venetian blinds and lace curtains are still popular, but many roofs have had their slates replaced by synthetic tiles. Smoke no longer rises from the chimneys (if there are chimneys) because few houses these days have coal fires. The most obvious change is that, of an evening, there are so many cars parked in the street it's difficult for callers to find a place, and recently a system of permits was introduced – in a street where once the only vehicle to be seen was that of a tradesman or doctor on his rounds. The street-lamps we played under on winter nights have long since gone. At any one time there may be seven or eight houses for sale and they go for anything between thirty and forty thousand pounds. The meadow, that green and golden field where we helped with the hay-harvest every summer, has been partly fenced off to make a rugby-pitch for the Catholic school. Only the Bute embankment remains to remind me of my bird-nesting, den-making, trout-tickling days.

Meadow Street and the streets around were a grand place for boys to play, winter and summer. There were gwlis, gardens, culverts, allotments, sheds, back lanes, a railway embankment, the sidings, a canal, and the long, high-roofed tunnel that took the feeder into the tinworks at Cilhaul, a dark, rank-smelling place inhabited by bats and frogs and owls and all manner of bwgi-bos. In season we played at marbles, conkers, hopscotch, bogeys, Dickie-show-the-light, peashooters, bows and arrows, and roller-skates. I was a champion skater and would spend all day at it, not even taking my skates off when I came in for meals.

One of my chief interests in those days was fishing. I don't mean fresh-water angling because there wasn't much fresh water where we lived, except Nant-y-fforest, the stream that came down off the Barry Mountain, through the grounds of the School of Mines and via a culvert under the railway line and then into the Bute woods, where we would put down night-lines in the hope of catching the occasional trout. There were eels, too, in the river, evil-looking things that we decapitated as soon as we caught them, and still they writhed. No, I mean coarse-fishing for roach and perch in the artificial lake at Abercwmboi, where a neighbour, Mr Harvey, used to take us of a Saturday afternoon. I was always astonished to see such beautiful silver-glistening, finely stickle-backed creatures coming out of the dark waters of what was, in fact, a feeder for the local pit.

Another branch of the Harvey family lived opposite us and they were the poorest in the street, the father being chronically unemployed. I don't know how many children there were, but I remember Roy and Howard and Esther and Alma (who was named after my mother) and Cyril, who was in the Pioneer Corps and used to come home from time to time while he was on the run. He always hid out in the Bute woods, in a den he'd made in the thickest part, and we boys would take him whatever food we could scrounge from our own homes. One night, from my bedroom window, I saw the military police waiting for him in doorways up and down the street and, when they pounced, he was caught and taken back to Aldershot. It was always a treat to go to the Harveys' house: I enjoyed going there, my mother tells me, because 'I could read the tablecloth' and was allowed to stick a knife into the jampot and drink straight from the milk-bottle. They had no clock in the house and the children used to come out onto their doorstep and call to my mother, 'Mrs Symes, whassa time?' This used to irritate my mother because, no matter how many times she explained her name wasn't Symes any more, they persisted in calling her by it. All the children have turned out well, she tells me.

I saw the name Sabrina H. Severn on an office door today; I

wonder whether her middle name is Hafren.

'The staircase of history resounds with the silver slipper coming down and the hobnailed boot going up.'

Pensées d'escalier. Escalator pansies.

Wednesday, 2 October

Kitty has brought us shopping at ZCMI, one of the largest of the Malls, and then to J. C. Penney's and Mervyn's in the University Mall, where Ruth bought shirts for Huw and a cardigan for herself. I'm writing this at a café table while they continue their shopping spree.

The unit of currency in Venezuela is the bolivar, named after (or for, as they say in these parts) Simón Bolivar, the great Nationalist leader who fought the Spanish colonists and liberated his country in 1821. When Wales is 'free, and prosperous and dull' what will our currency be called? The gwynfor, perhaps, with a hundred kinnocks to the gwynfor.

I've begun reading a copy of *Salamander* which John Davies (Prestatyn) sent me before I left home. It's the story of the Mormon forgeries that rocked Utah and the Church a few years ago. The title is a reference to the golden salamander which Joseph Smith claimed was guarding the plates when he found them on 'the hill Cumorah'. A Mormon antiquarian book-dealer, Mark W. Hofmann, claimed to have discovered original manuscripts pertaining to the early history of the Mormons, some written by Joseph Smith and his acolytes. The Church eagerly bought them up. When the supply of manuscripts ran out, Hofmann started forging them, so well that the Church and State archivists were completely taken in. The Church was particularly anxious to acquire the items which showed the Saints in a bad light; so was the State, and soon they were bidding against each other.

Several years passed before people began to grow suspicious of the documents from which Hofmann had now made a fortune. But a cop in Salt Lake City took an off-duty interest in the affair: he was convinced, without any proof, that Hofmann was a forger. So were a few other people but they were all blown up by bombs planted by Hofmann. He even went so far as to put a bomb under his own car – in order to draw suspicion away from himself. Eventually he was caught, exactly how I haven't yet discovered, and is now serving a life sentence in the State Penitentiary which I pass on my way to Salt Lake City.

The other thing I hear about Mormon society is that the blood feud still exists in some quarters. There have been several gory murders among people who believe in the old principle of 'an eye for an eye' – the Blood Atonement. This is the other side of the coin that presents Mormons as neighbourly, non-violent and forgiving.

On tv this evening they showed the famous clip of Leonard Rossiter, Eric Morecambe and Ernie Wise, dressed in wigs and American Army women's uniforms, singing 'He's the boogie-woogie bugle boy of Company B', which I never fail to find very funny.

In 1974, during the Edinburgh Festival, I saw Leonard Rossiter (who later made his name as the star of *Rising Damp*) starring in a performance by the Glasgow Citizens' Theatre of *The Resistible Rise of Arturo Ui*, Brecht's fable about Hitler. It was one of the most stunning theatrical performances I've ever seen. There's one line in it that still sends shivers down my spine: '*Der Schoss ist fruchbar noch, aus dem das Koch*', which was rendered in English as 'The bitch that bore him is on heat again.' Nor can I forget:

> If only we could look instead of gawking
> We'd see the horror in the heart of farce;
> If only we could act instead of talking
> We wouldn't always end up on our arse.

I once met the Kray twins in Cardiff. The occasion was a theatrical evening to raise money for the Aberfan Fund and it was organized by Ray Smith and Bill Meilen, the actors. A ghastly painting by Andrew Vicari – the shawled face of a lachrymose woman – was auctioned and the highest bid was from Reggie and Ronnie, who came up onto the stage to receive it and then announced they were giving it back to the organisers so that it could be auctioned again. I was introduced to them during the interval, after which Bill Meilen referred to them as 'real gentlemen'. This was about three years before the twins were sent down for life for the murder of Jack 'The Hat' McVitie. Bill Meilen, who was on the fringes of Plaid Cymru, went off to Canada, where the last I heard he was teaching Drama, and poor old Ray, who was an organiser for the Party for a while, died young a few years ago.

The people of Llantrisant are sometimes called the Black Army because, according to tradition, some of them fought for the Black Prince at the battle of Crécy. The village makes the most of this connexion: there is a tv and electrical goods shop on the square that claims to have been established in 1346.

It was while standing at the back bedroom window in Meadow Street the other day, and looking out over the field, that my mother confided to me that she's been worrying about what might happen to the house after she's gone. In the corner of the field workmen were busy making a children's play area, with swings and slides and roundabouts. This puzzled my mother because there are so few children living in the street nowadays. She went from top to bottom of the terrace, on both sides, identifying the occupants of almost all the eighty-odd houses, without calling to mind a single family with children young enough to enjoy the new amenities. No newly married couples, or couples with small childrern, have moved into the street for several years now. Indeed, most of the younger people – David Adamson's new Welsh working class – have moved out to places like Ton-teg, Beddau and Llantrisant (the hole with the Mint), where Wimpey and Barratt have been building new estates and giving their streets meaningless names like Chantry Close, Winchester Avenue and Kingfisher Way. Meadow Street has become a place inhabited by the middle-aged and elderly, or else the houses have been turned into accommodation for students.

This last point was causing my mother anxiety. What she wanted to hear from me was whether, after her days, the house that's been in our family for nearly a century (which is unusual in an industrial area) would be lived in by students from the Polytechnic of Wales, which is now beginning to creep up the hillside as its student numbers steadily grow. Most of the houses in Meadow Street and the streets around have already been turned into flats for students, and sometimes there are as many as ten to a house. The hostels put up by the Poly don't meet the demand for accommodation and more need to be built.

There is, quite understandably, growing resentment among the people of Trefforest at the effect this process is having on their community. Students tend to get blamed for all the evils of the night and day: windows are broken, walls are daubed with punk designs and graffiti, woodwork is smashed, grass and weeds are allowed to grow on pavements; there is rowdiness at night, cheek and foul language, loud music and cooking smells, punch-ups in the pubs, litter and vomit on the pavements, and so on. Many of the students are from England and there's a certain amount of anti-English feeling among local youths who are always spoiling for a fight, though this is often confused with the traditional proletarian hostility towards students and their lifestyles. There have also been some particularly gruesome muggings and rapes in recent years. Such incidents are too much for a small, old-established, working-class community which has always prided itself on its generally good behaviour and standards of decency, but which feels powerless to do anything about its new role as a student quarter. Neither the local council nor the Poly has so far shown much concern about the problem, as far as I know, and few of the academic staff, most of whom live elsewhere, are even aware there is a problem.

The staff of the French Department at Aberystwyth in my day were a mixed bag. The Professor, E. R. Briggs, a remote figure, had an atrocious accent and lectured drily on French scientific thought – people like Ampère and Pasteur. The Senior Lecturer, Margaret Phillips, known to undergraduates as Maggie Pip, was a charming old lady who taught Racine and Corneille. Killa Williams introduced us to the rare joys of Old French with military precision and a laconic manner. Dennis Fletcher, who looked a bit like Peter Sellers, specialized in the modern novel and Stuart John, a friendly man who supervised my dissertation on Emile Verhaeren, taught poetry. The Hoggans, man and wife, taught medieval literature and linguistics respectively.

The only lecturer who thrilled and entertained us with his impeccably racy French and outrageously left-wing opinions came to us from the History Department: the irrepressible, scatological

Richard Cobb was later to win fame as historian of the French Revolution and literary critic of the most erudite kind. I have several of his books, including *Promenades*, which deals with some of his and my favourite French novelists such as Marcel Pagnol and Raymond Queneau. If ever a Committee of Public Safety is set up in the Yookay (after the Revolution, that is), I wouldn't mind appearing before it as long as Richard Cobb is a member.

In my final Honours exams, despite having done well in the Literature paper, I got a Lower Second, largely because I'd neglected my Old French. My dissertation on Emile Verhaeren was given a very high mark, but that didn't matter because, as with Old English, a student had to do well in Old French, which consisted mainly of deciphering glosses in Latin manuscripts and reading some pretty dreadful early poems like the one about Saint Eulalie who lived in the cwtch unrecognized by his own father.

While waiting for Professor Briggs to announce the degree results in June 1961, I fell into conversation with a classmate who, though she'd done her dissertation on the role of the French Army in the first world war, clearly didn't know on whose side the Japanese had fought in the second. She was the only one of us in the Honours class to get a First.

One of the authors I read during my Honours year was Maurice Barrès, the novelist who had a great influence on Saunders Lewis. I wonder how many Welsh critics have done as much. Barrès, *hélas*, also influenced Charles Maurras and the *Action Française*.

When, after the death of General de Gaulle, someone asked Noël Coward what he and God might be talking about in Heaven, the master replied, 'It all depends how good God's French is.'

Moelwyn Merchant always used to swank to me about how he'd got Ezra Pound out of St Elizabeth's Hospital in America where he'd been locked up for about sixteen years on account of his alleged mental instability after the war, during which he'd sided with Mussolini. I've never been able to discover what exactly Merchant did; I suspect it was no more than sign a petition, with a few dozen others, prominent among whom was Robert Frost. He was a cousin of Gwyn Williams, the translator, and was brought up in the next street in Port Talbot, but they had very little in common and there was no love lost between them. I'm sure

Harri Webb had him in mind when he referred to the Reverend Dr Benghazi Goat in his poem about the arts festival Merchant used to put on at Llanddewi-brefi, much to the chagrin of local people.

Pound once referred to Verhaeren as 'the most boring man in Europe' – high praise coming from that old *fascisto*. I don't think Pound was quite sixteen ounces.

I sometimes think that one of the things I'd have liked to have done is drive across northern Europe in a tank in pursuit of the retreating Germans. It must have been exhilarating, except for the concentration camps.

Thursday, 3 October

While in the Cougareat this morning, we fell into conversation with one of the cast of *Barnum,* a conjuror by the name of Bruce Block. He and Huw had a long conversation about magic in which, it seems, there are as many technical terms as in quantum physics. The show is about Phineas T. Barnum, circus man and impresario, whose claim to fame is that he exhibited the midget, General Tom Thumb, in 1844. He later went into partnership with James A. Bailey and Barnum and Bailey's Circus became 'the greatest show on earth'.

When we attended the performance later in the day, Huw was thrilled to be invited up onto the stage to help Bruce Block saw a woman not in two but three, and we witnessed it with our very eyes. Afterwards I tried to get him to reveal how the trick was done, but he wouldn't – it was a professional secret. I wouldn't be at all surprised if Huw were now stage-struck.

During my student days I had a variety of jobs in the holidays. Every Christmas I used to work as a postman and at Easter I sweated in the bakery of Hopkin Morgan or in one of the factories on the Trading Estate. These jobs were a way of supplementing the annual grant I received from Glamorgan County Council. In the summer vacation I worked as a gravedigger in the cemetery at Glyn-taf. It was the healthiest job I've ever done: in the open air and sunshine, stripped to the waist, with our sandwiches and bottle of cider under the nearest cypress. I was one of a pair who could dig a grave in a day. Down we went, lifting the earth with a broad spade, then straightening the sides with a special tool and making the grave deep enough to hold three coffins. My mate was Reg Hooper, a great hulk of a man and a champion gravedigger. His secret, I think, was to spit on his hands before starting like a ferocious terrier to throw the earth up and place it in a neat pile on the edge of the grave.

Then we'd take a break, lying under 'the patient yew', and slaking our thirst with a mug of cider or cold tea. I spent every dinner-hour trying to teach Reg to read out of the *Daily Mirror*, without much success, I'm sorry to say, though I did help him understand the hands of a watch, more or less. He was a cheerful chap and used to say, 'This is the dead centre of the universe' and 'There's no slump in our trade' – time after time after time. Then it was back to work. If the grave was already occupied, the feat was to dig down without breaking through the rotten lid. Next day, we had to stand at a little distance during the interment ceremony, and when the mourners had gone we quickly filled in the hole once more and arranged the wreaths on the twmp of fresh earth.

When it was wet we worked in the crematorium, wheeling the trolleys to the furnaces as they came through the curtains. When I hear people discussing the choice between burying and cremating the dead, I can speak from my own experience, as it were. My opinion is that there isn't much difference in the end. It's only out of admiration for Dr William Price, the pioneer of the custom and much else besides, I tend to favour cremation.

> It's thanks to Dr William Price
> That modern corpses have the choice
> To linger in the mouldering clay
> Or go up the chimney straight away,
>
> Singing, I don't care a bugger
> What anyone thinks of me!

The most popular thing I've ever written is, alas, 'The Ballad of Dr Price'. When it's sung at folk clubs nowadays it's usually said to be 'traditional'. The song known as '*Y Mochyn Du*' had a similar popularity, especially after someone started adding verses about

Cosher Bailey. In the *DWB* its author, John Owen, is quoted as referring to it as 'a song that will continue to corrupt the taste of our young people when the tongue that first sang it will have long been silent in the grave. Forgive, O Lord, the sins of my youth!'.

In the summer of 1961, just after I'd graduated and was waiting to go on to Bangor to train as a teacher, I witnessed the funeral of the poet, Huw Menai, at Glyn-taf. What I recall is seeing, among the handful of mourners, 'the three Jones boys' – Jack, Glyn and Gwyn – walking solemnly behind the hearse. Even more memorable was the fact that Gwyn, my old English professor, the only one I'd seen before, was wearing a canary-yellow pullover and an open-necked shirt. Glyn, whom I recognized from the photo on the back flap of one of his novels, was in his usual mufti – green corduroys, blue shirt, cream jacket and red tie. Only Jack, whose face was familiar because I'd seen it in the papers so often, was wearing *dillad parch* – a dark suit and a black tie. I suppose it was the first time I'd seen a bevy of Anglo-Welsh writers in one place.

A few years ago Glyn told me, mimicking Huw Menai's Hyperborean accent, how, whenever he was about to meet someone for the first time, he'd tousle his hair to make himself look more bardic. He also told me Huw Menai once canvassed a number of famous English writers in the hope of receiving some award (a Civil List pension, I think), and that he received a reply from George Bernard Shaw so vitriolic it made him weep.

Glyn has given me a copy of *Caniadau Cymru* in a nice edition printed by Jarvis and Foster in Bangor in 1897. The book was once owned by John Cowper Powys, whose name is on the fly-leaf. He gave it to Huw Menai in 1956, who gave it to Gerard Casey in 1976 and then it passed to Glyn, who presented it to me in 1986.

It was in Glyn-taf I made my first attempts to read Welsh. In the old part of the cemetery most of the graves had inscriptions with words like *Er cof am . . . gynt o'r plwyf hwn . . . hefyd ei annwyl briod . . . a fu farw yn yr Arglwydd . . . hedd, perffaith hedd . . .* I used to read these words aloud, relishing their consonants which disturbed something deep inside me in a way I didn't understand at the time.

A few years ago John Ormond was telling a story to the effect that the body of W. B. Yeats is not in Drumcliffe churchyard near Sligo. He claimed to have evidence that after the poet died at Roquebrune in 1939, the body of a French Resistance fighter had been buried clandestinely in the same grave and that when the Irish frigate came to take Yeats's body back to Ireland after the war, it was the maquisard's body that was dug up. This story appeared in a book in 1988 and there was an anguished letter in *The Independent* from the poet's children, Anne and Michael Yeats, in which they provided proof that it was indeed Yeats's body that had been re-interred at Drumcliffe. A few days later another letter appeared over the signature of a Madge Cockman who claimed it was her uncle's body that had been brought home to Ireland, which couldn't have done anything to save the Yeats family further distress. Part of the confusion had to do with the fact that both men wore a truss.

When I was last in Dublin I was approached by a young woman who wanted me to sign a petition about the demolition of some Georgian building in the city. I did so, signing myself Leopold Bloom of 7 Eccles Street, and as I gave her biro back she said, 'Thank you for your support, Mr Bloom.'

My mother goes on fretting, not morbidly but out of pride in her home and all the hard work she's put into it over the years, and which would come to nothing, she fears, at the uncaring hands of students if our house were turned into flats. What she would really like to think is that a young couple would buy her house, and look after it properly, and bring up their children there, as she and my father did. The house will eventually belong to me and my brother, but I know there's nothing I can say to put her mind at rest, short of telling her I'll sell my own home in Whitchurch and move into 50 Meadow Street, which is unlikely. Nor will Lloyd ever come back to Trefforest from his thatched cottage in leafy Warwickshire. It isn't that I don't feel an emotional attachment to the house: 'All through the place there are voices and apparitions'. But if I say it will be sold, she wants to know to whom and whether they will keep the place tidy, and so on. So I avoid the question as much as I can, and when confronted by it, as I was the other day, pretend to make light of it. Be philosophical, I tell her, don't think about it. It is, after all, a question that an old woman shouldn't have to worry about, and one a dutiful son prefers to put off until such time as he can ignore it no longer.

I once tried to get W. H. Auden to read in Cardiff. He declined the invitation, saying he had to be in Oxford during the month I suggested for his visit. But about a fortnight later he died suddenly. Life, or in this case, death is what happens when you're making other plans.

I've often wondered whether it was Auden who wrote the lines:

> Not much remains, twelve winters later, of the hater
> Of purgatorial pains.

They are quoted in the first volume of Goronwy Rees's autobiography, *A Bundle of Sensations*. I've gone through Auden's *Collected Poems* and his verse-plays looking for them but without success. The lines have a touch of *cynghanedd*, but that's the only clue I have.

Friday, 4 October

This morning we set out early and southwards through Price and Moab. (Tom Swiftie: 'Yes, I shall go to Moab alone,' Naomi said ruthlessly.) Moab gives the impression of being a thriving little town with real people living in it, and has none of the blandness of Provo. We chatted with a gold prospector and admired the cowboy saddle, chaps and bandanas in the shops. We stayed the night at Prospector's Lodge, which is kept by a Chinese lady named Mrs Chen who grinned broadly at us and said not a word as she booked us in, as if we were an unmarried couple intent on a night of illicit passion, despite our having Huw with us.

Moab used to be the uranium capital of Utah and is the former home of Charles A. Steen, whose modernistic mansion can be seen from the road to the north of the town. It was he who discovered the Mi Vida uranium deposits in the 1950s. He and his wife used to throw huge parties, often attended by as many as 10,000 guests, on Discovery Day every year, or so we were told by a man we met at a garage. The town is now a recreational centre for those interested in the visual and performing arts.

When I was a schoolboy we had a Geography textbook in which the illustrations had unusually entertaining captions. Two I remember in particular. One was of an old timer sitting on a fence in the American West, to which the caption read, 'Sometimes Ah sits and thinks and sometimes Ah just sits'; the other was of an old man and little boy on the verandah of a porch somewhere in the Arizona desert, with the caption, 'Ah sure hope it's gonna rain. Not for my sake, you unnerstan'. Ah've seen it rain. But for this 'ere boy's sake'. I've seen several such people today.

I was once stopped by a neighbour in Whitchurch who asked me why the suburb is known in Welsh as Eglwys Newydd and not Eglwys Wen, the name used by the local school. I explained, without going into too much detail, that it had once been known as Eglwys Wen but then a 'new church' had been built, and the village had taken the Welsh form of that name. As this didn't seem to satisfy him, I added for good measure that, before it was known as Eglwys Wen, the village had been called Album Monasterium. 'Was it really?' he said, even more perplexed. 'That must have been before my time.'

He was a wine-salesman. One Boxing Day morning, we were having drinks in another neighbour's house when I spotted a portrait of Jeanne Hébuterne, cut from a Sunday newspaper supplement and pinned up on the wall. 'I do like this Modigliani,' I said, pointing to it with glass in hand. 'Do you?' he said. 'I can get it for two pounds a bottle, you know.'

In February 1963 I was among the demonstrators who sat down in the road at Trefechan Bridge in Aberystwyth in a bid to get bilingual summonses. It was the first time *Cymdeithas yr Iaith* had challenged the law in its campaign to win official status for the Welsh language. There were about thirty of us, if I remember rightly, and the protest lasted about forty-five minutes before it was broken up by a bunch of local yobboes and irate drivers. The police were nowhere to be seen and no one was summonsed. I found the episode thrilling: at last the Welsh were doing something about their language rather than talking about it. I have a small scar on my leg as a memento of the occasion, which I'm not averse to showing to *bona fide* students of the period.

Eisht!

Saturday, 5 October

We drove to Dead Horse Point, one of the scenic attractions in these parts. John Harris tells me the real name is Dead Whores' Point (the way he says it it sounds the same) because this is where the early Mormons disposed of the bodies of prostitutes, but I think he may be pulling my leg.

The Point perches on top of a rim of the Orange Cliffs escarpment, a magnificent line of sheer sandstone cliffs which trace a serpentine boundary of about 500 miles around an area where the Green and Colorado rivers meet. The view takes in the Abajo, La Sal and Henry Mountains, and the Aquarius Plateau, and down in the deep gorge the Colorado flows through a maze of buttes and mesas.

In the afternoon we visited Mesa Verde and saw the Anasazi rock-dwellings, a whole village cut into the side of the rock. The tribe that lived here, who were known as 'the Ancient Ones', are said to have just disappeared, though they are also thought to have moved south and been annihilated or assimilated by other tribes. It was a very eerie place, anyway. As we drove through this scenic area we saw chipmunks and prairie dogs.

We stayed the night at the Warsaw Motel in Cortez where all three of us had a jacuzzi under the stars. The only other bather was a very loud, highly pneumatic woman, dressed only in a brief bikini, who couldn't swim but was quite good at splashing. A floozie in the jacuzzi.

I was once in Leningrad (as it used to be called in what are now former times) with Peter Finch and Brian Morris. One evening, in my room, the telephone rang and I answered. The woman said her name was Tanya and she was an engineer. She engaged me in polite conversation and, on hearing we were poets from Wales, invited us to her flat. 'I have two friends,' she said. 'Very beautiful. We read Pushkin. You read Byron. We drink much vodka. We eat very much fish. We dance, we laugh, we enjoy.' I thanked Tanya for her invitation and said I'd have a word with my companions. Talking it over, I was all for going to meet Tanya and her friends, but Peter and Brian, more street-wise than I, advised against it, so I didn't ring back. I'd never heard the word engineer used as an euphemism before and for the rest of our trip we thought we spotted them everywhere.

On that same trip, in Moscow, we went to the mausoleum where they keep 'the eternal lightning of Lenin's bones', and standing in the queue I fell into conversation with Marilyn French, author of *The Women's Room*, which fortunately I'd read. When one of the guards told her to stop talking as we filed past the catafalque, she told him to fuck off – so loudly that the man pulled a pistol from its holder.

Once, in a bus from Whitchurch into the centre of Cardiff, a gorilla sat down next to me. I took no notice until a voice asked me for the time, and then said, 'Thanks, Meic'. It was Peter Finch going into town in the days when he liked to see how people reacted to his pranks. He's still the Alfred Jarry of Welsh letters.

Harri Webb always refers to the author of *Rape of the Fair Country* as Alexander Cor-blimey. I was once in a tv discussion with Cordell who'd taken exception to the fact that the Arts Council had given a prize to Eugene Ionesco. Until shortly before the programme started, Cordell was under the impression the money had been given to UNESCO. As a consequence, the discussion was a trifle unfocussed but he went on and on about public money going to 'piffling poets' and not to novelists like himself, which made John Tripp go for his throat. Cordell offered to put up several thousand pounds if the Council would organize a novel competition, but on condition he'd be the sole adjudicator. D. Tecwyn Lloyd blew a gasket when this proposal came up in Literature Committee and it was duly stamped into the ground. I think this is where Harri got the idea for his poem, 'Synopsis of the Great Welsh Novel'.

It was a dismal experience taking Ionesco around the University Colleges as recipient of the International Writer's Prize in 1974, and then Dürrenmatt two years later. On the first evening of Ionesco's visit we dined at the home of Aubrey Trotman-Dickinson, Principal of University College, Cardiff. Ionesco ate next to nothing throughout the sumptuous meal and, when asked what he'd like, he said, from behind that clown's mask of his, '*Une pomme*'. A maid was sent into the orchard to fetch an apple which Ionesco proceeded to cut into slices and eat very slowly as we all watched him. After the official toasts, including one to *La Reine*,

Ionesco rose to his feet and proposed a toast to *Le Collège de la Pataphysique*. I knew immediately this was a leg-pull, because pataphysics is a spoof science invented by Ionesco for comic effect in his plays. But the diners all got to their feet and dutifully intoned, *'Le Collège de la Pataphysique'*. It was his way of making fun of the absurd nature of the evening. I wouldn't have been surprised if he put us all in his next play.

As for Dürrenmatt, I recall very little of his visit, except that for most of the time he was sozzled. A week or so after his departure the bills started arriving for the vast quantities of the finest wines he'd been drinking at the various hotels where we'd put him up. He'd drunk so much on the day of the prize-giving he couldn't get out of bed for the ceremony at the Angel Hotel, and we had to hold it without him.

In Aberystwyth, I took the Ionescos to stay with Principal Goronwy Daniel and his wife, Lady Valerie, at Plas Penglais. Over sherry, Sir Goronwy thought he was entertaining us by challenging Ionesco to guess how much the antique oak furniture in the drawing room was worth. *'Comment coute ça?'* he would ask, moving rapidly from piece to piece, and when Ionesco ventured to answer, our host would say, *'Non, non, non, beaucoup plus, beaucoup plus!'* I'm bound to say Lady Valerie's French was much better than her husband's.

It was from Ionesco I first heard the expression, *'le zizi-pan-pan.'*

After Ionesco and Dürrenmatt it was a doddle taking Astrid Lindgren, Margaret Atwood and Derek Walcott around Wales – they were no trouble at all. I don't recall anything they said, except after a visit to the Folk Museum at St Fagans, Astrid Lingren commented about the man who had showed her around, 'He was a very nice chap but Oh, he wanted to tell me *everything!*'

On one of my trips to Moscow, with Roland Mathias and Harri Pritchard Jones, we met a group of Cuban writers and had a pretty riotous evening in their company. It was a bitterly cold night, the temperature at –22 degrees, and as we made our way back to the Peking Hotel at dawn, Roland and I suddenly realized we'd lost Harri. We became very anxious, imagining him freezing to death under a bush in a park. We needn't have worried because, next day, we found him in his room, fast asleep in the bath. One of the

Cubans, whose name was David Davies, had looked after him and brought him back to the hotel.

That was the time we were taken to Abkhazia and met young writers who were chafing against having to live under Georgian rule.

In Sukhumi I heard, one warm evening, a chorus of frogs that sounded exactly as Joyce describes them in *Finnegans Wake*: 'Brékkek Kébbek Kóax Kóax Kóax.'

I once received a letter from Kate Roberts, who'd been asked to read the typescript of *Marged*, the novel by T. Glynne Davies. She was strongly in favour of it and described it as 'a Welsh Ulysses', which was high praise indeed. But she also felt it was incumbent upon her to draw my attention to the fact that it included 'a description of the sex act' on such-and-such a page, and so it did.

It's a curious fact that so many of our most important writers, in Welsh and English, have either been unmarried or, if married, childless: Kate Roberts, D. J. Williams, T. Rowland Hughes, T. H. Parry-Williams, Robert Williams Parry, John Gwilym Jones, Caradoc Evans, Rhys Davies, Richard Llewellyn, David Jones, Gwyn Jones, Glyn Jones, Idris Davies, Gwyn Thomas, *et al*. Perhaps the greatest obstacle to genius is indeed the pram in the hall, as Connolly once observed.

At a committee of the Books Council in 1974, a number of candidates were being interviewed for a job. T. Glynne Davies's novel *Marged* had just appeared and the book had received a lot of publicity. One of the candidates, a recent graduate in Welsh, when asked whether she'd read *Marged*, replied, '*Marged pwy?*'

The Welsh names for Flat Holm and Steep Holm are Ronech and Echne, or perhaps the other way round.

'We are not interested in the crumbs or the size of the slice of the cake. We want the bakery.'

Karchima joss!

Sunday, 6 October

Today we drove to Four Corners, where the state boundaries of Utah, Colorado, New Mexico and Arizona meet. The place is way out in the desert but we weren't the only visitors. One of the attractions is that, at the precise spot where the state lines intersect – the only place in the whole of the US where this happens – you can put your hands down in two states and your feet in the other two, and that's exactly what we did.

The site is haunted (I can't help feeling that's the right word) by Native Americans, as they now call themselves, mainly Navajos, who sell their necklaces and bangles made of what looks like silver for a few dollars apiece. Among the precious stones they use I spotted onyx, malachite, turquoise, hematite and blue coral. They were not very communicative, at least not with Palefaces like us, but at one stall I got into conversation with a young man on the subject of the Navajo language, of which he seemed genuinely proud. He told me that Navajo has a sound that doesn't exist in any other language: the voiceless fricative lateral *ll*, as in *lli*, 'a horse'. When he challenged me to make the sound, I said 'Llanelli' and 'Llangollen', which took him aback a little more than somewhat.

I notice these people describe themselves as belonging to the Navajo Nation and that, although the American flag flew from many of the stalls, it was superimposed with the image of a brave in feathers and warpaint.

I'm not sure what the Mormons' attitude to the Native Americans is. In their Book, the Indians are the descendants of the dark-skinned Lamanites who wiped out the virtuous Nephites of whom Mormon was one. So I suppose they are the baddies in this neck of the woods. Yet I hear there are special LDS program(me)s for them, by which bright children are given a chance to qualify for education at BYU. Most go to the Hawaii campus, where research is done into the customs and culture of the Utes. On the other hand, I haven't seen anyone who looks like a Native American in Provo.

As we drove through the desert, through places like Ship Rock, Blanding and Aneth, one-*lli* towns all of them, we saw 'such quantities of sand', and many oil wells, their wheels rotating eerily. The only place that seemed to me to have any scenic interest was Arches, a natural sculpture park of red sandstone and deep, tortuous canyons. Nothing much grows there except thin grass, desert flora, cactus, pine and juniper. The wind has carved the salmon-coloured rock into amazing shapes, often arches and windows through solid stone, monoliths precariously balanced on their bases, chimneys standing on their own as we see so often in westerns and advertisements for cigarettes.

A father who lost two sons fighting on opposing sides in the American Civil War put these words on their gravestone: 'God knows which one was right.'

We passed several small reservations where Native Americans live in breezeblock houses. We called at a shop to buy bread and it was full of Navajos, young and old, who stared at us with less than polite curiosity. I wanted to tell them that, as a boy playing in the Bute woods, I'd always taken the Indian side against the cowboys and US cavalry, but it somehow didn't seem the right moment and we came away.

We drove back through Monticello, Moab and Price, the way we'd come because there was no other direct route back to Provo. Price is the coal capital of Utah and has an air of prosperity about it. The town was named after William Price, the Mormon leader from Goshen in the Utah Valley who explored the river's headwaters in the 1860s, and the area was first settled by the Saints as an agricultural community.

We reached Wymount Terrace at 11pm and the round trip was about 850 miles.

'And all shall be well, and all manner of things shall be well.'

Monday, 7 October
Tonight, the last of Ruth and Huw's visit, we had supper and a very pleasant evening at the home of Noël and Pat Owen. The holiday has gone very quickly and I shall be sorry to see them leave.

I spent eight years compiling and editing the *Companion*. Lowri was in the first form at Glantaf when I started it in 1978 and in her first year at Bangor when it appeared in 1986. The girls used to refer to it as 'the monster in the attic'. I worked on it almost every day, in the evenings and at weekends, often until late into the night, and I even took it on holiday with me. I was so committed to the project that even little Huw noticed: 'Dad's favourite book,' I once heard him tell a neighbour, 'is Dad's book.' I learned a great deal about the Reference Aesthetic from Dorothy Eagle, a splendid woman who had worked on several of the *Oxford Companions*. But I didn't receive a penny in royalties. As someone once said, 'Working for Oxford University Press is rather like making love to a duchess: one is more conscious of the privilege than the pleasure.' But *ware teg*, I chose not to be paid for the work as soon as it became clear the book's publication was going to require subsidy from the Arts Council.

It has often struck me what variation there is, in spoken Welsh, in the use of the second person singular pronoun *ti* and its plural equivalent *chi*. For example, Nain addresses all four children as *ti*, whereas Taid used to say *ti* to the sons and *chi* to the daughters. Differences in age and social status come into it, of course, but there is also regional variation: the egalitarian people of Rhosllannerchrugog, for instance, address everyone as *ti*, as many Welsh-learners do without noticing that some people bristle at it.

In English, of course, the use of 'thee' and 'thou' has all but died out, though I remember some of my grandmother's people in Cwm, Ebbw Vale, using it.

> Where bist that blackbird to?
> I knows where 'e be –
> 'E be up yon wurzel tree
> And I be arter 'e –
> Now 'e sees I and I sees 'e
> And 'e knows I be arter 'e
> With a ruddy great stick to larrup 'e –
> Blackbird, I 'ates 'e!

The only Mormon I know in Wales is Margie O'Mara, who claims to have been cured of cancer after her conversion to the faith. Her husband, Ron, who's not a Saint but nevertheless a good man, helps me with odd jobs about the house and garden. He has a phlegmatic way of approaching all problems. If I ask him whether he can do something for me, he says, 'Yes and no' or 'It's all according' – before pitching into it. By trade he's a ship's carpenter and it's good to be able to enlist the help of someone who can handle a hammer, chisel and saw. The O'Maras are very fond of animals and have a house full of pets. On one window of their car there's a sticker that reads, 'Dogs accept people for what they are'; on the other side there's a sticker that reads, 'Cats accept people for what they are'.

Tuesday, 8 October
Up early to drive Ruth and Huw to the airport in Salt Lake City by 10am. *'Boed teg yr awel ac esmwyth eu hynt.'*

After taking my class in the afternoon and attending a Creative Writing staff meeting, I spent the rest of the day in my office.

When I went to Paris to discuss Ionesco's visit to Wales I went by plane from Rhoose. The only other passengers on the flight were the Blaengarw RFC and their supporters who were going to France to see a rugby international. They were so boisterous, standing in the aisle and flapping their arms to help the plane get off the ground, and so on, that after about half an hour of high jinks the pilot stopped the aircraft and came out of his cabin to implore them to behave or else we couldn't take off. On the way back, their behaviour was much more subdued, Wales having lost, and just before we landed they passed a hat round 'for the driver'.

I had a visit today from a student called Sarah Cleaver. A sassy young woman, she's one of my best students and a Mormon from Maryland. She tells me she feels oppressed by the religious atmosphere at BYU and wants to transfer to another university. We had a frank talk about the theocracy that prevails here, in which I probably said too much about my own view of things, but no matter as I shan't be here much longer.

I wrote to John Pikoulis today to confirm that I wish to be considered for the *New Welsh Review* post, though not with much enthusiasm, and then I read more proofs for the *Oxford Literary Guide*. They are very clean, as usual. I remember when I was reading the proofs of the *Oxford Companion to the Literature of Wales* in 1986 I found only two typos: there was a reference to 'Duns Scotus, the medieval photographer' and another to 'Celtic millionaires crossing between Wales and Ireland in the sixth century'.

When I lived in Merthyr in the 1960s and was active for Plaid Cymru, the Treasurer of the local branch was an old-timer called Dai Jones, who was about 85 and a former bank clerk. He'd been a member of the ILP and had worked for Keir Hardie but had been converted to the Nationalist cause by Saunders Lewis who, during the Depression, used to hold classes for the unemployed in Dowlais. Dai Jones was fond of telling us stories about the old Merthyr, one of which has lodged in my mind these forty years. His great-grandfather, as a small boy, had been standing in a crowd in Penydarren one morning when a contraption emitting steam and making a loud clanking noise came down the tramroad. It stopped and a gentleman in a tall hat lifted him up onto the step of the machine, drove it a few yards and then put him down again, with the words, 'There, my boy, when you're an old man you'll be able to tell your grandchildren you had a ride on the first steam-engine in the world.' It was Richard Trevithick and the year must have been 1804.

Wednesday, 9 October
I rang home and heard that Ruth and Huw have arrived safely.

Talking, or rather listening, to John Harris today, I heard the one about St Peter showing a group of newcomers around Heaven. 'Those over there,' he said, 'are Baptists', and the Baptists waved their greetings. 'Those over there are the Methodists,' said St Peter, and they did the same. 'But before we come to the next lot,' he said, 'I want you all to be quiet. These are the Mormons and they think they're the only ones up here.' A bit like the *herren werin* back home. The fact that many religious sects believe they're the only ones who will go to Heaven and everyone else will be damned never fails to appall me.

'And here stand I, a suppliant at the door.'

Thursday, 10 October
It's warm by mid-day but there was a nip in the air this morning

when I went down to the campus. The place was swarming with middle-aged Mormons, alumni of the University, the men in dark suits and the women expensively dressed in the American way, all gold chains at throat and wrist, as in a scene from *Dallas*. This is one of the ways BYU raises its money, from wealthy former students. It's one of the doctrines of the Latter-day Saints that they're expected to make money and give a tithe to the Church. Godliness goes with financial prosperity, to which all are encouraged to aspire.

My mother's name is Alma. It's something I have in common with Doris Day. When I first came across the expression *alma mater*, I had some difficulty in not thinking it referred to my mother.

There's a Book of Alma in the *Book of Mormon*. He, yes he, was 'the son of Alma, the first and chief judge over the people of Nephi, and also the high priest over the Church'. Among other Books are those of Nephi, Jacob, Enos, Jarom, Omni, Mosiah, Helaman, Ether and Moroni. My copy of the *Book of Mormon* has a picture inside its front cover of a couple named Marsden from St George, Utah, who want me to know, 'We have prayed about it and know that it is true'; they also ask me 'to prayerfully read it' that I may find 'the great happiness' it has given them. H'mm.

Tonight the Y on the mountain behind Wymount Terrace was lit up with hundreds of blazing torches, part of the Homecoming ceremonies for the alumni of BYU.

When I was a lad, a wretched woman used to roam the streets of Trefforest and accost anyone who would stop to listen to her. 'Our Ken's in Col,' she would say, ''E've got a sustificate' – nothing more. Her son had gone to a training college somewhere in England and this was the only fact she could summon up in her deranged mind.

Late at night, after stop-tap, from my bed in the boxroom, I used to listen to Old Man Larkin making his way home from the Commercial Hotel (now called the Otley) at the top of Long Row. He used to talk to himself as he came down the street and would apologise to the neighbours for disturbing them, with the words 'I'm only Larkin'. I used to like listening for him because just as he was passing our house he would start whistling 'Lillibulero', always, without fail. He was a Catholic and this is the song they used when massacring Protestants in 1641: *'An lile ba léir é ba linn an lá.'*

When I lived in Merthyr, Catholics were known as *plant Mari*. In Dowlais there were people who were descended from the Spaniards who had settled there as iron-workers three generations before. Maria Fernandez, the wife of Gwyn A. Williams, was one of the 'Spannies'. Gwyn's story, 'The Funeral', which appeared in *The Dragon* when I was a student at Aberystwyth, is a brilliant evocation of their community. It describes the funeral of an old man, probably Maria's father, who had been a member of the *Partido Socialista Obrero España* – his card was stamped with the words 'Dowlais Branch'.

I remember publishing an article in *The Dragon*, which I edited at Aberystwyth in 1961, setting out the case for self-government, particularly in cultural terms and in the interests of creating a more progressive civil society in Wales. It was by Graham Hughes, a lecturer in the Law Department, and it had a profound influence on my thinking and on that of some of my contemporaries.

I'm still more interested in civil society, especially in our towns and urban areas, than I am in the *cefn gwlad*. In this I have no doubt been influenced by Raymond Williams and, more recently, by the writings of John Osmond, another Abergavenny man, who is among those helping to keep alive the idea of a Parliament for Wales. At the same time, I hope those who live in the Welsh-speaking areas will do all they can to protect and develop them, for the language needs a heartland and territory of its own. But in the mean while we must set up a Parliament and build the nation in civil terms.

My entry into student politics was in association with D. Ben Rees and his Socialist magazine, *Aneurin*, which ran for only a few numbers. My contribution to one of the early issues was an article about Nationalism from a left-wing point of view. Ben is an affable man, a native of Llanddewi Brefi, and he was one of the few *Cymry Cymraeg* whom I knew well as an undergraduate.

I found most Welsh-speakers in Aberystwyth pretty narrow, chapel-driven, clannish, old-fashioned and a little more than somewhat dull; this was, after all, the 1950s and the permissive mores and political unrest of the next decade hadn't yet begun. Male students weren't allowed in women's halls of residence and the scenes of frustrated desire that unfolded nightly on the pavement outside were quite something to behold. I once caused a brouhaha in *The Courier*, the College paper, by describing the railings in front of the hostels as 'more sinned against than sinning'.

Welsh social life at the College, including the student branch of Plaid Cymru, was the preserve of the *Cymry Cymraeg*, one of whom I was not at that time, though I did help to form the Alun Lewis Society, even winning a prize for a short story, three guineas I think it was, that I received from the hands of T.I. Ellis, no less. In those days about a third of the students were Welsh-speaking, another third were Welsh but without the language, and the rest were from outside Wales.

It wasn't until *Cymdeithas yr Iaith* started up in 1962, by which time I was in Bangor, that I realized the Welsh-speaking Welsh were capable of something a bit livelier. Among those I had admired most in Aberystwyth were Emyr Llywelyn and Cynog Davies. In Bangor, there was Gareth Miles and, in their first year, Robat Gruffudd, who refused to graduate while the College would not implement a fully bilingual policy in its administration, and Gruffydd Aled Williams, now a distinguished member of the staff of the Welsh Department. I introduced both Robat and Aled to the gentle art of painting slogans on the walls of the sleeping town. One night we painted 'Home Rule Will Come' on the long wall of Professor Brambell (brother of Wilfred Brambell who plays the part of Steptoe) and a few nights later an unknown hand added the words 'To Puffin Island'.

My first writings on Anglo-Welsh literature appeared in the paper *Lookout* and the magazine *Y Wawr*, the Plaid Cymru youth magazine, while I was at Bangor. I also won a small plaque for a group of poems at the Inter-College Eisteddfod during my training year. The adjudicator was Anthony Conran and the prize was presented to me by J. Eirian Davies, whom I later came to admire greatly.

Perhaps the most taciturn writer I've ever known was Ivan Malinovski, whom we met when Ruth and I went to the Poetry

Festival in Rotterdam in 1973. The Malinovskis came to stay with us in Cardiff shortly afterwards and, during our trip to Sweden in 1976, we spent a week with them in their house in the depths of a pine-forest somewhere in the south of the country, the nearest town being Reftele. Ruth Malinovski was an artist-craftsman who designed and made beautiful wall-hangings, and she was extremely vivacious. But it was as if Ivan had taken a vow of silence. When I asked him what he did all day in the lonely place in which they lived – the nearest house was forty miles away – he said he went out into the forest and sat on a stone until the sun went down. His poetry, which was highly acclaimed in Denmark, was minimalist and one sequence was entitled 'A Critique of Silence', about which he seemed to know a lot. Ruth and Ivan were Danes and Marxists who had met as teenagers during the war when they'd been working for the Resistance; they had both killed a number of Germans at point-blank range. When we stayed with them that summer, with the children, they fed us on frozen elk, wild ducks' eggs and jellied eels, all shot, gathered or caught in the forest.

I wonder whether Edwin Markham's poem, 'The Man with the Hoe', which was inspired by Millet's painting, had any influence on the making of Iago Prytherch:

> Bowed by the weight of centuries, he leans
> Upon his hoe and gazes on the ground,
> The emptiness of ages in his face,
> And on his back the burden of the world.
> Who made him dead to rapture and despair,
> A thing that grieves not and that never hopes,
> Stolid and stunned, a brother to the ox?

Black Bess. Rosinante. Marengo. Vic. Silver. Copenhagen. Trigger. Bucephalus. Magnolia. Fubuki.

Friday, 11 October
I spent most of today in my office, finishing the OUP proofs and writing an article about Wales, Utah, for the *Western Mail*.

Just after lunch I had a visit from a student named Alana

125

Kindness. She writes poems that are rather appealing in their naivety, and I've called her 'the Grandma Moses of Mormon literature', which seems to please her. She didn't want to discuss any problem, which makes a change, but simply to say Hi! She is courteous, well-read, bespectacled, beaming, and dressed in a jacket that seems to be made from milk-bottle tops, except they don't have milk-bottles here.

I had a 'phone-call from Lowri this evening and also spoke to Brengain and my mother who are staying with her and Gareth at their new home in Bethesda. Lowri's wedding last August was a very happy day and she and Gareth seem to be well suited. No man is a liberal when it comes to his daughters, but I'm content with the match. *'Lowri dan wiail irion.'*

This evening I watched the latest instalment of the Clarence Thomas hearing. A black man, he's been nominated as a High Court judge but is accused of sexual harrassment by one of his female staff, also black and very beautiful. He's clearly a very intelligent bloke and radiates integrity, but the evidence is piling up against him.

When I was about to publish Gerald Morgan's book, *The Dragon's Tongue*, in 1966, I wrote to about 300 people asking them to buy a copy in advance, as a way of raising money to pay the printer. Almost all responded, some buying more than one copy, and D.J.Williams bought a dozen copies. Only one person refused: Sir Ifan ab Owen Edwards, who wrote me a mean little note beginning, *'Torchwch eich llewys, ddyn ifanc.'* The phrase has become something of a running joke between my brother-in-law, David Meredith, and me.

Ruth and I once had dinner at the home of Professor A.O.H. Jarman, the Gododdin scholar, and his wife, Eldra. She's of Romany stock and I get on well with her. When the meal was brought in from the kitchen, it seemed to consist of a very small animal baked in what appeared to be clay sprinkled with nuts. 'Squirrel,' said the deadpan Eldra, and I gulped audibly. But it turned out to be duck, and delicious.

On a visit to the Soviet Union a few years ago, as part of the Pushkin Festival, we were taken by bus by train and bus to a place called Pskov, way out on the steppes; and those who came to

Pskov remained to pray because there was no way of getting out of it. During the very long train journey I met a Bosnian poet named Izet Sarajlic. Neither of us had much of the other's language but we got on well together; he looked rather like John Ormond, whom I always found good company. At one point in the journey, Izet said to me, 'Meic want woman.' I assured him it was not so but, intrigued to find out what he really meant, I resorted to doodling on the steamy window-pane. After a while it became clear what he meant was, 'Meic is missing his wife.' A man says in a foreign language what he can say, not what he wants to say.

It was on that trip I bartered a few cheap paperbacks for an ikon. It's a 'Mother of God, Pray for Us' ikon and was said by the man who swapped it to be from the monastery at Novgorod, which I visited. As I went through Customs at Moscow airport, I wrapped the treasure in my raincoat and tried to look as nonchalant as possible, only to walk through the 'Something to Declare' gate. Fortunately, I was waved on and the ikon came home with me.

'Agenbite of inwit. Inwit's agenbite.'

Saturday, 12 October

I went for a long drive north to Heber City today and then on to Evanston in Wyoming up the Dwight D. Eisenhower Highway. It wasn't very scenic – just rolling hills and a few ranches, and I came back through Kamas. Evanston is a very undistinguished place, a bit like Tregaron only not so exciting; it's a railroad centre, pretty rough and rundown. The road was littered with the stinking carcases of skunk and deer. The only thing I saw that made me smile was a sign outside a barber's shop: 'Hair cut while you wait'.

I've had several letters from readers of my column in *Planet* in response to my appeal for information as to the origin of the word 'Rodney', signifying a disreputable man. My grandmother used to call my grandfather 'a proper Rodney' when he'd had a pint too many, but I always thought that was a reference to the fact he'd been brought up in Rodney Street, Pentonville. The last train up the valley, late at night, was known as 'the Rodneys' special'.

According to Ifor Williams, in his book *Enwau Lleoedd*, the old name for Rhondda was Rhodni, which the professor believed was a reference to the 'rowdy' river. Leslie tells me it came from the name of an American ship which docked at Cardiff during the first world war: the crew went on the rampage and all hooligans were known thereafter as Rodneys. Today I received a letter from Tom Ellis, the former MP, a most genial man, who says he has no idea where the word came from but it was current in Rhosllannerchrugog when he was a boy. Ian MacDonald writes from London to say the word comes from Rodney Parade, the football stadium in Newport, and the unruly behaviour of the crowd as they made their way home after matches. Yet another says it's from the name of Admiral Rodney, but he seems to have been a thoroughly respectable naval gent. It certainly has nothing to do with the younger brother of Del Boy in *Only Fools and Horses* because his name is Dave.

For many years it was generally believed that the Mary who had a little lamb was, in fact, a Welsh girl by the name of Mary Thomas, who lived as a child at Tŷ Isaf, a farm near Llangollen. According to family tradition, the rhyme was written for her by an American lady named Miss Buell, a schoolteacher and poet, who'd stayed at the farm in 1847, when Mary Thomas would have been about five. One day, watching the girl being followed across the yard by a cade lamb, or *oen swci*, the visitor is said to have recited what was to become one of the best-known verses in the English language. The story appeared regularly in English newspapers during the first decades of this century and, for the last time, in 1931 on the occasion of Mary's death.

Alas, it's not true. I found a reference book in the Library here the other day which tells me the verse first appeared in *Juvenile Miscellany* in 1830 and was reprinted, in the same year, in *Poems for our Children*, both by Sarah Josepha Hale (1788-1879), a writer and editor of the *Boston Ladies' Mirror*. It must therefore have been written at least twenty years before Mary Thomas was born.

But wait for it. Mrs Hale's maiden name was Buell and, being an early champion of women's rights, she often used it. It's also known that she was in North Wales in about 1847. So what might have happened is that the American visitor, staying at Tŷ Isaf, inadvertently gave Mary, or perhaps her parents, the impression that the verse had been specially composed for her. Be that as it may, Mary went to her grave believing she was the Mary in the rhyme. One of her grandchildren, now in his nineties, lives near us in Whitchurch.

Ruth tells me I'm to be considered for the *New Welsh Review* job, along with Herbie Williams and Robin Reeves.

Some of my happiest moments have been spent in Soviet Georgia. If it's true that all men are brothers, as I'd like to think, I often had that feeling in the Caucasus. Despite the lack of a common language, I seemed to understand instinctively what the villagers and farmers were telling me, and took to them enormously. I made several speeches about international understanding which, through my interpreter, caused some of them to weep openly and then to propose toasts to me that were outrageously flattering. I made one hit by referring to a beak-nosed, white-haired old lady as La Pasionara, which pleased her enormously. Of course, Georgians are known as rogues and bandits, but I found them kind, generous, tender-hearted and altogether hospitable in much the same way as the ancient Celts were said to be.

Sunday, 13 October

Today I had a chance to reread a long letter from Glyn Jones, typed with his left hand now that his right has been amputated, and mostly about an exhibition of his work during the Cardiff Literature Festival, which is to go on to his beloved Llansteffan. Going into some detail about his Carmarthenshire ancestors, he writes: 'What genealogy seems to teach is that everybody is related to everybody else, and so what?' *Eitha reit, 'ed.*

Glyn has been presented with a framed copy of an *englyn* by Alan Llwyd:

> *Hwn yw'r un na châr rannu'i wehelyth*
> *Yn ddwy hil : mae'n mynnu*
> *Nid deuoliaeth mewn teulu*
> *Ond dwy iaith o fewn un tŷ.*

Singing in the bath this evening, as one does, I suddenly realized the first verse of that grand old sea-shanty, 'The Good Ship Venus', is a perfect *triban*.

It's a coincidence that Glyn Jones was born and brought up in Clare Street, in Merthyr, where Bobi Jones's grandfather also lived. I get on well with Bobi and admire him as a writer. When he's in Evangelical mode, which is often, I find him pretty hard to take, so we keep off religion. But as a writer he's always lively and I find his poetry repays the trouble one has to take over it. I'm told his long poem, *Hunllef Arthur*, which takes up a large book, hasn't sold a hundred copies since it appeared five years ago, though that won't deter Bobi in the least, so devoted is he to writing in Welsh. He's an important writer and a serious one in the sense that writing, for him, is an essential part of living and praising his God.

The definition of a Splott breakfast, according to Owen John Thomas, is 'an airf of dairk an' a mairmite sairnie'. During the campaign for a Welsh tv channel in the late 1970s, I attended a meeting at the Reardon Smith which was chaired by Lady Plowden. At one point in the proceedings, which were pretty rowdy, she turned to the audience and remarked, 'I don't know whether it's I who am being stupid, or you . . . ' at which Owen John Thomas piped up, 'Let's take a vote.'

Monday, 14 October

When I lived in Garth Newydd with Harri Webb in the early 1960s, Keidrych Rhys was a regular visitor. I had a somewhat exaggerated respect for him as the former editor of the magazine *Wales*, that is until I got to know him. He dealt mainly in innuendo about unspecified people and would ask me rhetorical questions such as, 'Tell me, dear boy, who's the glittering dustpan of Anglo-Welsh literature?'. He also dispensed bits of useless advice like, 'Never trust a Welshman who signs himself, Yours ever' and 'Get yourself a pair of suede shoes, dear boy'. Although I never did anything to offend him, as far as I know, and even dedicated an anthology to him in 1969, he wrote me many strange letters during my first years at the Arts Council. He also wrote to the Welsh Office informing them I was leader of the Free Wales Army. When he was given a bursary to write his memoirs he claimed that, together with his best shirts, the typescript had been stolen from his flat by Bryn Griffiths. He must have been off his rocker. Gwynfor Evans, who's his literary executor, once told me that Keidrych (aka Ronald Rees Jones) lost his job at a bank in Llandeilo 'after an incident with a shotgun', and left Carmarthenshire for London because he couldn't get on with his father.

The Arts Council's bursary scheme was, on the whole, successful. I know it was abused by some writers but it helped a great many more. A few wrote their books in advance, some didn't give up their jobs, as they were supposed to do, and some just didn't write the books for which they had received awards. But many good books were written with the aid of bursaries and the scheme helped many writers. It also had the effect of bringing writers back to Wales, among them John Tripp, Ned Thomas and Roland Mathias.

We also had three Bretons staying with us at Garth Newydd for weeks on end. Padrig ar Goarnig was on the run from the French police for some misdemeanour that was never divulged to us. His parents were famous in Brittany for having refused to register the births of their dozen children for as long as it wasn't possible to give them Breton names. We met Padrig, who was only 16, at the Celtic Conference in Cornwall in 1962 and brought him back to stay with us at Garth Newydd while the trouble blew over. He was a very robust boy with hair down to his waist and he later became a champion exponent of *la lutte bretonne* and a fine sculptor. Yann-Ber Piriou was a French-language assistant in Aberdare and used to stay with us whenever his girlfriend came over to visit him. He was a Breton poet and became one of the founders of the *Union Démocratique Bretonne* and a scholar of some repute; he now teaches with Per Denez in the Celtic Department in Rennes. The third Breton was Paol Keineg, also a poet, who was the father of Judy Gurney's two children, Goulven and Katell.

When, in 1976, I was made a White Robe member of the Gorsedd of Bards, I chose the name Mihangel o Gwm Taf. I haven't taken part in its ceremonies since, except in 1982 when Ioan Bowen Rees and I attended the Gorsedd held at Cilmeri to mark the seventh centenary of the death of Llywelyn Ein Llyw Olaf. It was, I thought, the least I could do.

'Mae marc y Cwm fel nôd ar ddafad arnaf.'

Tuesday, 15 October

I spent an hour this afternoon with Sally Taylor, who has an office next door but one to mine. She's a pleasant woman, of Welsh descent but a bit vague about where her ancestors came from. A poet, she gave me a copy of her most recent book.

Tom Swiftie: 'Send the prisoner down,' said the judge condescendingly.

Wednesday, 16 October

I spent the morning in Provo's four second-hand bookshops, in each of which I was the sole customer, and bought three books: the *Collected Poems* of Robert Frost, *A Literary Guide to Europe*, and *The Golden Apples of the Sun* by Ray Bradbury, whom I've long admired for his short stories.

Reading the Robert Frost, I came across a reference to Thomas Jefferson in a poem entitled 'The Black Cottage' and to his famous dictum that all men are created 'free and equal':

> That's a hard mystery of Jefferson's.
> What did he say? Of course the easy way
> Is to decide it simply isn't true.
> It may not be, I heard a fellow say so.
> But never mind, the Welshman got it planted
> Where it will trouble us a thousand years.
> Each age will have to reconsider it . . .

It's a well-known but poorly documented fact that eighteen of the fifty-six representatives of the American colonies who signed the Declaration of Independence in 1776 were of Welsh descent, or so I've read somewhere. True, the list includes such names as William Williams, Robert Morris, John Adams, William Floyd and Stephen Hopkins. Even Jefferson, the author of that splendid document, has been claimed as one of us, mainly on the grounds that he once wrote: 'The tradition in my father's family was that their ancestor came to this country from Wales, from near the mountain of Snowden (sic), the highest in Great Britain (sic again). My father's estate on the James river was called Snowden, after the supposed birthplace of the family.'

I also found the couplet by Frost: 'Forgive, O Lord, my little jokes on thee/And I'll forgive thy great big joke on me.'

I remember Derek Lloyd Morgan as a fresher at Bangor in 1961, speaking brilliantly in favour of the motion 'Good fences make good neighbours', and thinking he was destined for great things. As Derec Llwyd Morgan he's a fine poet and now Professor of Welsh at Aberystwyth.

Derec once told me a story about Waldo Williams. The poet, when he was wandering in England after the death of his wife, found lodging for the night in a shelter for down-and-outs. He had only ten shillings to his name, which he left in his jacket hanging beside his bed. In the bed next to him was a rough-looking man, so he took the note from his jacket pocket and placed it under his pillow for safekeeping. But this, for Waldo, seemed as if he didn't trust his fellow man, and so after a bit he got up and put the note back in his jacket. It was still there in the morning.

I spoke to Ruth on the 'phone this afternoon. The news is that HTV has managed to keep its franchise, but only by paying some £20 million for the privilege; the only other serious contender was C3W, but Euryn Ogwen failed to pull it off. Bang goes my chance of writing a documentary about Ivor Novello, a synopsis of which was part of C3W's application. I expect HTV will continue to be a lame duck, especially now it's had to fork out so much to keep its franchise.

This evening in the BYU bookstore I bought John Hollander's book on traditional poetic forms, *Rhyme and Reason*, and have dipped into it with great pleasure. It's all about alcaics, cinquains, leonine rhyme, monostich, pantoums, rhopalic verse, skeltonics, verbal mimesis and zeugma. I wonder why the Americans, who have led the English-speaking world in literary experimentation, are also good at writing ballades, villanelles and sestinas. Perhaps because there are so many of them. I often think that what we in

Wales need most (apart from an East Coast) is a few million more people in addition to the three we have.

I've always liked the response by an Embassy official in London when Spike Milligan asked him whether he could become an Irish citizen: 'Ah, Jaysus, of course you can, we're always a bit short of people.' Nationality is largely a matter of personal choice and should not be contested.

One of my favourite limericks I heard from the Irish poet, John Montague, whose stammer made it all the more delicious :

> There was a young girl named Miss Tuck
> Who ran into a spot of bad luck:
> She went out in a punt
> And fell over the front
> And got poked in the eye by a duck.

It was John Montague, when he was living in the Rue Daguerre, who took me to see the grave of Oscar Wilde in the nearby Père Lachaise.

I remember, in the days when I was editor of *Poetry Wales*, receiving a letter from Robert Graves, in which he complained at great length that his book, *The White Goddess*, hadn't received any attention from Welsh scholars. It went on and on, in the most barmy way, and there was a good deal about Taliesin and Arianrhod and Dylan Eil Ton that sounded to me like the most magnificent tosh. The postscript was pithier: 'I know all the rules of Senghenydd.'

Clarence Thomas has been confirmed as a judge by the Supreme Court. This evening in the Cougareat, where I had a burrito (or was it an enchillada or a torquilla or a taco?), I heard someone say of him. 'There ain't enough oos in "smoooth" to describe that guy.'

I spent a year at the University College of North Wales, Bangor, in 1961/62, training to be a teacher, partly at the Grammar School in Rhyl. I don't remember attending any classes in the Education Department and I did my dissertation on the teaching of English poetry, rather than on anything to do with French, and nobody said a word. I used to get up very early to catch the train to Rhyl and wouldn't be back in Bangor until about six o'clock.

I felt a bit isolated from student life in Bangor, having come up from Aberystwyth, and the only writer I got to know well was Tony Conran, who at the time was unmarried but constantly in pursuit of some Muse or other. I was a frequent visitor to his flat and we drank many cups of coffee and ate many a Marmite sandwich together, talking over the literary situation in English-speaking Wales, such as it was. I thought much of what Tony said about the nature of poetry was highfalutin but it was he, together with Gerald Morgan and Harri Webb, who encouraged me to think of launching *Poetry Wales*.

In Bangor I took a few Welsh lessons with Islwyn Ffowc Elis. The book we read in class was O.M. Edwards's *Cartrefi Cymru*. My admiration for Islwyn has grown ever since.

'Pessimismo della ragione, ottimismo della volunta.' Bene, Antonio.

Thursday, 17 October
A letter from Mick Felton, glum as ever but nicely sardonic too. He says Swansea Council is hoping the Year of Literature will be held in the city in 1995, and is casting its net widely, with Robert Minhinnick (Porthcawl) and Tony Curtis (Barry) being lined up as star attractions. The Head of Leisure Services, an expatriate Yank, is pressing for the inclusion of Mark Twain in the programme – and why not?

Also a letter from Bryan Martin Davies. We've always been good friends, even after discovering we'd both competed for the Arts Council job in 1967. T. J. Morgan, it seems, wanted to appoint Bryan but Gwyn Jones wanted me and, since Gwyn was Chairman, he had his way. It's made no difference to our warm friendship, although I haven't seen as much of Bryan as I'd like because he lives in Rhiwabon, where I don't often go.

Bryan tells me he was recently at an Academi do in Gregynog. Among the speakers were Bobi Jones, who went on in Calvinist mode, Selyf Roberts, 'as sinister as Al Capone', and Harri Pritchard Jones, who drank a lot of red wine during his talk. The only bright spot in Bryan's estimation was Gwyn Thomas speaking with delightful irony about his own work. Irony is in short supply at meetings of the Academi, both sections. This was the first Academi meeting for Bryan to attend in ten years and he says the next time will be in 2001. The letter ends with a dire warning not to grow sentimental over Wales while I'm in America. No fear of that, Bryan *bach*.

One of the things I did during my last months at the Arts Council was find a house for the writers' centre that Gillian Clarke and I wanted to establish in Wales. Eventually I located Tŷ Newydd at Llanystumdwy near Cricieth, the home of Sally Baker and Elis Jones. I wrote to a number of people, including Sally Burton, the actor's widow, and managed to raise about £15,000 for the Taliesin Trust. I also spent several weekends working on the house and, on my last visit, did various jobs like painting the common room and finding long oak tables for the refectory.

I spent three hours in the Genealogy section of the University Library today, in the hope of finding out more about my Radnorshire ancestors on the fiches so assiduously kept by the Saints. I already have dates for most of the Lloyds, going back to about 1760, but it was a pleasure to see them all listed here. I was nonetheless surprised to see they'd all been baptized by proxy into the Mormon faith in 1973 and their marriages 'sealed for eternity' in the celestial kingdom to which all good Mormons believe they will go. When I called the attendant over to ask him to explain what exactly this meant, he informed me that the Lloyds now had the chance to enter the Mormon Heaven. I found this all the more ridiculous because the Lloyds spent their terrestrial lives as devout Anglicans, some of them as churchwardens.

The Mormons believe the dead can achieve salvation through baptism by proxy. If dead souls accept the invitation to become Latter-day Saints, they can be reunited with their families in the Mormon Heaven. It's estimated that to date about 200 million dead people have been baptized in this way. They include Buddha, all the Popes, Shakespeare, Walt Whitman, Einstein, Freud, Anne Frank and Elvis Presley – in fact, thousands of famous people from all over the world. The insensitivity of baptizing Jews seems to me particularly crass, but the whole thing is gobbledigook, anyway.

Genealogy is important to the Mormons. The Church teaches that family relationships exist not only for this life but for 'the eternities'. Members are encouraged to research their family tree and there is an extensive Church programme which helps them in this task. Each member has to trace at least four generations, that is as far back as their great-great-grandparents. Having identified their immediate ancestors, they can perform baptism and marriage ceremonies for them in the Temple, by proxy. Those in the next life are then able to accept or reject the work done on their behalf. The dead who are baptized or married in 'the Mormon Heaven' are not counted on the membership records of the Church, *ware teg*.

Just to the south-east of Salt Lake City there's a complex of caves which have been bored into the granite of the mountains to provide a safe home for all the records gathered by the Church and put onto microfilm.

Whenever I ask Nain, who's immensely proud of her family's long connections with Cwm Cynllwyd in Merioneth, how long they've been in the valley, she replies, *'Erioed'*, which I take to mean always, before the Romans.

Geraint Bowen wrote an *englyn* about Nain's father, John Jones of Blaen-y-cwm:

> *Fe gerddai lle canai côg – cyweiriodd*
> *Aceri'r ceirch brigog;*
> *Caled oedd fel clwydi og*
> *A mwyn fel gofer mawnog.*

I intend asking Jonathan Adams, Sam and Muriel's son, who's a gifted calligrapher, to paint the letters of this *englyn* for me and I shall have it framed. I met John Jones shortly before he died: he showed off his knowledge of English to me by saying, 'Keep death off the road' – one of the few phrases at his command.

This afternoon I was visited in my office by a woman called Magdalena, about whom I've been warned. She's a strange woman who spends her time calling on people and talking to them in a stream of quasi-Joycean language which proceeds by word-association and quotations from the Bible, the *Book of Mormon* and English literature – rather like this journal, I suppose. She also has a bit of Professor Stanley Unwin about her: deep joy, thinkley odder-oh. I listened in astonishment and with some enjoyment for about half an hour and then made strenuous efforts to be rid of her, even getting up and showing her to the door a couple of times, but she persisted for nearly an hour, spouting the most fantastic nonsense, and then suddenly subsided, as if she'd run out of steam, and left me in peace. I've never come across this phenomenon before but there's probably a clinical name for it. Logorrhœa, perhaps, and she's a logodædalist.

The Duke of Edinburgh, presenting his awards to a group of young people in Cardiff, asked one where he came from. 'The Gurnos Estate,' was the reply. 'Oh, really,' said the Duke, 'what's the shooting like up there?'

Now that John Tripp is dead, there's a growing number of stories about him that make people laugh in the retelling. He could be good company when he was on his best behaviour, but he was often not. I saw a lot of him because for many years he and Fay Williams, my secretary, were going out together. After a while I had to stop asking them to our house because John used to pocket various things, from spoons to more valuable items. He would also ring me up in the middle of the night and demand I go and fetch him – wherever he happened to be. Once, after I'd given him a lift home from Aberdare, he vomited over the dashboard of my car and then, without a word of thanks or apology, disappeared into the night.

He wasn't averse, either, to pinching lines and sometimes whole poems from other poets. His poem, 'Welcome to Wales', for example, is a direct lift of D. J. Enright's 'Welcome to Sunny S'. But the most disgusting story about him is that, one Christmas Eve, he called at the home of Peter Finch and his wife, Val, and begged to be allowed to spend the night on the sofa. When the Finches came down on Christmas morning, Trippo had gone. But across the chimney breast he'd written, in lipstick, 'Thanks, Pete and Val – you're my friends, Happy Christmas!' Also gone were the entire contents of their drinks cabinet. Very funny now, but hard to take at the time.

Among the hardest tasks I had to face at the Arts Council was dealing with the Evans brothers, owners of *Y Faner*. The difficulty arose from the fact that they not only owned the paper but printed and published it as well. Despite protracted attempts, we couldn't get any reliable circulation figures or printing costs out of them: every time we enquired they'd be different. In the end the Literature Committee insisted that all periodicals receiving grant-aid would have to be printed by someone other than the publisher, so that a true picture could be gained of how much they cost to be produced. We didn't believe the *Faner* was selling three thousand copies, or a thousand, or three hundred – in fact, we had no idea what the print-run or sales were because the figure kept on changing according to the tactics employed by the Evanses for their own advantage. The new rule called their bluff and eventually the Council stopped its grant; I don't think it had any alternative. The ensuing controversy generated more heat than light.

Friday, 18 October
I rang home this morning and spoke to Brengain, who's decided to come out to Provo for a holiday; she's very excited about it.

A letter today from Marie-Thérèse Castay in Toulouse. We've known her these many years and it was she who arranged for us to exchange houses with her colleague, Maurice Levy, about ten years ago. She sends me all the new French stamps and I send her Welsh books in return; she reads, writes and speaks Welsh well. Among the people she knows in Wales is R. S. Thomas, whom she calls Ronald, and with whom, she tells me, she usually discusses Theology and Philosophy. She always gets anxious about him when she hears he's been delivering political opinions, wishing he'd stick to writing poetry; quite.

I had a long talk with Eugene England today about the difficulties he's got(ten) into with the Sanhedrin. A genial man, he talked about being 'a renegade Mormon' but at the end of our chat I wasn't much clearer as to the exact nature of his views than I was at the beginning because he wasn't willing to go into any detail. Eugene asked me to interview Leslie for a book he's planning in honour of him, and I shall do so with pleasure.

I read in *The Mormon Experience* that Eugene is reckoned to be among the best contemporary Mormon prose-writers; two others who get a mention are John S. Harris and Douglas Thayer, both members of the English Department's staff. The only other name I recognize in the Mormon Pantheon is May Swenson, whom I've seen in various anthologies. Also listed are scores of painters, dramatists and musicians, but none of their names means anything to me. But then, how many Welsh artists are known here? Perhaps the most famous Mormons are the Osmonds, just as Tom Jones is the most famous Welsh singer.

As I walked home this evening the BYU brass band was practising in the carpark for the Cougars' game against Hawaii tomorrow and when they saw me coming they struck up 'O Shenandoah, I love your daughter . . . '

Music here is intended to spur the home side on to greater glory. But it also has the power to leap over international boundaries. I once read in Villemarqué's *Barzaz Breiz* that during the Seven Years' War, at the battle of St Cast in 1758 to be precise, there were Breton and Welsh soldiers fighting in the French and English armies. The Welsh went into battle singing one of their marching-songs, *'Rhyfelgyrch Capten Morgan'*, at which the Bretons, recognizing the tune as one of their own, refused to engage 'the enemy' and joined in the song. The Welsh, too, stopped in their tracks and, despite commands from their officers (in French and English, no doubt), neither side took part in the action that day. Tradition does not say what happened afterwards.

The year I spent in Quimper seems a long time ago now. I didn't see much of Brittany because I was too poor to get around, but I used to go on the back of one of the *pions'* motor-scooters to Rennes, once a week, where I managed to get a *Diplôme de langue française* from the University. I also made the acquaintance of Per Denez, who has remained a friend, and of Joël-Jim Sevellec, the artist who taught at the town's *lycée* and who designed the plates we still have on the dresser at home. Unfortunately, Per-Jakez Hélias, the man who wrote *Le Cheval d'Orgueil*, was in hospital that year but I met him at the Poetry Festival in Rotterdam in 1973, and I was to meet Guillevic in Finland a few years later. By chance I met the novelist Louis Guilloux in a café in St Brieux and later enjoyed *La Maison du Peuple* and *Le Sang Noir*. I also made the acquaintance of Maodez Glanndour, the poet who translated the New Testament into Breton; I was able to invite him and Ronan

Huon, the editor of *Al Liamm*, to the Taliesin Conference held in Cardiff in 1969.

I can still remember the names of the *pions* at the *Ecole Normale*: Marcel Le Floch, Paul Madec and Jean Lozach. It was in Quimper I started putting on weight, mainly on account of the *pommes frites*, meat and red wine that were served daily. The Breton Movement at the time was still struggling hard to come out from under the smear of collaboration with the Germans and among the staff and students at the *Ecole Normale*, a bastion of Jacobinism, despite the fact that most were Bretons, there was no sympathy or interest in the plight of their country.

I remember visiting David Jones in his 'dug-out' at Harrow-on-the-Hill and he signed my copy of *In Parenthesis*. That was the occasion I saw a copy of *The Welsh Nation*, Plaid's paper, on his desk and asked whether he didn't find it a bit extreme and he replied that it didn't go far enough in his opnion.

The first world war continues to haunt us. One of the most poignant stories I know is about the mother of Mary Webb, the novelist, who in 1914 told a neighbour that her son had gone to France, assuring her that he'd be safe enough: 'They have trenches over there, you know.'

Harry Secombe once gave a concert for the inmates of Wormwood Scrubs, reducing his audience to tears of laughter with his rendering of 'Bless this House', particularly when he came to the lines, 'Bless this house, O Lord, we pray, make it safe by night and day.'

A few years ago my friend Paolo Pistoi, a lecturer in Sociolinguistics at Turin University, arrived in Aberystwyth with the intention of doing some research. One warm summer's evening he went up Constitution Hill and fell from the cliff onto the beach, about a hundred feet, and was killed. I had the awful task of meeting his parents and step-mother off the train in Cardiff and driving them to Aberystwyth, where we were joined by Ned Thomas, another of Paolo's friends. Together we took them to see their son's body in the mortuary and then to talk to the policeman who'd found him. It was one of the most heart-rending things I've ever had to do.

I once talked to an old man in his nineties named Arthur

Watkins and living at Llaneigon, near The Hay, who told me his regiment had been posted, in 1916, to Dublin at the time of the Easter Rising. One evening he'd been sheltering in a doorway when he saw two men walking down the street with a white flag. They had, he said, the side of their hats turned up like Australians and one, the shorter of the two, had a boss eye. He immediately called the sergeant who went out to see what the men wanted. They had come to surrender. The one with the boss eye must have been Patrick Pearse. I asked Mr Watkins whether he knew what had happened to the insurgents. He didn't, and when I informed him that sixteen had been executed by the British, he was quite astonished. 'But didn't you hear?' I asked him. 'No,' he replied, 'as soon as it was all over they sent us back to Macedonia.' When, a few weeks later, I went to see Mr Watkins again with a view to recording him, I was told by a neighbour that he'd died.

A copy of the Proclamation of the Irish Republic hangs above my desk at home: 'Irishmen and Irishwomen: In the name of God and of the dead generations from which she receives her old tradition of nationhood, Ireland, through us, summons her children to her flag and strikes for her freedom . . . ' It was the beginning of the end for the British Empire.

The first time I gave a public lecture was in 1962 at the Plaid Cymru Summer School in Pontarddulais. Its title was 'The Matter with Wales' and it subsequently appeared in *The Nationalist*, the only number of which I edited before it folded for lack of support. Gerald Morgan was kind enough to say he'd heard 'the voice of a new Wales' in what I had to say, though it proved too iconoclastic for some of the traditionalists like J. E. Jones, the Party's Secretary, with whom I never got on.

Blith draphlith triphlith traphlith.

Saturday, 19 October
Up early and drove to Salt Lake City and then on the Dwight D. Eisenhower Highway along the southern shore of the Great Salt Lake. The salt flats shimmered in the sunshine and stretched as far as the eye could see.

I saw the Bonneville Measured Mile where they break the land speed record, often, then went on to Wendover on the border with Nevada, a horrible little place, dusty and dilapidated, set in the most desolate landscape I've seen so far. The mountains in the distance seemed to be carved out of dust, colourless and formless, and the valley was totally barren, with no vegetation at all, and the road ran straight ahead endlessly. I continued for about forty miles into Nevada and the landscape grew even gloomier, especially as the sky was gunmetal grey. Coming back on the same road, I turned south to Grantsville and Tooele and Fairfield, rejoining Route 15 at American Fork. Apart from these small towns, I saw no sign of human habitation all day, and I drove for about 450 miles. It wasn't a very interesting trip but I can now say I've 'done' seven States: Utah, Wyoming, Idaho, New Mexico, Colorado, Arizona and Nevada. 'The lone and level sands stretch far away.'

'*Aca nada*,' as the man said when he first saw Canada.

On returning to the flat I cooked myself a huge nosh of fried sausages, as I used to at Garth Newydd in the 'sixties, though I didn't know then that *nosh* is the Russian for 'fork'. I remember Harri Webb doing the same, except the sausages always managed to leap out of the frying pan when he cooked them and then he would kick them about the kitchen and out on to the landing, cursing them and stamping them into the floor, beside himself with the rage that overwhelmed him from time to time. Harri once told me his nerves had been affected by the pounding of the guns on the warship with which he served in the Mediterranean during the war.

Every man is a desert, according to Mauriac.

Another letter from John Pikoulis about *The New Welsh Review* in response to mine indicating I was willing to be considered for the editor's job. He informs me a number of candidates will be interviewed on 28 October and I shall be considered *in absentia*, as he puts it. He asks me to let him have my thoughts on two points in particular: how, if appointed, would I envisage my relationship to the editorial board and would I be content to leave the magazine's office at 49 Park Place? I dashed off a note indicating that neither of these matters presented any difficulty as far as I was concerned and gave him what assurances I could. I still can't summon up much enthusiasm about editing the magazine, though.

Sunday, 20 October

I rang home, then went to have lunch with Sally Taylor and her husband, Dave; their daughter-in-law was also there with her children, Candice and Carlton. The meal was excellent and my hosts charming but, at about three, the visit came to an abrupt end and we all left: we'd been invited for the meal, not the afternoon, in the American way.

I once had lunch in the Park Hotel with Richard Llewellyn, who wanted a bursary from the Arts Council, which in due course he got. He struck me as a very anglicized Welshman, military in his manner, entirely concerned with himself, totally out of touch with Wales, highly phoney, absolutely convinced he was the greatest writer in the world, and would I pay the bill, old chap? I was extremely embarrassed when, in 1975, his novel, *Green, Green My Valley Now*, the sequel to *How Green Was My Valley*, appeared: it was dedicated to Sir William Crawshay, Chairman of the Arts Council, and me.

I've noticed several Mormons wearing the Garments – John Harris was today. From what I can glimpse of them at neck and ankle, they look like a tight-fitting vest and Long Johns and are decorated with small symbols, or so I'm told. I don't know what the significance of this apparel is, but I shall enquire. They look as if they're very hard to get into and much harder to get out of.

There's a comic story concerning the Garments. In 1977 a Wyoming beauty queen, Joyce McKinney, kidnapped a 21-year-old Mormon missionary and handcuffed him to her bed in the hope of having sex with him and becoming pregnant. After he'd been released, the young man told reporters that the Garments had kept him chaste.

I was once asked to leave Lear's Bookshop in Cardiff after pointing out to the manager that a copy of a book, *The Pound Era*, should have been on the Literary Criticism shelf and not in the Finance section.

Many of the apartment blocks around Wymount Terrace are lit up with pumpkins for Hallowe'en. I'm surprised the Church allows such superstitious nonsense. But there, once people stop believing in the orthodox religions, they can believe in anything, including witches and spooks and the planet Kolob.

'The death of reason produces monsters,' said Benjamin Franklin.

Monday, 21 October
Today Brengain arrived for her holiday. Her visit started inauspiciously. First, I mislaid my coat in the airport café where I'd been having a snack, only to find it half an hour later in the Lost Property office – where else? Then I waited at the wrong gate, rushed to another, didn't see Brengain coming out and was told by a steward she wasn't on the flight and was probably still in Dallas. Then, as I was trying to get through to British Airways, I heard my name being called over the loudspeaker. But I still couldn't see Brengain. About forty-five minutes later she appeared on the ground floor, to my great relief, and none the worse for the mix-up. We were back in Wymount by ten and she went straight to bed.

I stayed up for an hour to read a copy of *Green Armor on Green Ground* by the American poet Rolfe Humphries and found this in the introduction: 'What we know of the Welsh seems mighty little, compared with what we think we know of the Scotch (sic) or Irish. An invidious nursery rhyme; some lampooning, not without rough admiration, in Shakespeare; what else? A contumacious people, they seem to have been, the Cymri, confederates never any longer than they had to be, fighting with, and beaten by, Romans, Saxons, Normans, Danes, Irish, turning around, as often as not, and mauling their oppressors, coming home victorious, to betray their leaders and fall to feuding, repeating the cycle.' Who, us?

I'm glad we gave the name Brengain to Brengain. I found it in Denis de Rougement's book, *L'Amour et l'Occident* when I was an undergraduate. Brengain is the handmaiden of Trystan and Esyllt and it's she who gives the couple the magic potion that causes them to fall in love, with such awful consequences. Some of our friends and relatives found it a bit unfamiliar at first – the name didn't exist 'in or out of the Mabinogion' – but they've all got used to it now, though some pronounce it Bren-gain whereas in the family she's known as Breng-ain. There's even a pop-song, sung by Bryn Fôn, in which she's mentioned by name.

The name Heledd was almost as rare when we gave it her in 1968. The only other Heledd we knew at the time was the daughter of Thomas Jones, the Mabinogion man, but by today the name is quite common. I'm proud to think Heledd is now teaching at the *Ysgol Gymraeg* in Pont Siôn Norton, Pontypridd.

As a devoted Hibernophile, I've long since grown tired of Irish jokes. It's not only the Irish who go in for illogical sayings: the Welsh are just as prone to it. Here's one that springs to mind: 'If Aneurin Bevan were alive today, he'd be spinning in his grave.' On the Rhigos mountain above Aberdare, at the highest point and on the steepest bend, someone has painted the words: 'Yes, you can't.' A councillor in Treorchy is famous for the remark, 'I'm not a bloody bird – I can't be in two places at once.' The late Lord Heycock will be remembered for his comment after the Referendum of 1979: 'The way forward for Wales is the *status quo*.' The most damning comments I've ever heard on a colleague are: 'Deep down, he's shallow' and 'Trust him, he'll always let you down.' When I was a boy my grandmother used to say to me and my brother, 'You two are a pair if ever there was one, too.'

I recall standing next to Aneurin Bevan at the National Eisteddfod held in Caerffili in 1950 and being impressed by his pinstriped suit.

Tuesday, 22 October
Leaving Brengain in bed, I went down to my class. She came to my office at about three and we had a late lunch in the Cougareat, where we happened to bump into the ubiquitous Clint Graviet.

Then we drove up to Sundance and on to Timpanogos Lodge, which belongs to BYU, where the staff and students of the English Department were having a social. I always feel the name Timpanogos ought to have an asterisk after it, like Combrogos*, the Celtic word from which *Cymry* is derived, and which I intend using for the name of my literary agency when I go home. We listened to some of the older members of faculty reminiscing about 'the good old days', then to a barber shop ensemble which sang songs like 'Heart of my Hearts', and then there was a barn-dance. I was struck by how beautiful Brengain is, with her curly red-golden hair and lovely smile that's so reminiscent of my mother's. *'Do, fe alwyd ar angylion i hollti aur yn wallt i hon.'*

'Fame is rot – daughters is the thing.'

We were back in Wymount by ten, and now I have a severe cold.

When D. J. Williams died in January 1970 he'd just been speaking to villagers in a chapel at Rhydcymerau, his native place. His last words were *'O bobol, cerwch Gymru'*, and then, as he took his seat, he collapsed and died. Margaret, Ruth's sister, who knew him well from the time she and Ioan lived at Maenclochog, wrote a fine poem about him in which she refers to his devotion to the national ideal and to his *'bywyd crwn'*. D.J. has a special place in my affections because it was he who suggested I should change my name from Michael to Meic, which I did in about 1958 after a visit to the Bristol Trader in Fishguard. I have used the form Meic for so long now that my mother uses it too and I barely recognize myself as a Michael. I can't think of another Welsh writer who was loved as much as D.J. was and I count it a great privilege to have known him.

Scripta manent, as they say in Trediflas.

The poem I'd like to have written about my father I found in one of the Norton anthologies today. It's by Robert Hayden and called 'Those Winter Sundays'. The poet describes, in just a few lines, how his father used to get up early to clean the family's shoes and light the fire. It ends with the words: 'What did I know, what did I know of love's austere and lonely offices?'

'Que sçais-je?'

Wednesday, 23 October

There was thunder and lightning in the night and the sky was lit up for what seemed like minutes on end. This morning the temperature has dropped to 52 degrees and a storm is blowing up.

We spent the day in Salt Lake City. Brengain went on a guided tour of Temple Square, which is *de rigeur* in these parts, and then we went around the ZCMI shops. For lunch I had a clam chowder and Brengain a huge chicken sandwich. At about five we drove up Capitol Hill and looked out over the city. The sky was blue again but it was too cold to stay out of the car for long. We then drove for about fifty miles along the shore of the Great Salt Lake until it grew dark and we came back to Provo for an early night.

A letter from Don Dale-Jones today in which he recalls a whole day which he and I spent with Mike Parnell at our home in Whitchurch earlier this year, when Ruth kept us amply supplied with tea, *bara brith* and plates of ham sandwiches with plenty of mustard. I remember being deliciously exhausted by these two Olympian talkers.

Don expresses the view that we in the Yookay have acquired our freedoms at a very high price and they are illusory anyway. He says the average citizen cares nothing for 'free speech' and that human nature, when allied to cash, is incapable of democracy. Democracy means in practice the power of the rich and big business to oppress the poor under a smokescreen of doing it in their name. This is Don's way of getting at the Tory government of John Major, elected by about 35 per cent of the electorate. Don is particularly vehement about Major's recent announcement (at the Tory Party's conference) that he's going to do away with the class system, pointing out that to do this he'd have to abolish public schools, private medicine and the House of Lords, for a start. Don is a left-winger and I see what he's driving at.

He ends by saying that, although agnostic, he believes in the power of prayer, not because he thinks any hypothetical deity might be influenced but because it's psychologically good for both the one who does the praying and the one prayed for. He doubts whether anyone puts in a prayer for him and asks whether I could manage one or two on his behalf. He must be pulling my leg. But 'whereof we cannot speak thereof we must remain silent'.

Also a letter from a Dr Robert Bratman inviting me to visit him and his Welsh wife in Cupertino, California. They've seen my column in *Planet* and have several of my books. I rang them to accept the invitation.

Between the temperaments of my father and my grandfather there was a difference, an antipathy perhaps, that as a growing boy I couldn't help being aware of. This curious reversal of the usual stereotypes – the phlegmatic, fastidious, rather gentlemanly Welshman and the excitable, easy-going, extrovert Englishman –

might have had little effect on me if the paradox had ended there, although I recognize something of both of them in myself. But there was this difference, too: whereas my father's work left him time and energy only for the most mundane things – his Union, walking his dog, Guto, and so on – my grandfather encouraged me to listen to the wireless and talked to me about whatever happened to be the serious news of the day.

He'd lived through the Boer wars, two world wars and the Depression in between, so he had a lot to reminisce about. Among his heroes were Keir Hardie and Aneurin Bevan (with a nod in the direction of Lloyd George and his pension), and he spoke of the Tonypandy Riots and the Senghennydd Explosion as if they'd happened only the other day. On the subject of Tonypandy he was particularly adamant, summing up the vexed question of whether or not Churchill had sent the troops with the verdict, 'Even if he didn't, he did!' and he was among those who swore to having seen a glow in the sky above Senghennydd, just over Mynydd Meio from Trefforest, on the night *before* the disaster at the Universal Colliery. It was this talk about local history, however highly coloured, that fascinated me. Soon I was hearing about some of the famous people who'd been associated with the district. There was, for instance, the eccentric Dr William Price – neo-druid, Chartist and cremationist – who used to parade through the streets of Trefforest in his Davy Crockett hat and with burning torch in hand, and whose memorial is the crematorium at Glyn-taf, 'across the river', as we used to say, as if the Taff were the Styx.

The village and district were rich in industrial archaeology: we had a canal, feeders, foundries and railway sidings, all derelict but splendid places for boys to play. At the bottom of Meadow Street stood the ruins of Crawshay's tinworks, around which the village had originally grown. About a mile upstream, the story of the Old Bridge was waiting to be told and I remember being taken to see, in Ynys Angharad Park, the monument to the composers of *'Hen Wlad fy Nhadau'*. In this way I was introduced to what my grandfather sometimes called 'John Jones's Country': that small part of Wales – industrial, English-speaking but nonetheless Welsh – which he knew and evidently wanted me to know about too.

I don't think it's possible to understand Wales, to see it whole,

149

without knowing something about both its languages, both its literatures, the history of both its Welsh and English-speaking people.

I took my Veldschoen to be repaired today in a small shop where the proprietor said her name was Guildenstern. I half expected her to say she had a partner named Rosencratz, but she didn't; perhaps he's dead.

Thursday, 24 October

On my way to campus this morning I bought some medicine for my cold and, after my class, Brengain and I went to see the Monty L. Bean Museum, which is full of geological exhibits and stuffed animals. After my afternoon class we went to the University Mall, where I bought a rather nice blue-grey, herring-bone jacket for $97 (half price).

This evening Brengain went with Katie Owen, Noël's eldest daughter, to a 'pot-luck' dinner organized by the women's section of the Mormon Church, while I drove to Salt Lake City to hear Leslie read his poetry at Westminster College. He's a magnificent reader and received thunderous applause from the students.

Welsh MPs, Tory and Labour alike, were always carping about the political element in the magazines that were published with the financial support of the Arts Council, especially *Barn* and *Planet*.

'We gave our masterpiece to history in our country's MPs.'

I'm aware that for those who take the language to be the *sine qua non* of Welsh nationality, my Wales may not be recognizable as Welsh at all. Such a view fills me with dismay, for it seems to deny or ignore how the people of Wales, or the greater, English-speaking part of them, have lived during this century, but it doesn't leave me entirely cast down. Wales is a small country and the Welsh, even at three million, are a small people, yet not so small that they don't have to rely on diversity for whatever unity they might, on occasion, wish to claim. We come to see ourselves as Welsh, and to make our commitment to Wales, for different reasons and in different ways, and there seems to be little point in falling out over it. Perhaps, instead, we should now try to accept, even enjoy the differences, and go on to explore what we have in common and what we might yet make of it. The time will come when we shall have to try again to establish the political means of governing Wales in a more democratic way. Nationalists and Socialists of all parties will have to work together to that end.

'Pacienca y barajar!'

As for myself, I've known for many years what I want for Wales. Just after my grandfather's retirement in 1945, the Electrical Trades Union, of which he'd been a member for many years, presented him with a gold medallion, 'for services rendered'. I remember the pride with which he first showed it to me, drawing my attention to the motto inscribed on it: 'Light and Liberty'. Today that medallion, together with his Oddfellows' badge, is one of my most precious things and, more and more in recent years, I've found myself contemplating the meaning of those words.

'How vain it is to sit down to write when one has not stood up to live.'

Friday, 25 October
After getting antibiotics from the clinic for my cold, which is now turning to 'flu, I drove south with Brengain through Gunnison, Salina, Richfield, Panguitch (where we had a sanduitch for the sake of the rhyme), then via Ruby's Inn up the Red Canyon to see Bryce Canyon. The mountains here are flamingo pink and decorated with snow which glistens in the sunshine. We were now at about 9,000 feet. There were ravens on the buttes and deer in the woods and chipmunks in the lay-bys.

Continuing through Hatch and Dixie National Forest and Glendale, we stopped at a trading post called Apache Fort where Brengain bought a jacket and I a necklace for her. Outside there was a lifesize model of a covered waggon and two horses. We played with a white kitten which followed us around. A few miles down the road we stopped again at a petrol pump and, to our great surprise, heard a Mkgnao! and found the kitten under the car. It must have taken a ride on the chassis. So we drove back to the trading post and left the mite where we'd found it. We took a room for the night in Mount Carmel at the Golden Hills Motel for $34.

Tomorrow we shall see the Grand Canyon! I hope it's still there.

Before we set out today there was a letter from Mary Parnell, very sensible and dignified. I'm touched to hear that she asked for three of Mike's best friends to write about him in the *New Welsh Review*, of whom I was one. Mary tells me Mike had a rare vascular catastrophe which was totally undetectable and immediate in its effect: he died instantly as he was coming out of the sea and waving to her.

She's heard that I've shown interest in the editorial job with the *Review* and says, if I get it, she'll gladly come in and help on the administrative side with no remuneration. I was in Aberystwyth at the same time as Mary and we both read French but it's only in recent years I've got to know her, initially as Mike's wife, but I'm bound to say she has sterling qualities. She ends her letter with the words: 'I know Mike was a lovely man, but it helps to hear others say so.'

My father was a bastard. He wasn't in any way unkind or unpleasant. On the contrary, he was good-natured and mild-mannered and always ready to do a good turn. No, what I mean is he was illegitimate – he was born to an unmarried woman and never knew her or his father. In other words, he was conceived on a pack-saddle bed and born out of wedlock, on the wrong side of the blanket, without benefit of clergy, misbegotten, baseborn, a bantling, a by-blow, though he wasn't a love-child.

Saturday, 26 October

After breakfast we drove south through the mountains and forests via Kanab and Fredonia, reaching the entrance to the Grand Canyon at about 11am.

What can be said about the Grand Canyon, except that it's more than 250 miles long, between four and eighteen miles wide and reaches depths of a mile? It must be one of the most breathtaking places on earth. We viewed it from Bright Angel Point, Point

Imperial and Cape Royal and were overwhelmed each time.

The top of the Canyon is flat, with meadows and forests – whereas I'd expected desert. We stopped for coffee out of a flask (and my antibiotics) and then drove on through some of the most enchanting scenery I've ever seen. I've seen the Alps and the Pyrénées, and Svaneti in the Caucasus, but nothing quite like this.

Svaneti I remember as a country of stunning beauty. The main village, Mestia, situated high up a deep valley, with steep, snow-capped mountains on either side, serves as a supply base for the ascent of Elbruz, the highest peak in the Caucasus at over 18,000 feet. Until about 1945 the place had nothing that worked on wheels and the people worshipped the sun and spent their days prosecuting blood-feuds. Although there are only about a hundred thousand of them, they still have their own language, spoken only in these narrow valleys. Tall towers, built for defence purposes, dot the landscape. Some are still inhabited and we were taken into one for refreshments.

Only the menfolk sat at table: the women stood against the walls, giggling when I spoke to them. There were ibexes in the main street and the people seemed very poor. The old women were dressed all in black but many of the younger women were making efforts to doll themselves up with head-scarves and heavy make-up. For a few hours after our arrival we had to rest while our lungs grew used to the rarefied atmosphere.

When a group of villagers gathered outside the small hotel in the hope of seeing the visitors, I went out and tried to speak to them, but they were very shy. The only one who was willing to talk was a tall, handsome man dressed just like the others in leather boots, baggy trousers, white tunic and astrakhan hat. He spoke perfect American English and said he was a pilot with Aeroflot, home on holiday with his people. It seemed incongruous in this remote, primitive place.

Brengain and I reached Page, a new town at the head of Lake Powell, at about six, found a room at the Page Boy Hotel, had a splendid supper of fresh trout, then turned in for the night. The lake, which is about 185 miles long, lies behind the Glen Canyon Dam and is named after Major John Wesley Powell who led the first exploratory expedition through the canyons of the Colorado river in 1869.

I remember the maxim by Don Marquis that publishing a book of poetry is like dropping a rose-petal into the Grand Canyon and waiting for the echo. Most Welsh poets, in whatever language they write, know what he meant.

I have a dim recollection of seeing the Republicans on Market Square in Pontypridd when I was a schoolboy in the early 1950s. They were shouting the odds about Wales and I stopped to listen for a few minutes as I made my way home from school. If only they'd burned the Union Jack on that occasion, as they often did, I'd have remembered it much more vividly. If I'd been a little older I might have joined the *Gwerinaethwyr*. They must have been great fun and, in their way, courageous, though it's hard to see, forty years on, what exactly they achieved. The Republicanism which they hoped would appear up and down the Valleys of Glamorgan and Gwent just didn't show itself.

During the 1960s, when I was in Merthyr, a group of dissident Nationalists led by John Legonna, Harri Webb, Emrys Roberts, Meic Tucker and Roger Boore formed the New Nation Group, bringing out a magazine called *Cilmeri*. Harri tried hard to recruit me but I was put off by the apocalyptically right-wing views of Legonna (*née* Brooks) and the group's bitter antipathy towards Gwynfor Evans, whom they detested. Nothing came of the *groupuscule* and it will be remembered only as a brief footnote in the history of Plaid Cymru, if at all.

On Saturdays when I was in Form VI and had pocket money for the first time, I used to go to Cardiff for the day. It seemed a long way from Trefforest and took about forty minutes by bus or train. I'd go to the market for a plate of cockles, then to the bookshops, especially Beti Rhys's in one of the arcades, then to the Kardomah for a meal of chicken-in-the-basket, and end up in the Globe Cinema in Wellfield Road, where I saw all the classic French films like *Les Enfants du Paradis*, *La Grande Illusion*, *Le Jour se Lève*, *Le Salaire de la Peur* and *Le Mouton aux Cinq Jambes*. My parents let me go to Cardiff on condition I didn't stray any further than the bridge at the top of Butetown, because south of that point, they said, in the old Tiger Bay, there were Lascars and I might be shanghaied. I'd return to Trefforest on the Rodneys' train, well content with my day out, and all for ten bob.

'Say, can that lad be I?'

My father was brought up in Heolgerrig, on the hill above Merthyr, by the village policeman, William Stephens, and his wife, Elizabeth. PC Stephens already had a son, Billy, and two daughters by a previous marriage – my Aunties Gwen and Annie, who were always said to be my father's half-sisters when in fact they weren't related to him by blood. William Stephens's first wife had been a Rebecca Giles, whose family kept the pottery at Rumney, near Cardiff.

Sunday, 27 October
We left Page early this morning and drove south-east through Kayenta and Kaibito. It was now raining heavily and we couldn't see much but we had the impression this is wild country. We stopped a few times to buy Indian trinkets, as we thought this was one way of showing our sympathy for the plight of these dispossessed people. I understand that alcoholism, unemployment, illiteracy and disease are rife among them. Some listen to their language on the local radio and it's taught on some reservations, but the young tend to speak American these days.

In my first year at Aberystwyth the controversy caused by Goronwy Rees was at its height. Like most of the student body, I was strongly pro-Principal, not least because one evening while I was waiting for a girl to turn up at the Belle Vue, he bought me a dry sherry. He didn't know me: this is what he habitually did for all students if he happened to meet them socially. I took part in a huge demonstration in the quad of the old College during which the student body made its views known. We had no idea about the charges of spying and the internal wrangling which was going on in the College. Alas, we'd fallen for the silver-haired charm, the suede shoes and white polo-neck pullovers which seemed to us the height of intellectual chic. *Ah, si la jeunesse savait . . .* Little did I know at the time that one of those in the anti-Goronwy camp was J. E. Meredith, one of whose daughters I was to marry. I could never get Taid, who'd been on the College Council at the time, to speak about this episode, so painful was it for him. There was speculation that Rees had been involved with Guy Burgess and Donald Maclean in spying for the Soviet Union. Be that as it may, he took his secrets to the grave in 1979.

Just before I left home a doctor told me I have the first signs of diabetes.

What, still alive at fifty-two
And weighing more than eighteen stone?
Lose some weight, lad, if I were you,
And leave the alcohol alone.

To fats and sugars say goodbye,
Eat more carbohydrates, lad,
Give up puddings or you'll die,
On jam and marmalade declare jihad.

Life may be sweet but from now on
Guinness is a mortal sin,
Scrape the butter from your scone,
Or next you'll be on insulin.

Look your last on all things luscious,
Go easy on the currant cake,
Apple tarts may be delicious
But they are a big mistake.

Take my advice: diabetes kills,
You're too young to go to heaven,
Take those blue remembered pills
Or else you won't see fifty-seven.

Cut out chutney, cheese and chocolate,
The wines of Portugal and France,
Or you'll get a one-way ticket
To the isles of Coxsaikie & Langerhans.

Take your blood count every morning,
Then some strenuous exercise,
Let me give you this dire warning:
First it affects your feet and eyes,

Then, if you don't pay attention,
Hæmorrhage in heart and head;
Soon, I must not fail to mention,
You'll end up a statistic – dead.

But there's life beyond the gravy,
Don't complain and never grouse, man,
Try to live a life that's savoury –
And give up reading A. E. Housman.

Monday, 28 October

We got up early to find a blizzard blowing, with the snow half way up our window and the car buried by it. The snow of Utah is supposed to be 'the greatest snow on earth' – the slogan to be seen on car registration plates here. It falls in large, fluffy flakes and soon sticks, having been dried as it comes in across the Nevada desert. The blizzard persisted until we reached Price, where we had coffee and pancakes, and it was still heavy as we went over the mountains in the direction of Provo. The road was covered in snow and there were deep drifts in some places but the Chevrolet proved to be up to such hazardous conditions. I hate to think what might have happened if we'd had an accident as there was no one else about and we didn't pass any other vehicles for hours on end. Nor did we have an air-bag.

Eventually we reached Provo in the late afternoon and, after a rest, decided to take another look at the shops in Park City. The snow in this part of Utah wasn't as heavy and the ploughs had been out all day. We had T-bone steaks and beans in Texas Red's and then came back to Wymount.

An exciting day was rounded off with a letter from Ifor Owen in Papua-New Guinea and one for Brengain from Aron Evans. She was delighted and it looks as if something's going to come of this romance. Ruth and I are glad because we both like Aron, who's nearly finished a Fine Art degree at Cardiff. If they get married we shall have to refer to Lowri and Gareth, who are also Evanses and live in Bethesda, as Evans Above, and to Brengain and Aron as Evans Below.

When Huw was four or five he went through a phase of calling people by strange names. For a few weeks he used to call me Tex and Ruth Lassie. I asked him recently whether he had any recollection of it, but he hadn't.

On his retirement from the police force in 1919, when my father would have been nine, William Stephens took his wife and the boy to live in Lower Ruspidge, near Cinderford in the Forest of Dean, where they had relatives. About a month later, my father was on his way home from school one afternoon when he happened to meet the village milkman. 'You'd better get on home, lad,' he said. 'Your father's dead.' William Stephens had died of lock-jaw after injuring his hand while cutting firewood in the backyard; he was buried with his first wife in Rumney. Soon afterwards Elizabeth Stephens married a man named William Christmas Llewellyn. They lived first in Duffryn Road, Rhydyfelin, and later in Oxford Street, Nantgarw, where my father grew up. It was William Llewellyn who got him a start in the power-station at Upper Boat in 1924. Elizabeth died when I was a few months old but I remember her second husband: he died in a 'flu epidemic during the winter of 1950/51, which also carried off his daughter and grand-daughter.

Tuesday, 29 October

Ruth rang today with the news that Robin Reeves has been appointed editor of *The New Welsh Review*. I'm not in the least put out, but astonished the editorial board should choose Robin before Herbie Williams, who is a good poet and experienced journalist. Perhaps Herbie didn't want the job either. I know of Robin only as a journalist with, I think, *The Economist* and latterly the *Western Mail*, and I've never thought of him as a literary man. Perhaps he'll use the magazine as a mouthpiece for his political views, which fortunately are strongly in favour of a Parliament for Wales. We shall see what sort of fist he makes of running a literary magazine.

I taught my classes today while Brengain went to hear a public lecture on inner-city problems in Chicago (she did, after all, take a degree in Sociology at Bangor). All three of my daughters graduated at Bangor. Our family's connection with the College goes back to Ruth's father's day. Taid was President of the Students' Union and later of the NUS. During his term of office in the 1930s he led a delegation to Rome where he met, on the same day, both the Pope and Mussolini. He once told me that what he remembered most about Il Duce was that as he bent over a paper he was about to sign, he had a huge mastoid on the back of his neck that seemed to throb with the effort he was making.

I had a letter from John Davies (Prestatyn) today, sending his best wishes for my Semester among the Mormons. He was my predecessor and spent the whole year here, with his wife and children. I'm told he made contact with some backwoodsmen who make carvings of birds, and that John is now a dab hand at it. In fact, it has become his *violin d'Ingres*. 'As for Mormonism,' he writes, 'I always veered between admiration for people whose faith gave them such cohesion and purpose, and amazement at finding myself amongst grown-ups who believe in fairies.'

'Forsan et haec olim meminisse iuvabit.'

My father didn't learn the facts about his birth until shortly before his marriage to my mother in 1935, when a sister of William Llewellyn's, a woman named Janet Dyke who also lived in Nantgarw, revealed the secret to my mother's mother in a fit of temper and to spite Elizabeth Llewellyn, with whom she'd fallen out. My grandmother told my father, who immediately went to see Gwen and Annie in Merthyr to find out whether it was true and they told him it was. The news that the man and woman he'd always regarded as his father and mother weren't his real parents shocked him and he spent a week in his bedroom, unable to speak or eat. My father's illegitimacy made no difference to my mother's love for him, of course, and later that year they were married.

Wednesday, 30 October

The skies are blue again but there's heavy snow in the mountains. We set out in a northerly direction on the way to Salt Lake City, then Ogden and up the canyon through snowy forests to Woodruff and into Wyoming. We just had to stop to take pictures of Brengain standing under the 'Welcome to Wyoming' sign. Among the animals we saw were deer, a golden fox, buzzards, wild horses and a giant skunk.

At one point we had to stop while men on horseback drove a flock of sheep down the road in front of us, just like in Wales, except there were a lot more sheep and these men had guns in their holsters and lariats across their saddles and were wearing wide-brimmed hats, bandanas and spurs, just like in the John Wayne films. I asked one how many sheep were on the road. '3,742,' he snapped.

Despite this laconic response, we struck up a conversation. On seeing the sticker on the rear of the Chevrolet, he asked what it was. I told him it was a red dragon. 'Are there many of those critters where you come from?' he asked. 'Not as many as there used to be,' I replied. 'Waal,' he drawled, 'I guess that ain't no loss to the country.' And with that he galloped off in a cloud of dust, as fabulous a vision as anything we saw in Wyoming.

According to statistics published by the Welsh Office just before I left home, the number of sheep in Wales has reached a record 11 million, about four times more than the number of people. I heard recently of a young teacher, newly arrived in Builth, who learned a lot about sheep in a most graphic way.

She was using flash-cards to stimulate interest among a class of seven-year-olds. 'Policeman, Miss' and 'Orange, Miss' and 'Teapot, Miss' they called out eagerly. Then she held up a card with a sheep on it. Silence. 'Oh, come on,' she coaxed, 'surely you know what this is.' So she asked one of the brighter pupils to hazard a guess. At last came the cautious reply. 'Well, Miss, I'm not sure. It could be a short-horned Kerry or it may be a black-faced Beulah. I'll ask my father and tell you tomorrow.'

Buffalo Bill once visited Builth with his circus, elephants and camels and all.

'And how do you like your blue-eyed boy now, Mr Death?'

I once spent a miserable hour on a wet Sunday afternoon in the car-park of the mart in Lampeter, waiting for a friend to whom I'd promised a lift. All the shops were shut and there was nothing to do but sit there, watching the downpour. Desperate for something to read, I could find only a hand-painted sign hanging askew on a corrugated tin shed. It said, 'We stock Thibenzole, Flukanide and Ranizole.' These words meant nothing to me but, try as I may, I don't think I shall ever forget them.

Since the weather was so fine and driving conditions so good, we pushed on to Garden City and Bear Lake and into Idaho, then over the mountain to Logan and back through Brigham City and Ogden to Salt Lake City, and were home by nine.

My father was given the name of his mother when Gwen and Annie showed him a copy of his birth certificate, which they'd found in a family Bible after their father's death in 1919. Her name was Annie Sophia Lloyd and her home address was shown as 'Blanebeddoe, Glescombe, Radnorshire'. It was thus my father learned the name of his mother and that his surname was, in fact, Lloyd. He'd been born at The Green in the village of Walton, near Old Radnor, on 25 February 1910, the home of his mother's aunt and uncle. He hadn't been adopted by William and Elizabeth Stephens, so he wasn't legally a Stephens. The reason why the Stephenses took him into their home was that Elizabeth had had three miscarriages and badly wanted a son. Gwen and Annie told my father he'd arrived in Heolgerrig, with his mother, 'a tall, fair-haired, well-dressed, softly spoken lady', at Christmas of the same year, when he would have been ten months old, and that she'd brought with her a hundred gold sovereigns. She'd continued to visit the Stephenses in Heolgerrig for a couple of years, often bringing butter and eggs from the country, but as the boy began to grow she'd stopped coming and they never saw her again.

Thursday, 31 October
A letter from John Barnie, editor of *Planet*. He's had the unenviable task of sifting through the entries for the Rhys Davies Short Story

Competition before the main adjudicators saw them. The standard, he says, was pretty low. He's heard on the grapevine, a hardy bloom in Wales, that some reputable practitioners put in a story but failed to impress.

On one of my trips to the Soviet Union I was met at the airport in Moscow by a young woman who greeted me with the words, 'Goodbye, I your interpreter am.' Her name was Titsiana and she asked me to call her Anna, which of course I was happy to do.

I had a long talk today with John Harris on the subject of nostalgia (which ain't what it used to be) as expressed in popular songs. Of course, John knows a lot more American ditties than I do, but there was remarkable agreement between us as to the causes of nostalgia: advancing years, economic depression, social change, homesickness, war, and so on. We sang quite a few songs we had in common: 'Peg o' my heart', 'My grandfather's clock', 'Pennies from heaven', 'Home on the range', 'Red River Valley', 'Cool, clear water', 'The Yellow Rose of Texas', 'Moon River', 'I'll take you home again, Kathleen', and a favourite of mine: 'Once I built a railroad, now it's done . . . Buddy, can you spare a dime?' This last was written by Yip Harburg, the man who wrote 'Somewhere, over the rainbow'.

One of the things I heard from John during our sing-song was this from his Army days: 'The Sergeant rides in a jeep, the Corporal rides in a truck, the General rides in a limousine, and we are out of luck. Sound off! One two! Sound off! Three four! . . . '

John Barnie's reference to Alun Richards called to mind an anecdote Alun once told me about an RAF pilot, an old boy of Pontypridd Grammar School, who in 1947 was invited to speak to Form VI. 'We were flying over Berlin,' said the hero, 'when these two fuckers came out of a cloud and started firing at us,' whereupon the headmaster, Piggy Thomas, quickly interjected with, 'I think you ought to know, boys, that the Fokker is a type of German aeroplane.' Back came the airman, 'No, no, Headmaster, these fuckers were Messerschmidts!'

Brengain went to an LDS barndance in Timpanogos Lodge this evening and I stayed in to do some marking and catching up on correspondence. It's Hallowe'en and many students have dressed up in witches' costumes and are roaming the quad. Some of them came to my door and asked for 'trick or treat', much to my bafflement and their amusement. I gave them dollops of icecream and wafers from the fridge and they seemed content.

As a boy I was told my father had been born and brought up in Heolgerrig and I never thought to doubt it. But then, in 1962, while staying with one of my Auntie Gwen's daughters in London, she inadvertently let slip that my father had been 'adopted' by William and Elizabeth Stephens and that his real mother had been from 'up in the hills of mid-Wales'. I paid little attention to this information at the time and, as usually happens, I didn't begin to think about it until I was married and had children of my own. But as the years went by it began to intrigue me as to who my father's parents, my grandparents on the spear side, were.

Friday, 1 November

We drove south through Thistle to Wales, so that Brengain could see this strange little place and I could have a second look at it. There were a few more people about this time, though not many. Among the villagers we met was Gene Taylor, a retired teacher, whose great-grandfather, a Merthyr man by the name of Rees, had built the village store, now boarded up. He took us to see Mathel Anderson, the woman who wrote the booklet on the history of the village, and she was pleased when I told her a copy would be deposited at the National Library of Wales.

As we went down the Sanpete Valley, a cop-car overtook us, with its lights flashing and siren wailing, and when I stopped I was informed I'd driven through a village at 67 mph; I hadn't even noticed the village. The cop looked as sinister as they always do here – he had a gun and was wearing sunglasses – but this one was polite, *ware teg*, and let me off with a warning.

The nastiest brush I've ever had with the police was in Paris in 1959, at the height of the war in Algeria, when I was pushed up against a wall by three members of the *CRS* and frisked. *'Foutez le camp!'* was a phrase added to my vocabulary on that occasion.

In 1963 I was escorted down to the Merthyr police-station for questioning after the sabotage carried out by Emyr Llewelyn Jones in Cwm Tryweryn. I think the police were interviewing Plaid Cymru members indiscriminately. My finger-prints were taken and I was asked whether I knew anyone with the initials E.R. When I said, 'Elizabeth Regina,' one of the detectives grabbed me by the throat and had to be restrained by the other.

A letter from Sam Adams awaited me on our return to Wymount. The ceremony for the award of the Rhys Davies short-story prizes went off well, with Dai Smith doing an excellent job as chairman and Nerys Hughes reading extracts from the winning entry. Leslie and Barbara Hardy were the main adjudicators.

Sam and Muriel took Lewis Davies on a trip to the Rhondda, including Blaenclydach, where Lewis and Rhys were born and brought up. They also visited Gilfach Goch, where Sam was born, and a pint at the Bog (aka the Griffin), kept by his sister. I'm very glad Sam looked after Lewis in my absence. Lewis has, after all, been extraordinarily generous in funding the Rhys Davies Trust, a unique act in the small world of Welsh letters. When I went to see him in Lewes last year he wanted to make me a personal gift of £100,000. I thought it would be better to form a Trust, into which the money was subsequently paid, and it will now be used to keep the memory of his brother before the public and help sponsor Welsh writing in English.

In Glamorgan visitors are invited to help themselves to sugar to put in their tea; in Carmarthenshire they are asked whether they want one lump or two; in Cardiganshire they are told to give their cup another stir.

Not all mean people in Wales are Cardis. Gwilym R. Jones once told me of a quarryman in Dyffryn Nantlle who was so mean he'd bring an orange to work and peel it in his pocket so that his workmates wouldn't see it and ask for a slice.

Aron, Brengain's boyfriend, told me a story that takes the biscuit for parsimony. In the house where he was living as a student in Cardiff there was an old codger whom he used to help in various ways such as putting out his refuse bins and fetching his daily paper. One day this chap gave him a large paper bag of Brazil nuts which Aron dipped into from time to time. A few weeks later he met on the stairs a woman who turned out to be the old man's daughter. They struck up a conversation and he told her about the gift of nuts. The woman was horrified. 'Oh no!' she exclaimed, 'they're the chocolates I bring him every week. He can't eat the nuts because of his false teeth so he licks the chocolate off and puts them in a paper bag. Sorry!'

When I was teaching at Tonypandy in December last year, one lunch-time Jeff Powell and I went over the mountain to Maerdy, where we took part in the ceremony marking the end of coal in the Rhondda. It was a moving occasion, with a lot of sentiment and clenched fists, and I decided there and then I'd like to compile an anthology of verse and prose about the Valley. *On verra*.

> For I am like Zamyatin – I must be a Bolshevik
> Before the revolution, but I'll cease to be one quick
> When Communism comes to rule the roost.

One of the curious things about teaching French at Tonypandy was having to deal with the local dialect. They say 'I do sing' and 'I do go' – the teachers as well as the pupils. I had two girls in Lower VI who were doing French at A Level and they would write sentences like *'Je fais manger'* (I do eat) and *'Je fais dormir'* (I do sleep). The last straw was when one of them wrote *'Je fais faire mes devoirs'* (I do do my homework). When I mentioned this to one of my colleagues he said, 'I know, mun, these old French verbs do do their 'ead in'; he was the English teacher.

I used to be entirely comfortable in French. In France, despite or perhaps because of my difficulty with the ulvular r, I was often taken for a Walloon. I can think of only a few famous Walloons: Georges Simenon, René Magritte, Jacques Brel, Henri Michaux, Françoise Mallet-Joris . . . though all these are usually taken to be French. Emile Verhaeren, although he wrote in French, was in fact a Fleming and spoke the Flemish dialect of Dutch. I can still read French without difficulty and write it fairly correctly, but my spoken French is rusty now and I'm much more fluent in Welsh, which chronologically is my third language.

Adèle Foucher. Lydia Bunbury. Leah Lee. Anna Birch. Julie Charles. Jennie Gobillard. Marie Dorval. Annie Playden. Jeanne Duval.

I've often wondered about the three Welsh sea-captains who, during the Spanish Civil War, tried to break the blockade of Bilbao by Franco's forces. They were known at the time from the cargoes they carried: Potato Jones, Corncob Jones and Ham and Eggs Jones, though they may also have been running guns; Potato Jones had a ship called the *Mari Llewellyn*. They are mentioned in Hugh Thomas's magisterial history of the war, but no further details are given there, and when I met him at Oriel a few years ago I didn't have a chance to ask about the Joneses because he was button-holed by Hywel Evans, who wouldn't let anyone else get near him.

It takes a lot of history to make a little literature.

The only writer who ever asked me for money *yn blwmp ac yn blaen* was Caradog Prichard. He came up to me on the Field of the National Eisteddfod and boldly asked me to write him a cheque for £300 to pay the rent on a cottage in Cornwall where he intended taking a holiday the following week. When I explained the Arts Council didn't work that way he was quite put out.

'*Chi serva al cumüm, nun agradesch'ad ingün.*'

There's a chip-shop in Pontypridd called The Golden Dap.

In 1979, without telling my father what I knew, I started looking for his mother. I didn't know whether she was alive or dead, so I decided to proceed with the greatest caution. First I checked out Heolgerrig, then Devauden in Monmouthshire, of which William Stephens was said to be a native, and then Ruspidge in the Forest of Dean, but found no trace. There are a lot of Stephenses in the churchyard at nearby St. Arvans and a haulage contractor of that name has premises in the village, but I haven't made any enquiries locally.

I then hit on the idea I should have had in the first place: I wrote to the Registrar General and, about a week later, received a copy of my father's birth certificate. On it were written the same particulars as my father had been given by Gwen and Annie in 1935. There was a blank space where the father's name should have been: it was the old story – *pater semper incertus, mater certissima est.*

Saturday, 2 November
We spent this morning in Salt Lake City, where Brengain visited Trolley Square.

I've often wondered who it was Rhys Davies couldn't name when he related in his autobiography, *Print of a Hare's Foot*, how he once discovered 'one of the revered Welsh Doges, a married academic visiting London for a solemn conference,' in bed with the famously accommodating Nina Hamnett. I seem to recall Glyn Jones telling me the man in question was W. J. Gruffydd, who was by all accounts a bit of a ram, though not so discriminating.

'Come nebo me and suso sing the day we sallybright.'

In 1967, just after taking up my post at the Arts Council, I organized an open letter to the Court of the National Eisteddfod calling for the retention of the All Welsh Rule. It went out in Harri Webb's name and was signed by about sixty Anglo-Welsh writers who made it clear they wouldn't take part in any English competitions under the aegis of the Eisteddfod, which they thought should be maintained as a Welsh-language event. The move went some way to improve relations between the two literary camps in Wales and shortly afterwards I was able to discuss with the Academi the creation of an English-language section.

'In the Wales in which we live, there is no literary answer to the literary problem. The crisis that is disturbing the nation is caused by political pressure; it must therefore be resolved politically.' One of the *obiter dicta* of the Old Man of Aberdaron to which I can readily subscribe.

The best of intentions are sometimes misunderstood. The wife of one of our Labour MPs was buying apples in a corner-shop. Anxious to avoid any that were ideologically unsound, she made a point of asking the shopkeeper to tell her which ones came from South Africa so that she could avoid buying them. She was about to make her choice when another customer, who'd heard her fussing, plucked at her sleeve and in the nicest possible way said, 'That's right, love, you can't be too careful. You don't want to go buying anything those blacks have been handling.'

I don't think we went on holiday as a family more than two or three times when I was a boy. If we did, I have no recollection of it whatsoever. I remember spending a wet, windy week in a caravan among the sand-dunes of Porthcawl and there are snaps of us on the promenade at Brighton, I think it was, or perhaps Worthing, but that's all. My father's idea of a day out was to take us on the bus to Merthyr to see my Aunties Gwen and Annie. Gwen was the widow of a man called Leyshon who had owned a fruiterer's business in the town and whose lorries are still to be seen about the place. Annie kept a small grocer's shop known as Sunclad Stores in the High Street of Cefncoedycymer, opposite the war memorial. The shop, with its smell of fruit and vegetables and the advertisements for Fyffes Bananas and Outspan oranges, was for me a place of delight that I savour again whenever I enter a grocer's shop all these years later.

It was on our frequent trips to visit these members of Merthyr's shopocracy I first became aware of social class. Annie's husband,

Enoch Chappell, worked in a sub-power-station, so I suppose they were working class, just like us. Uncle Enoch was a genial, muscular man whose way of amusing me was to lift me up until my head bumped the beams of their small living-room at the back of the shop and to shout 'Cato pawb!' in mock-horror. Their son, Howard, had served in the war as a navigator with the RAF and used to regale me with tales about Gremlins and bombing raids over Germany. Their daughter, Bernice, was a good-natured, buxom girl who was kind to me; she later married John Price, the Brecon egg-merchant.

Although we were always made welcome by Auntie Annie and Uncle Enoch – I spent many a weekend at their house, during which I swam in the Blue Pool and walked over to Ponsticell – I began to feel somehow we were the poor relations, to be entertained to tea as lavishly as possible as if we couldn't afford to eat properly at home. The Chappells were certainly better off than we were, on account of the shop, and they had a few things like silver teapots, bone china, linen tablecloths and ringed serviettes that I'd only ever seen in their house. Whenever they came to visit us in Trefforest, my mother and grandmother would put on a good show, making apple-tarts and sponge-cakes, and serving ham sandwiches and *bara brith*, but somehow it never seemed quite as grand as what was laid on for us in Cefn. Perhaps it was the salty Carmarthenshire butter they always spread on their thinly sliced bread or the cinnamon sprinkled on their bakestones that made the Sunday afternoons we spent there seem so superior to what we had at home. Be that as it may, the difference in our situation was driven home to us when my parents were not invited to the weddings of their son and daughter.

Remember Sir Andrew Barton – he laid him down to rest a while then rose to fight again.

Many things do not matter much and most do not matter at all.

Sunday, 3 November

I took Brengain to lunch at Sundance and Clint Graviet came with us. Leslie was there with Peter Florence, the man who runs the Hay Literature Festival.

Katie Owen called at the flat to say goodbye to Brengain, for she's going home tomorrow.

The next time I became aware of social class was when I started going to see a girl in Cadoxton, Barry, whom I'd met while on a sixth-form course at Dyffryn in the Vale of Glamorgan. Her parents, Tom and Olwen Yeoman, were invariably kind to me and I must have seemed to them a very callow youth. Their house was quite small and modestly furnished – they were both primary-school teachers and leading members of the Labour Party in Barry – but it was there I saw silk cushions, carpets, polished block floors and a bathroom for the first time. My friendship with their daughter, Siân, dragged on for another four or five years, on and off, and I became a regular visitor to her home, but I was always conscious of the difference between her social class and my own.

Siân's parents once took me for Sunday tea at the home of Aneirin Talfan Davies in Pencisely Road, Llandaf, to whom Olwen, a Welsh-speaker, was distantly related. The visit was memorable for two reasons. There I met Owen Talfan, Aneirin's elder son, a suave young man and a student at Oxford at the time, who was later killed in a car-accident in Scotland, and his brother, Geraint Talfan, then a schoolboy, who is now Controller of BBC Wales.

The other reason was that Aneirin Talfan showed me a cheque signed by Dylan Thomas. He'd had it framed and it hung on the wall of his study; it had bounced, of course, he told me with a broad grin. I later became a great admirer of Aneirin Talfan for his work as a literary critic who was keenly interested in Welsh writing in English. His book, *Yr Alltud*, was the first book I ever read about James Joyce.

'Tun pretelthanks corbunci heafleode gradinlinc.'

The first story I covered as a cub reporter with the *Western Mail* was about a Newport man, a circus performer, who had been killed after falling from a high wire into a tub of water – his head had hit the side and he'd drowned before he could be fished out. I had to interview his widow but failed to do so because several large men were standing at the gate of her house and turning

170

away all visitors. When I got back to Thomson House the news editor, John Humphries, gave me a bollocking for not getting a quote from the bereaved woman.

'Apart from that, Mrs Lincoln, how did you enjoy the show?'

There's a pub in Cardiff with the words *Floreat Ecclesia Anglicanum* painted on the front wall; the Church of England in its cups, as it were.

I must have about 140 Welsh ballads in English now and hope to put them into a book one day. Some of them I copied from a small collection of original broadsheets that Eirian Davies once lent me. Most are about murders and executions, pit-disasters, strikes and lock-outs, and a few refer to events such as elections and shipwrecks. But none has the power of the verses that begin :

> You've heard of the Gresford Disaster
> And the terrible price that was paid –
> Two hundred and sixty-two colliers were lost
> And three men of the rescue brigade.

The disaster happened in 1934 but no one seems to know who wrote the ballad.

Huw's first attempt to write a whole sentence in English was: 'ai opend dde dor an ai fel on dde flo'. He used to make up the most delightful words, among them *enfach* for 'tiny', on the model of *enfawr* for 'huge'; he always referred to breaking wind as *'prog'*. When he acquired a little English (by going to the *Ysgol Gymraeg*) he used to say things like 'flicking hep!' and 'good gorgeous me!'.

In the Spring of 1980 I went to Glascwm, a small village in the hills of the old cantref of Elfael a little to the north of Builth, and then, from the Hundred House side, walked up over the Giant's Tump and into a small valley to see Blaenbedw. The house had 'gone down', as they say in Radnorshire: its upper floor had been removed and the building was being used as a store for cattle feed, but the fireplace was still intact and the glass of the windows was still in its frames. There were Charlie trees planted in a row in front of the house and a broad drovers' road ran past it down the valley.

A Glasgwm a'i eglwys ger glas fynydd,
gwyddelfodd aruchel, nawdd ni echwydd.

In the village I looked through the parish registers and talked to several old people who could remember Annie Lloyd, including the couple who owned Blaenbedw, Mr and Mrs Stan Jones, who also kept the village sub post office and shop. They told me it was known she'd had a 'by-blow', the Radnorshire word for an illegitimate child, when she was about twenty, but had never revealed who the father was. She'd lived with her brother, Hugh Lloyd, who had farmed Blaenbedw and worked at the Mill in Hundred House until about 1945, but in the same year as the birth of her child she'd moved away and hadn't been seen in the district since. They also told me that, a few years previously, a man had been in the village asking about Annie Lloyd and looking for a photo of her, but no one had been able to help him; that was my father.

Going through the church registers, I discovered that Annie Lloyd, at the age of 17, had been in service at The Court (also known as The Yat), the 'big house' in Glascwm. I immediately thought her child might have been fathered by one of the Vaughans who lived at The Court and so I did a good deal of research into the family, even publishing a list of their twelve children in the newsletter of the Kilvert Society. One of them, John Dyke Vaughan, had been the baby 'baptized in ice' by Kilvert at Bettws Clyro on St. Valentine's Eve 1870. But this proved to be a false trail.

Elsa Triolet. Thérèse Levasseur. Juliette Drouet. Marthe Massin.

Man is born free and everywhere he is in chinos.

Monday, 4 November
I drove Brengain to the airport at Salt Lake City. We've had a most enjoyable holiday together and have done just over 2,000 miles during her time here.

In the afternoon I went into the Department and had a long talk with Leslie about an interview for the book about him that Eugene England is compiling.

172

I remember taking Jack Jones by car to a conference at Gregynog and asking him, among other things, whether he was a religious man, to which he replied, 'I pray more times in a day than a Muslim.' I got to know Jack quite well when we lived in Rhiwbina, as he did. Our house was first in Lôn y Rhyd and then in Clos Bryn Deri, near the Butcher's Arms, where he was a regular. He would call on us for a glass of stout on Saturday mornings before going over to the pub. When the Arts Council gave him a prize in 1970 he began his speech with the words, 'Ladies and gentlemen, I've come this evening without my braces . . . ' Shortly after his death later in the year I went to see his widow and she gave me two of his oak bookcases as a souvenir of a remarkable man and writer.

Another occasion when Ruth and I were supposed to spend a night at Gregynog comes to mind. Late at night, while I was attending a meeting of the Press's management board, Ruth, on her way to bed, tripped on a frayed carpet and fell headlong down the stairs, dislocating her shoulder. There being no doctor on call, I drove her across country to the nearest hospital – in Shrewsbury. We returned to Gregynog just as dawn was breaking, with Ruth still in great pain. After an hour's rest, and deciding to go home before breakfast, we were dismayed to find a bill for the night's accommodation awaiting us. Friends and colleagues urged us to sue Gregynog for the disrepair of its carpets, but we let it pass.

After my first visit to Glascwm I spent about a year trying to find trace of Hugh Lloyd, Annie's brother, as a way of locating her. He'd been married three times and had four daughters by his first two wives. One of them, Dolly Lloyd, had died in Gladestry in 1944 and in her funeral report in the *Brecon and Radnor Express* I found a list of mourners, including a Mrs A. Parsons of Leominster, who was described as her aunt. I then went looking for a woman of this name in Leominster, without success. The surname turned out to be a misprint for Passant. I found it in a report of Hugh Lloyd's funeral in *The Hereford Times* in 1968, in which there was a reference to a 'Mr Alfred Passant, also representing Mrs Passant, sister', and among the wreaths had been one 'from Annie and Alf, Hanwood'. The same report also stated: 'Mr Lloyd was a member of a well-known Radnorshire farming family and was formerly vicar's warden at Glascombe (sic) for 14 years'. It was thus I found my father's mother: she had become Mrs Annie Passant of Great Hanwood, just outside Shrewsbury.

How many miles, how many, from Leominster to Llanllieni?

I got the idea for Dial-a-Poem, a scheme by which poets were invited to read a poem over the telephone every week, during a trip I made to Friesland with Alun Creunant Davies in 1972. We picked up several good ideas in Leeuwarden/Ljouwert, including the *Bro a Bywyd* series and an annual Books Festival.

Mother Tongue. Mother Carey. Mother Goose. Mother Church. Mother Bear. Mother Bunch. Mother Brown. Mother Courage. Mother Shipton. Mother of God. Mother of Pearl. Mother of Thyme. Mother of Invention. Mother of Parliaments. Mother of the Free. Mother of all Battles. Mother Wit. Queen Mother. Mother Macree. Motherwort. Mother Superior. Mother Moll. Mother's Pride. Mother Marvel. Mother Teresa. Mother's Day. Mother's Boy. Mother's Mark. Mother's Ruin. Old Mother Hubbard. Old Mother Riley. Mother Russia. Mother Earth. Great Mother.

The first time I met Harri Webb he saved me from going up in smoke. We were standing in the saloon bar of the Old Arcade in the Hayes, one of the last of Cardiff's pubs to have preserved some measure of its Edwardian charm. It was all mirrors and mahogany, there was sawdust on the floor, a coal fire, a spittoon, and women were allowed only in the snug. As we stood there chatting and drinking the draught Guinness, I noticed from the corner of my eye that we were being observed. Presently, an elderly man got up from his table and came over to us. He had the air of an old soldier, suggested by his beeswaxed moustache and rather stiff bearing, and he carried a cane with which he tapped Harri gently on the shoulder. Then, with a smart salute, he said quietly, 'Excuse me, sir, your friend's on fire.'

So I was. I'd been leaning on the counter, my elbow just touching one of the small gas-jets that were used to light cigars, and the leather patch on my schoolmaster's jacket had begun to scorch and the tweed to smoulder. Flapping my arm, yet feeling nothing, I tried to inspect the damage, but couldn't see what was going on. There was a smell of singeing in the air. Harri now intervened. He didn't quite leap into action (that wasn't his way), but his thinking was quick enough. With one hand he held my wrist and from the pint-glass in the other he slowly and solemnly poured his Guinness down my upturned sleeve. The fire was doused and not a head had been turned. I thanked the old gent for raising the alarm, and so discreetly, bought him a tot and a new glass for Harri, and we resumed our conversation at the counter.

It was the late summer of 1962. Just down from the University, I was about to take up a post as French master at the Grammar School in Ebbw Vale, and Harri was on a half-day's excursion to the city from Dowlais, where he was branch librarian. I can't remember what exactly we talked about on that first conflagrative evening, but I know we took a shine to each other there and then. It may have been because we had a good deal in common, despite a difference of some eighteen years in our ages. For a start, both our fathers had spent their working lives in electric power stations, his at Tir John and mine at Upper Boat, so our family backgrounds were quite similar – staunchly proletarian with roots in rural, English-speaking Wales. We had both taken degrees in Romance Languages, and I recall our conversation grew more and more macaronic as that first evening drew to a close. We found, too, that we liked the same poets – Lorca, Prévert, Neruda, Eluard, MacDiarmid – and shared the same views about language, literature and politics. Both members of Plaid Cymru, we nevertheless thought of ourselves more as Welsh Socialists than traditional Nationalists and were primarily committed to the Party's progress in the industrial south-east, the only part of Wales we really knew. These shared interests, and Harri's profuse quotation from writers I admired, made for a headier brew than anything served in the Old Arcade that evening, and by stop-tap I was his liege-man.

On the last train up the Valley that night, before getting off at Trefforest, I accepted Harri's invitation to meet him in Merthyr Tydfil on the following Saturday, with a view to my taking a room in Garth Newydd, the house at the bottom of the Brecon Road at the junction with Bethesda Street, where he'd been installed for about two years. The prospect of living in Merthyr held great appeal for me. As a boy, I'd often paid visits to the town to see my Aunties Gwen and Annie, so I knew my way around its streets pretty well. The place was associated in my mind with Dic Penderyn, Charlotte Guest, Thomas Stephens (no relation, alas), Henry Richard, Keir Hardie, Glyn Jones, Jack Jones and Gwyn A. Williams, the last of whom I'd come to know in Aberystwyth. I liked especially the egalitarian spirit of the people, despite its rough edge, and was interested in the rich industrial archaeology to be found there before they started knocking the old Merthyr down. Meeting Harri at his library, which was housed in the stables of the Guest ironworks, I was shown around the furnaces, the tramroad and the limestone tips with an enthusiasm I found infectious. Harri seemed to know everybody and it was that afternoon, on being introduced to some of his many borrowers, I heard the Welsh of Dowlais, a form of *Gwenhwyseg*, for the first time. Its peculiar phonology and vocabulary, which Harri had cultivated and used with a certain panache, lent just that final spot of local colour to a place that already had me in thrall.

I've always liked the image of a turbine. When I take my seat in the House as Lord Trefforest I shall have a coat-of-arms and headed notepaper with a turbine on it and two pink pigs flying across it and the words *'Cato pawb!'* emblazoned underneath.

In 1983, still proceeding cautiously, I made some enquiries in the Hereford County Archives and the Shrewsbury Crematorium, where I discovered that Alfred Cornelius Passant and his wife, Annie Sophia, had lived at 1 Vine Cottages in Great Hanwood, but that she had died on 15 April 1971 at the age of 81.

I then went looking for a solicitor in Shrewsbury, to enlist help in making an approach to Mr Passant. I had no idea of his circumstances and thought it prudent to ask a third party to act on my behalf at this stage. As I was ushered into the solicitor's office, I immediately recognized Delwyn Williams, who used to be the Tory MP for Montgomeryshire. I explained what I was about and, a genial man, he kindly agreed (for a modest fee) to go to Hanwood. In due course, after calling at Vine Cottages, he reported that Alfred Passant still lived there but knew nothing about Annie's having had a child.

I'd failed to find my grandmother alive but now I knew she was dead I could press on with greater speed to find out more about her. I sometimes wonder what would have happened if she'd still been alive: would I have had the courage, or the moral right, to contact her and would my father have wanted to meet her and she him? Fortunately, perhaps, we'd been spared all that.

Tuesday, 5 November
Guy Fawkes is unknown here.

I received a letter from John Pikoulis today informing me Robin Reeves has been appointed editor of *The New Welsh Review*.

I spoke to my classes today about Anglo-Saxon, of which they were only vaguely aware. When I asked where the English language had its origins, one student thought it had been brought to England by the Romans and another that it had grown out of Norman French.

The reason why I read French at Aberystwyth was that, in the 1950s, when Gwyn Jones was Professor, for a student of English to fail the first-year English paper (which I did) was to be debarred from ever entering the Honours English class. However harsh this rule seemed, and many of us chafed against it, the paper had to be sat again and the year repeated before even a pass would be allowed. So that's what I did, following again exactly the same syllabus in my three subjects as before, despite the fact I'd passed all the other papers, except this time I made sure I didn't fail in Old English.

As a consequence, I had a highly convivial extra year at Aberystwyth, writing for the *Courier*, the College newspaper, getting involved in politics, and going out and staying in with quite a few women to whom I shall always be grateful. My extra year also made me ineligible for military service which, by the time I graduated in 1961, had been abolished, though I'd signed a preliminary statement with a view to being a conscientous objector on political grounds. I often wonder how I would have managed if I had refused to be conscripted or, worse, had been obliged to serve.

My repeat year, and then my year in France, also meant I had a chance to read voraciously in both English and French and to work my way through the collection of books by Anglo-Welsh authors in the Library. The only effort I made during the year was with my Anglo-Saxon. To this day I can still conjugate Old English verbs and recite, if given half a chance, passages from Henry Sweet's *Anglo-Saxon Reader*: 'Ochthere told his lord, King Alfred, that he of all Norwegians dwelt the furthest north . . . '. I can even remember how Caedmon's Hymn begins: '*Nu sculon herigean heofonrices weard, metodes meahte and his modgethanc . . . '*. It might come in handy one day, though not here in Utah.

Having learned so much by rote, I was given a very high mark (I think it was 96 per cent) the second time round. But too late: my copybook had been blotted and there was no erasing the stain. The following year it was with gratitude I accepted a place in the French Honours class, taking English thereafter only as my auxiliary subject. I went on to enjoy every part of my degree course – except Old French – and today I'm glad things turned out as they did. Otherwise, I shouldn't have read Villon, Ronsard, Racine, Baudelaire, Verlaine, Apollinaire, Eluard, Breton or Aragon in their own language.

I've always been tickled by the story about a sergeant introducing a speaker to a class of Army squaddies in the days when conscription was in force. 'Now our guest this morning,' he said, 'is going to speak to you about Keats and Yeats. I bet none of you ignorant sods would recognize a Keat or a Yeat if you saw one.'

I moved into Garth Newydd about a week after meeting Harri Webb in the Old Arcade. It was a large, Victorian, ironmaster's house, one of the oldest in town, with a dozen rooms on three floors and another two in the attic which I chose for myself and where, after a little refurbishment, I soon settled in. The remarkable thing about my tenancy, Harri explained, was that although I was expected to share the cost of the usual amenities, I would pay no rent since the house was not owned by anybody. More precisely, as I was to learn in due course, the property – formerly the home of Dr Biddle, Merthyr's first charter mayor – had been presented to the town by Lord Kemsley, one of its more untypical sons, during the grim years of the Depression, and had been used for various social and philanthropic purposes ever since. The local branches of the Women's Voluntary Service and the Red Cross still had a presence in one of the wings and there was a large wooden hut in the backyard that was sometimes used for public meetings.

In 1959, however, having stood vacant for some years, the old house had been occupied by a small group of pacifists who'd thought to lead a life based on Sarvodayan principles and good works in the community. Harri had become acquainted with these hopelessy impractical people, mostly middle-class English do-gooders, and had taken up residence because it was roomy, congenial and free. No pacifist himself, he had nothing but cold contempt for his hosts, although it was from them, I'm sure, he acquired his taste for the pungent curries which he cooked and consumed with such gusto. When, after a while, the Fellowship of the Friends of Truth, as they called themselves, began to quarrel and fall apart, Harri found himself the sole occupant of the house. By this time all the original trustees were dead and he'd assumed what amounted to squatter's rights, living in Garth Newydd and now inviting others to join him there.

This evening the Norrises gave a party for Peter Florence, where I met the Parkinsons, the couple next door.

I don't like kissing women. I hope that doesn't make me a philematophobe. What I mean is I don't like the custom which seems to be fashionable, both here and increasingly in Wales, of greeting women with a peck on the cheek, especially if they aren't relatives or old friends. If there must be flesh-contact, I'd much prefer the old French aristocratic habit of kissing, or nearly kissing, the lady's hand. It's much more elegant and flattering, and at least the man doesn't come away with cosmetics on his face. What I dislike most is when women, as they are kissed, go 'Mmmmmmmmm–ah!' – as if this gob-smacking adds something to the experience. Perhaps after 1992 there will be grants from Brussels to encourage the technique of hand-kissing.

About 55 million people lost their lives during the second world war.

In Moscow I saw the huge monument, about twelve miles from the centre of the city, that marks the spot where the German tanks ran out of petrol and local people came out and butchered the invaders.

I've been trying to think in French all day today. 'Dysgais yr *eang Ffrangeg, iaith dda, iaith deg.'* A pretty ugly woman is not the same as *une jolie laide, un mariage blanc* is not a white wedding and *feu le roi* does not mean fire the king.

I've had a jab against the 'flu because an epidemic is expected in the Wasatch Valley. I try to recall how many times I've been seriously ill. I don't remember being operated on by Dr Gwyn Evans, our family's GP, on the kitchen table when I was one, as my parents once informed me, nor have I ever been able to discover what was wrong with me on that occasion, unless it was a suspected case of meningitis: the doctor put a needle into my spine, or so I'm told.

The cures to which we had recourse when I was a boy now seem to smack of witchcraft. Bread poultices and goosegrease were applied to the affected parts and a bunch of keys on the nape of the neck was supposed to stop a nose-bleed. Brimstone and treacle were given to children who were constipated. A coal fire was always lit in the bedroom of a person with pneumonia and the patient encouraged to inhale the steam from boiling kettles. Among the commercial remedies I can remember are Beecham's Pills ('worth a guinea a box'), Scott's Emulsion, Zambuk ('for speedy relief of muscular pains'), Parrish's Food, Snowfire ('soothes chapped hands') and Brooklax ('keeps you regular').

In 1984, during the miners' strike, I drove into a herd of runaway horses on the motorway on my way to Llandysul and had to spend ten days in the East Glamorgan Hospital while recuperating from lacerations to my face. One of the horses was killed in the collision but I received some small compensation from its owner. I still get pain in my neck and shoulders from the jolt of the accident.

The only time I can remember being ill was when, in 1965, I caught glandular fever ('the kissing disease'), shortly after my engagement to Ruth. I come from a sturdy line of Radnorshire hill-folk and artisans and I enjoy robust health, which is a piece of great good fortune.

I decided to go to Hanwood to see Alf Passant and talked to him on the pretext I was doing research into the Lloyds, the family of bonesetters to which his wife had belonged. It was strange sitting on the hearth where my grandmother had lived for so long and my mind raced in thinking about the circumstances of her child's birth and her subsequent life here. I didn't have the heart to reveal to Mr Passant what my real motive and true identity were. It was clear his wife had never told him about the child she had borne in 1910 and I felt it was best not to betray her secret to the man she'd subsequently married.

He was quite ready to talk about his late wife, informing me that he'd courted her for seventeen years before marrying her in 1936, when she would have been 46 and he was 36. They'd been happy togther, he said, and had enjoyed going for trips on a motor-bike. This had been their only marriage and there had been no children. The reason why they'd taken so long to marry was that Annie had been content with her lot at Weston, a farm at Priestweston, near Chirbury, the home of a Mr and Mrs Harry Davies; the hamlet, like Walton, is within a hundred yards of the border with England. Before that, Mr Passant said, she'd worked for a cattle-breeder named John Watkeys Jones at Sheep House, a large farm on the road between Glasbury and The Hay. Mr Passant, a tall, spare man with an Edwardian moustache, also told me he'd been a builder by trade and that his firm, Higley's of Pontesbury, had built the King's Hall in Aberystwyth. I didn't get another chance to talk to him because he died of a heart-attack in 1986. He was buried with his wife in an unmarked grave in the churchyard, at a spot pointed out to me by the vicar.

Fluctuat nec mergitur.

Wednesday, 6 November
'Happy the hare at morning, for she cannot read the hunter's waking thoughts.'

Peter Florence asked me today to drive him down to Salt Lake City where Amos Oz was speaking at the University of Utah. Peter wants him to appear at the Hay Festival and Oz said he would. I can remember nothing of his talk except that he began by saying, 'If ever the University of Utah establishes a Chair in Extremism, I shall want to be considered a candidate for it.' I should think there'd be plenty of other candidates, mostly Utahns.

I told Peter the story about Goronwy Rees meeting an

aristocratic young Englishman in the buttery of his College during his first week at Oxford. On being asked, 'Tell me, do you know the Angleseys?', Rees was perplexed and could only reply, 'Do you mean there's more than one of them?'

In one of Nancy Mitford's books, when asked what it had been like in France during the war, she replies: 'My dear, it was frightful – we couldn't get books by Charles Morgan!' How many read Charles Morgan nowadays? Rather fewer, I think, than Anthony Powell – to whom I may be very distantly related. I've long intended to look into the matter by writing to Powell (Pole); like me, he's a member of the Radnorshire Society and keenly interested in his family-tree. My great-grandmother, Martha Powell, lived at Gwernybwch, near Huntington, a little to the north of Michaelchurch-on-Arrow, and not far from The Traveley, the house near Brilley where Anthony Powell's forebears lived. The Powells are still at Gwernybwch; I know because they win prizes at the Agricultural Show in Builth every year.

I bet the Marquess of Anglesey would know who said, 'In battle the cavalry lends tone and dignity to what otherwise would be a bloody mess', but I can't remember who it was. Is this the first sign of onomastophesia?

It was Glyn Tegai Hughes, rather surprisingly, who told me a man knows he's growing old when he starts forgetting people's names and peeing on his shoes. I don't know whether Glyn was speaking from experience, but I think he was right on the first point. He and I started off on the wrong foot after he joined the Literature Committee, mainly on account of a paper I wrote about the creation of a National Publishing House for Wales. It offended his Liberal *laissez-faire* principles, I think. But as we came to know each other better our relationship improved and I got on quite well with him, particularly after he became Chairman of the Committee and we managed to revive the Gregynog Press in 1974.

The board that ran the Press was the most glacial in its progress I've ever attended. It was chaired by Lord Kenyon, a keen bibliophile, who insisted on telling us all about the fine editions he'd acquired for his extensive library since our last meeting. To make matters worse, his Lordship was short-sighted and deaf, so it was difficult to draw his attention to anything. The other members, who included two of the most erudite and urbane men in Wales, deferred to him in the most craven way. I chafed at every meeting, but I was there only as an observer on behalf of the Arts Council, so I tried to say as little as possible. At one meeting the old Tory and Grand Pontiff started running down Ioan Bowen Rees, Chief Executive of Gwynedd County Council, on account of his support for self-government, and wouldn't be shut up. Unlike everyone else present, his Lordship was unaware that Ioan is my brother-in-law. When the attack subsided, they all looked at me as if expecting me to go for Kenyon's throat. All I said was, 'Chairman, I think you're being scurrilous. I suggest we move to the next item on the agenda.' He didn't hear me and the others just grinned sheepishly and shuffled their papers.

Ça ira, ça ira, ça ira . . .

I had a hand in getting B. S. Johnson a Fellowship at Gregynog. I'd known him since our undergraduate days when we were both involved with *Universities' Poetry*. Bryan had stayed at our home and I at his in London; he lived quite near Rodney Street in Pentonville, where my grandfather was brought up. He was very happy during his time at Gregynog and got on well with Glyn Tegai. In his novel *House Mother Normal* there's a passage in which the first letters of successive paragraphs spell out the name of Glyn Tegai Hughes and those of his wife, Margaret, and their sons.

I had no idea of Bryan's suicidal tendencies. I knew he had an unusual interest in death and in cancer, from which his mother had died, and he once pointed out to me that the design on the jacket of his novel, *The Unfortunates* (the one in which the chapters can be shuffled and read in any order), is based on cancer cells. But I always found him good company and of a sunny temperament. I was really shocked in 1973 when told that he'd killed himself. I liked him very much. He was one of the few English writers with whom it was possible to have an intelligent discussion about things Welsh. Bryan drank a bottle of whisky before slashing his wrists in the bath and when he was discovered they found 'This is my final word' daubed in blood on the tiles of the bathroom wall.

Gerallt Jones is at Gregynog now: a good man and a fine writer. I got to know him well during a trip to the Soviet Union a few years back with Gillian Clarke. We went first to Tbilisi and, on our last day there, I caught too much sun while bathing in the pool on the top of the Iveria Hotel and was quite ill. By the time we arrived in Tashkent I was really groggy and in Samarkand I had to take a bath in yoghurt to cool my body down.

Glyn Tegai Hughes once told me that when he was National Governor of the BBC in Wales he was attending a meeting in London when a message was sent up from reception about a man who had an urgent complaint to make. During a coffee-break the Governors agreed to see him. It turned out this poor chap wished to complain that he was receiving the Third Programme through his false teeth, the steel wires of which were picking up radio signals. It was driving him potty and he wanted to know whether the BBC engineers could do anything about it.

During that first winter of 1962/63 at Garth Newydd, for much of which we were snowbound, there were five of us in the house. For a while we tried to run it as a commune. Judy Gurney organized a rota of domestic chores, the household accounts were in the capable hands of Tony Lewis, I painted and papered the rooms, Neil Jenkins gave us Welsh lessons, and Harri presided in an avuncular sort of way.

Within a year, we'd been joined by Rodric Evans, Dave Buckel and Peter Meazey, later the owner of Siop y Triban in Cardiff, although so many people came to stay with us, often for weeks at a time, it wasn't always easy to say just who the residents of Garth Newydd were. One of the features of our occupancy was that we felt obliged to keep the door on the latch for anyone who wanted a bed for the night, especially political activists or writers from other parts of Wales. Some of these visitors wrote their names in our guest-book – Gwynfor Evans, Keidrych Rhys, Phil Williams, Trefor Morgan, Chris Rees, Emrys Roberts, David Pritchard, Twm Jones, John Daniel, Gareth Miles, Tony Conran – while others, prudently perhaps, declined to leave any trace of their sojourn under our roof.

I've often been asked whether Harri Webb is homosexual. I've even heard a rumour, from Doreen Jones, to the effect that one of the reasons why the marriage of Keidrych Rhys and Lynette Roberts broke up was that Harri and Keidrych were too 'close'.

From what I know of Harri I can say without the slightest hesitation that he's certainly not homosexual or bisexual. He's been emotionally involved with several women, often young actress types, though nothing has ever come of these brief affairs, and that may have caused the speculation. Harri has given me his journals, which span some forty years, and in one of them he names the women with whom he's had sex, some ninety in all, though I suspect most were one-night stands and some were definitely prostitutes. What people don't know is that in the 1950s Harri had a common-law wife and at least one daughter – though that's no proof of his sexual orientation, of course. It was in an attempt to escape from this unhappy relationship with the woman, whose name I know, that he went to Cheltenham where he became a librarian. There's certainly a streak of misogyny in him.

The cause that bound us together was that of Plaid Cymru. We were active on its behalf in Merthyr and neighbouring constituencies, and Harri was doing a stint as editor of *Welsh Nation*, the Party's newspaper. I used to help Harri put the paper to bed and learned a lot about typography and printing in the process. More generally, among the things we thought were good ideas was a Secretary of State for Wales, as a step towards an elected Parliament, and in the mean while we were in favour of any public body that might be charged with responsibility for the cultural or economic life of Wales.

'We go to win a little patch of land that hath no profit in it but the name.'

The events that dominated the thinking of many Nationalists in the 1960s were the unsuccessful campaign to save the Tryweryn and Clywedog Valleys from being used as reservoirs for English cities, and the birth of *Cymdeithas yr Iaith*. The two were not unrelated: the political parties' failure to defend the interests of Wales, despite all the oratory, had led to a call for 'direct action', particularly among the young. We wanted to do something rather than talk about it. We at Garth Newydd were on the side of the new militants and a contingent from Merthyr was usually to be found in the thick of the fray, as at Trefechan Bridge in February 1963. But I don't think any of us, least of all Harri, was ever involved in anything more felonious than the painting of slogans, although it was he who devised the symbol, based on the White Eagle of Eryri, which later became the badge of the Free Wales Army.

Harri also took part in some of the emissions of Radio Free Wales, the pirate radio set up to circumvent the Government's refusal to allow Plaid Cymru broadcasting time. It's difficult now to imagine a Wales in which Plaid Cymru is banned from broadcasting. Peripatetic, but with a very weak signal that confined its message within a radius of a few miles, the radio went on the air just as BBC television was closing down. 'Do not switch off,' Harri's unmistakable voice would be heard to announce just as 'God save the Queen' faded. 'You are listening to the voice of Free Wales.' Among others who took part in the broadcasts were Glyn James, Alf Williams, a veteran Nationalist from the Rhymney Valley, and Ray Smith, the actor.

One night, as the others went on the air from my attic room, two policemen called at Garth Newydd. They were in the habit of doing so because they knew they could count on a chat and a warm by the fire before going out again on their beat. Harri didn't turn a hair at sight of our late-night visitors, but made them toast and a cup of tea and kept them talking for half an hour while the operators of Radio Free Wales packed up their equipment and made their way on tip-toe out into the night.

I recall a mysterious incident at Garth Newydd. I was in bed with 'flu and alone in the house one morning when two strangers in suits walked into my room. They had come, they said, because they'd been told I might be interested in forming a Welsh counterpart to the Boy Scouts. After a while it became clear that the movement they envisaged would consist of clandestine cells of boys in their teens who would learn drill and the use of firearms. I was in no state to discuss the matter and, after about an hour, they left. I have no idea who they were and never saw them again, but I'm inclined to think they were *agents provocateurs*.

I did my bit to draw attention to the iniquitous ban on Plaid Cymru from the airwaves. One dark night in 1963, with Bill Williams, the Plaid councillor in Dowlais, I painted a slogan on the wall of Cyfarthfa Castle: 'Lift the tv ban on Plaid Cymru'. A passing police car spotted us and we were subsequently taken to court and fined £12 each. We refused to pay the fine, arguing that we hadn't defaced the wall but improved its appearance, and after a few weeks of stalemate, an anonymous sympathiser paid it for us. Bill Williams lost his seat at the next election.

The only time I was in trouble as a schoolboy was after an incident involving Al Jolson. It was shortly before the first lesson of the afternoon and Form IVA were waiting for our teacher to arrive and call the register. There was just time for a spot of light entertainment and it was my turn to make the class laugh. So I went out to the front and, going down on one knee, began singing.

'Maaaamy! Maaaamy! The sun shines east, the sun shines west . . .'

The other boys watched as I clasped one hand to my chest, the other fluttering in the air and my eyes rolling like Al Jolson's, except I didn't have a blacked-up face.

'But I know where the sun shines best . . .'

Some of the boys were standing on their desks and clapping and cheering wildly as I went through the famous routine.

'I'd walk a million miles for one of your smiles . . .'

It occurred to me at this point that perhaps the others were beginning to lose interest but I was determined to carry on to the crescendo.

'My Maaaamy!'

There was no applause except for a single pair of hands clapping slowly, irregularly, in mock-appreciation of my performance. The classroom was hushed and the boys were making sheepishly for their seats. When I looked up I saw what they could already see: Mr P. R. Jones, whom we called Nap because he used to keep his right hand tucked inside his jacket, standing poker-faced in the doorway.

'Stephens,' he said, 'come and see me at four o'clock. You ain't heard nuthin' yet.'

Astonished as I was to hear him using Hollywood slang, I knew only too well what an invitation to his study at four'o clock meant. I spent the afternoon in keen anticipation of six of the best.

'Enter!' he called when I knocked at the door.

The study smelt of fresh polish and stale cigar-smoke and there was a vase of gladioli on the windowsill. The Headmaster made a show of tidying some papers on his desk and didn't look up as I came in and, well out of the reach of his right arm, stood shifting uneasily from one foot to the other, expecting the full weight of Mr Jones's authority to descend on me at any moment. When he eventually deigned to notice me it was with a weary sigh, whereupon he seemed to relax and a wan smile flickered over his stern countenance.

'Well, Stephens, it seems you're fond of the cinema.'

'Yes, Sir.'

'Mmm . . . Do you go often?'

'Yes, Sir, every week, Sir.'

'Mmm . . . where do you go?

'The White Palace, Sir.'

'Mmm . . . and what films have you seen recently?'

'*The Count of Monte Christo*, Sir.'

'Mmm . . . What about *Mrs Miniver*? They tell me it's good.'

'No, Sir.'

'Mmm . . . what else have you seen?'

'I saw *Michael Strogoff*, Sir, when it came to the Cecil, Sir.'

'Mmm . . . did you like it, boy?'

'Yes, Sir, but it was all in Russian, Sir.'

'Mmm.'

The exchange of critical opinion between the two film-buffs didn't seem to be leading anywhere. The Headmaster shuffled some papers and when the large clock on the marble mantelpiece struck the half-hour, stared at it as if in utter disbelief.

'Off you go, boy, or your parents will be wondering where you are.'

'Yes, Sir. Thank you, Sir.'

'Oh, and Stephens . . . don't let me catch you fooling about again, will you?'

'No, Sir. Sorry, Sir.'

It was a strange experience to revisit the school a few years back and see how small the headmaster's study was, and how nondescript.

Thursday, 7 November

Today I read the typescripts of essays by R. S. Thomas and Peter

Lord in my *Changing Wales* series. Peter has it in for the Art Department of the National Museum and musters some pretty convincing arguments for a radical reappraisal of its policies regarding the visual arts in Wales. The title of Thomas's essay is *Cymru or Wales?*: it's his usual gripe about the anglicization of our country. One of the things he objects to is the practice of naming children John, but more generally, I think, he's against the 20th century – tv, the cinema, tourism, the internal combustion engine, towns and cities, political parties, the English language, democracy . . .

The most succinct reader's report I ever received was an *englyn* by T. Arfon Williams on a book about R. S.Thomas:

> I read it and liked it, alas I feel
> It fails to encompass
> Our esteemed R. S. Thomas;
> Yet I opine, let it pass.

When R. S. Thomas was vicar of Eglwys-fach he used to write to Taid just before Christmas every year asking whether he could arrange to get rid of the manger set up near the Town Clock by the Chamber of Commerce. It was, he thought, 'vulgar'. Hoity-toity Thomas.

What gets my goat is adulation of the man and poet by those who do not fully understand what he is saying about Wales and the Welsh and, even if they did, would do nothing to work for the Wales he wants. I can't take his ultra Nationalism seriously: he married an English woman and sent his son to school in England and chose to bring him up English-speaking. It's easy for R.S. Thomas to castigate the Welsh for failing to live up to the impossible ideals he enunciates but which he himself fails to live up to. His politics are the politics of the apolitical.

Peter Paul Piech has asked me to write a short poem to go on a poster depicting R. S.Thomas. I wonder whether this squib will do:

> A patriot is a happy man,
> His love of country makes him glad;
> Come on, Mr Thomas, why so sad?
> Let's see you smile for Cymru – if you can.

This afternoon I found in a secondhand bookshop in Provo a copy of *Teague, Shenkin and Sawney* by J. O. Bartley, who is described on the title-page as a Lecturer in English at the University College of Swansea; it was published by Cork University Press in 1954 and must be quite rare. It's a study of the Irish, Welsh and Scottish characters in English plays and is dedicated 'to Hugh Owen Meredith, Guide, Philosopher and Friend'. In a chapter on the Stage Welshman, 1592-1659, the book examines the play *Match at Midnight* (1607) by William Rowley, in which one of the female characters says of the Welsh hero, 'The sight on's eyes is enough to singe my little maydenhead'. I shall suggest to the University of Wales Press that it should consider bringing out a reprint of this fascinating book.

I've been trying to find out more about an anonymous poem entitled *Llywelyn: a Tale of Cambria in Four Cantos* and published by G. H. Huttman at the Military Orphans Press in Calcutta in 1838. It's significant, I think, because Llywelyn is depicted not as a rebel against the English Crown but as a Welsh national hero. I'd dearly like to know who wrote it. It must be a rare book because the National Library doesn't have a copy. I bought mine for a shilling at a secondhand bookshop in Cardiff and I've had it bound in leather.

Another book I bought for a few shillings is *Barddoniaeth Dafydd ap Gwilym*, the first printed edition of the poet's works, edited by Owen Jones (Owain Myfyr) and William Owen and published in 1789.

Glyn Jones has given me a copy of *Gorchestion Beirdd Cymru*, edited by Rhys Jones o'r Blaenau and published in 1773. It belonged to Glyn's grandfather, Llwch Haiarn (David William Jones), and among the subscribers was Dr Samuel Johnfon. Rhys Jones (1713-1801) belonged to Ruth's mother's family and some of his bawdy verses were once in their possession.

This evening I went to see a musical put on, in a very amateur way, by staff and students of the English Department and based on *The Rape of the Lock*. Oh, my aching sides!

Another letter from Bryan Martin Davies today in which he says Gwenlyn Parry has died. I didn't really know him because I wasn't one of his boozing pals, but I always found him genial and

I admire his plays. I shall always remember introducing him to Ionesco at the BBC in 1972 and the look of veneration on his face.

Those were halcyon days for Harri at Garth Newydd in the early 1960s. A gregarious man, he revelled in the company of younger people and the less abstemious of his own generation, many of whom were first attracted to Plaid Cymru by his wit, erudition, iconoclasm and conviviality. I can see him now, holding court in The Lamb, one of Merthyr's grottier pubs, where a band of pint-pot patriots and assorted nutters used to gather nightly. It was very much a case of 'The Revolution begins at stop-tap – just time for another'. Among them was a group calling itself the Free Wales Navy who were reputed to train on the waters of the lake in the park at Cyfarthfa. A frequent visitor to the pub was Julian Cayo Evans, Commandant of the Free Wales Army, whom I always found to be a most amiable lad and an excellent accordion-player. Whenever we meet nowadays he greets me with the words, *'Codwn ni eto.'*

Harri's political views in those days were left-wing and quixotic. He was a vivid public speaker – I sometimes thought he looked a bit like Lenin – who could be hyperbolic and acerbic by turns, reserving his most scathing invective for the Labour Party (of which he'd once been a member) but also quick to turn on his own party when it failed to give the lead he expected from a movement of national liberation. One of his *bons mots*, not altogether original, was to the effect that Plaid Cymru's economic policy consisted of 'two acres and a Welsh-speaking cow'.

He wasn't a practical politician and the mundane aspects of electioneering were not for him. The role he preferred was that of Welsh Bard, rallying his people against the foe, whether foreign or native-born, and as such he had a part to play. Verbally inventive, he had a puckish sense of humour to which he gave fullest rein in the column he wrote for *Welsh Nation* under the pseudonym Robin Clidro and later in a regular feature about the goings-on in a Valleys town, run by Labour, that he called Cwmgrafft. He was particularly good at coining sobriquets for eminent Welshmen, several of which have stuck, and it was he, I'm pretty sure, who first referred to our Hyperborean countrymen as Gogs. *'Beirdd byd barnant wr o galon.'*

Via ambro nenian malkresku.

When Lenin was asked by students at Moscow University to give them a succinct definition of Marxism, he said (in Russian, of course), 'Who whom?'. I used this today in explaining to my students the difference between a sentence's subject and its object. The word 'whom' seems to have fallen into desuetude here and the Yookay will probably soon follow suit. The same could be said for will/shall and would/should. There's a rude limerick about a queer and a lesbian of Khartoum which would have also served my purpose today, if I'd dared to use it. It ends with the line, 'Who does what, with what and to whom?' Why, I wonder, are limericks usually so bawdy?

One of the few limericks I can remember that are not bawdy goes like this :

> There was an old Bolshie called Lenin
> Who did one or two million men in;
>   That's a lot to have done in
>   But where he did one in
> That old Georgian Stalin did ten in.

I recall my first visit to Georgia in 1970 when we went to Gori, Stalin's home town. There were many photos of him in taxis, restaurants and the windows of houses. The only thing I could get Georgians to say against Jugashivli was that he hadn't attended his mother's funeral. One of the most shocking things I heard was that when his son was captured during the war, the Germans offered to release him in exchange for a thousand of their own men. Stalin refused and the son died in prison.

Among the Georgian poets I met on that trip were Josef Nonashvili and Grigor Abashidze. Both were charming men who went to a lot of trouble to make me welcome and show me around Tbilisi. Josef was a Deputy of the Supreme Soviet of Georgia, Chairman of the Georgian Peace Committee, and Secretary of the Georgian Writers' Union. But I've since discovered that what he and Grigor Abashidze wrote was pretty primitive stuff. Even so, that Josef was famous as a poet was attested by the fact that as we strolled along Khartaveli Avenue, people kept coming up to us and, bowing and addressing him as *'Batoni'*, kissed his hand.

The Welsh language has come a long way since the 1960s. I heard the other day of a man in Cardiff, a member of the city's Pakistani community, who approached the Headmaster of a Welsh-medium primary school with a view to sending his son there as a pupil. The headmaster was delighted, of course, but happening to know the man was also the father of three daughters, ventured to ask why they hadn't been sent to the Welsh school. 'Ah, you see,' came the reply, 'they are only girls. For my son I want the best.'

In 1983 I went with my brother, Lloyd, to see the brother and sister-in-law of Alf Passant at his home in Shrewsbury. Despite their astonishment at hearing that Nancy, as they knew her, had had a child, Roy and Mary Passant received us with tea and sympathy and provided what little information about her they could. They were struck by the strong facial resemblance between Nancy and me and between her and Heledd, my second daughter, whose photo I showed them. They said Nancy had been 'very reserved' and had hardly ever left Hanwood in all the years they'd known her, never taking a holiday and never having visitors to the house. She'd been at Priestweston from about 1914 until her marriage to Alf Passant, was very fond of animals and had the knack of restoring them to health. Mary Passant said there was 'a deepness' in her sister-in-law that she'd never been able to fathom. She also hinted at the possibility that, some time in the 1930s, she may have had a second child, perhaps by Harry Davies: she had left Priestweston for a year and gone home to Glascwm, with no reason given. I haven't followed this up, but it has occurred to me that there may be someone else looking for his or her parents or grandparents in the same quarter as I've been searching all these years.

The Passants gave me a photo of Nancy which had been taken at Priestweston. This was the first time I'd seen what she looked like. The resemblance between her and Heledd really is striking, especially the straight blond hair and what I can only call a Leonardo face. They also gave me Nancy's copy of *Mrs Beeton's Cookery Book*, with her name written neatly on the inside cover.

Friday, 8 November

Today I received a visit, or perhaps a visitation, from Clinton F. Larson, the *soi-disant* Poet Laureate of BYU. He must be one of the Three Chief Bores of the State of Utah. He asked me to give him copies of my books and told me all his are on sale at the Bookstore. I don't think I shall bother to go looking for them.

In the evening I went with Noël Owen to what we thought was going to be a dinner for Honours English students at Aspen Grove, but it turned out to be a brown bag affair, with everyone bringing their own food, and as we'd brought none we didn't stay very long. Instead, Noël drove me around Provo and showed me some of the best places to eat. We had a frozen yoghourt with fresh fruit and then a long talk about Mormonism, in which he believes unquestioningly, accepting all the orthodoxies as if he learned them as a child.

I've started counting the days until I go home. I could have come here for the full academic year but I know now it was wise to accept the post for just the Fall Semester. Zion does not have all that much appeal for me. I prefer humanity in all its lovable imperfection.

Among the things I look foward to seeing again are my books and paintings. We bought a Will Roberts, a John Elwyn and a Kyffin Williams shortly after we married and had to think twice about spending £40, but these things have given us immense pleasure over the years. My books, too, are a source of great solace. I must have about 12,000 now. Perhaps it's time to get rid of some of them because I've reached the point in life when I'm not going to read them again. But I can't bear the thought of parting with any of them, especially my collection of books by Welsh writers in English, which must be one of the largest anywhere outside the National Library.

The French composer and pianist Charles Alkan was killed when a large bookcase fell on top of him.

There was never any distinction in Harri's mind between politics and poetry: that they could be complementary seemed to him to go without saying. This conviction I helped him express in writing a number of ballads and topical songs, and in the publication of *Triad*, a booklet of poems in which we collaborated with Peter Griffith (now Gruffydd), that appeared in 1963. By then I was running the Triskel Press from Garth Newydd and, two years later, with a modicum of help from Harri, I launched *Poetry Wales*. Some of Harri's early verse had appeared during the late 1940s but I'm proud to think he was to find his mature voice and win his reputation as a poet in the pages of my magazine. It may be for his squibs he's become best-known – things like 'Ode to the Severn Bridge' – but he is capable of a more subtle lyrical note, combining a sense of history with contemporary realities, as in 'A Crown for Branwen', one of his best poems. Some of his poems have the authentic quality of folk-song, for example *'Colli Iaith'*, which is so hauntingly sung by Heather Jones. On the other hand, he hasn't always managed the 'sonorous utterance' to which he generally aspires and that is heard most clearly in his Welsh translation of Neruda's great poem, *'Alturas de Machu Picchu'*. I used to rib him on this score, urging him to write less doggerel and more of the other kind, but with no effect as far as I know.

I still visit Harri in his flat at Cwmbach. He doesn't see many of his old pals these days because he's fallen out with most of them, and he's not much interested in poetry or politics, but I do what I can to help him in everyday matters, and he's appointed me his literary executor. He spends his time reading reference books and watching tv. The last time I went to see him, last summer, he wanted me to find him videos of films starring Bette Davies, on whom he seems to have an erotic fixation.

In 1989 I attended a Lloyd family reunion in Cheltenham organized by John Stratton of Llandrindod, whose 90-year-old mother was a Lloyd. At the lunch I was invited to say a few words about my connection with the family and I did so, setting out the basic facts about my father's birth. I also asked anyone present who could shed light on it to speak to me afterwards, but none did.

Some of the Lloyds, a numerous clan, are mentioned, albeit not by their real names, in J. J. Duggan's book, *The Unforgotten Valley* (1926); the Duggans once owned the Mill at Hundred House where Hugh Lloyd worked. This is a rare book but after tracing the author's descendants in Canada I was sent a dozen unbound copies.

Saturday, 9 November

Yves Montand died in Paris today at the age of 70. Over a cup of coffee in my flat I sang one of his songs, *'Le P'tit Cordonnier'*, in his honour: *'Aux marches du Palais, y a une tante belle fille . . . '*, the only song I know in which every line is sung twice.

Today is the anniversary of the death of Dylan Thomas and also of Ceri Richards. Strange to think they met only once, in 1953, on the day before Thomas left Laugharne and went to America for the last time.

By 1965 the time had come for us all, except Harri, to leave Garth Newydd. I went to live in Twynyrodyn after marrying Ruth in August of that year, although I still saw Harri regularly and, despite his high regard for S. O. Davies, he came out during my campaign at the General Election in the following spring. Soon he was once again living alone in the cavernous hulk of Garth Newydd and he stayed on there for another six years, by which time he'd become Librarian of Mountain Ash. In 1979 the old house, by then derelict, was claimed at last by the town council and, probably much to the relief of the local Labour Party, demolished. I happened to be in Merthyr the week the bulldozers were set to work. As I watched the battering of those sturdy walls and heard the shattering of glass, I saw the elegant mahogany staircase dangling in mid-air and caught a glimpse of the William Morris wallpaper I'd put up in one of the rooms, just before it all came crashing down into a heap of rubble.

'Dust in the air suspended marks the place where a story ended.'

Tonight is Kristallnacht, the night in 1938 when the Nazis, ordered by Goebbels, destroyed thousands of Jewish homes and shops all over Germany as a reprisal for the shooting of a German diplomat in Paris.

I've been thinking about ambiguities in English. I've never been clear as to what the construction 'The field holds nine hundred if not a thousand sheep' means. Does it mean the field holds nine hundred and perhaps a thousand sheep or does it mean the field holds nine hundred but not a thousand sheep?

Trawsfynydd is a good place to come from.

I shall waste no time in reading your poems.

'Let him have it, son,' Bentley called to Craig, as the policeman cornered them on the factory roof, meaning, 'Give him the gun'. But Craig thought he meant, 'Shoot him', so he shot the policeman. He was too young to hang, so they hanged Bentley.

'Who would have thought that purple tie goes with your yellow shirt and red jacket?'

'Go across the road and ask how old Mrs Thomas is,' said the mother to her little boy.

'Hello, Mrs Thomas, Mam wants to know how old you are.'

Mae'r dyn wedi torri ei wddw – does that mean the man has cut his throat or broken his neck?

'How many people work at the Welsh Office?'

'Oh, about half.'

At the funeral of Raymond Williams in February 1988 I remember seeing, *inter alia*, Glyn Jones, Ned Thomas, Walford Davies, Ioan Williams, John Osmond, Hywel Francis, Kim Howells, Dai Smith, Gwyn A. Williams, Terry Eagleton and Tariq Ali. It was a cold day and it snowed intermittently. Just as the coffin was lowered into the grave the snow stopped and there was a brief burst of wintery sunshine. I suppose the serendipity would have been wasted on Williams, but it struck all present as somehow apposite.

France has Marianne, the Irish have Cathleen ni Houlihan, England has Britannia, and Wales – Dame Wales. She was usually depicted as a homely old woman dressed in a cloak, starched apron, and tall black hat, with granny specs and an ample bosom, and she made her début in cartoons in the mid-19th century. Still around in Lloyd George's day, the Welsh Mam used to appear regularly in the *Western Mail*, especially in the cartoons of J. M. Stanniforth, and she survived into the 1940s as a brand name for flour. She's seen only rarely these days but we haven't found any other woman to replace her as a symbol for Wales. It's a bit late in the day, I suppose, for romantic national heroines – and yet, and yet.

When Harri was a member of the Literature Committee, under T. J. Morgan's chairmanship, he once walked late into a meeting wearing a striped sloppy joe (this was before they were called T-shirts) and garish canvas shoes, and with a huge ice-cream which he proceeded to lick voraciously, oblivious to the stares, as the minutes of the previous meeting were received and signed as a correct record. It was during that meeting, while we were considering a grant-application from a Welsh publisher (it was either Bacon or Bungay), that he passed me a squib he'd just composed:

> Behold the accounts of Mammon Press
> Which show a big deficit:
> The arts in Wales are in a mess,
> Not worth the taxman's visit.
>
> But no, let tribulation cease
> And fear and doubts stop biting,
> For this is just another piece
> Of good creative writing.

I happened to see a copy of Clinton F. Larson's poems, *Sunwind*, in the BYU Bookshop today. The most remarkable thing about the book is that it has a smashing photograph of the Geneva Steelworks on the cover and was published by the Geneva Steel Corporation. The poems aren't up to much and I was able to resist the temptation to buy Larson's book.

My next call in the search for Annie or Nancy Lloyd or Passant was on Joan Whittaker, the niece of the people for whom she'd worked at Priestweston, who had been described in her funeral report as 'a very close friend'. She lives at Mounton, near Chepstow. Having virtually been brought up by Lloydie, as she called her, she was able to give me a lot more information about her, as well as several photos. She had many fond memories of her and called her 'my heroine'. There had clearly been a bond between them and Mrs Whittaker was only too pleased to talk to me about my grandmother. One of the things she could vividly recall was being taken by Lloydie in a trap from Priestweston to Montgomery on market day. She also remembered her once saying, 'It's not always the bad girls who get caught.' Lloydie had been jolly and kind-hearted and a capable worker on the farm. She was known locally as a 'dangerous' woman, in the sense she could turn her hand to anything and was particularly good with animals.

Mrs Whittaker also gave me a great deal of detail which, after I'd corroborated it with later informants, turned out to be highly relevant to the fact that Annie had had a child in 1910. She admitted that local rumour had it that for many years Lloydie had been the mistress of Harry Davies and she too could remember her leaving Priestweston for about a year in the 1930s. Alf Passant had eventually married her after Harry Davies, greatly put out by the courtship, left the district to work as bailiff on the estate of Sir William Fitzherbert at Tissington in Derbyshire.

Sunday, 10 November
This evening I watched a tv documentary about the drowning of Johnstown in Pennsylvania in 1899. It was a largely Welsh town built around the Cambria Steelworks and some 2,200 people lost their lives when a dam broke and flooded the area.

I remember the story Kyffin Williams told me the last time we met. He'd been out painting in the fields of Anglesey. On returning to his car he found it was stuck in a rut. The noise of his engine revving brought down the lane a man who offered to help. After much effort, the car started. Kyffin, grateful for his help, took out a drawing he'd made and presented it to the man, who stared at it, pushed back the peak of his cap, gave Kyffin an old-fashioned look, and then folded the drawing neatly into four before stuffing it into his pocket.

When Heledd, *'y ferch dawel wallt felen'*, was a little girl she once said to me, 'Dad, I've got Jesus Christ in my stomach.' I assured her that wasn't possible. 'It's Dafydd Iwan, then,' she insisted. I thought it best at this point to ask her what she meant. 'Well, whenever I take a bite of my sandwich it goes down into my stomach and half an hour later I'm hungry, so someone must be eating it.'

I went back to Glascwm several times. On one visit I talked to Mrs Renée Harley Davies who was related to Hugh Lloyd's first wife, Florence Harley, who had died in 1918. When I told her what I was about, she exclaimed, 'You must be Mr Stephens's son!' She went on to tell me how my father had called on her twice during the 1960s. He'd been wanting to find a photo of his mother, he said, and was hoping one of his grand-daughters (that is, my daughter, Heledd) might look like her, as Mary Passant had observed and as is indeed the case. After my father's visit, Mrs Harley Davies had written to one of Hugh Lloyd's daughters, Dilys Pickersgill, who lived near Blackpool, asking whether she had a photo of Annie, but her reply had been, 'Why has he waited so long?' and she'd refused to help. My father's response, on his second visit to Glascwm, had been that he didn't know whether his mother was still alive and had no wish to embarrass her, especially if she'd married. Mrs Harley Davies thought this response 'perfectly honourable' and told me, 'I could have hugged him!' The identity of the father of Annie Lloyd's child, she said, was never revealed to villagers, though some had been puzzled why she hadn't married Billy Davies of the Mill at Hundred House, who was courting her at the time.

Monday, 11 November
In the English Department common room today I found a tape of Carl Sandburg reading his poetry at BYU in 1956. I admire his work very much, especially 'The People, Yes'. I wish we had a similar poet in Wales, one who could tackle what happened in the Valleys during the Industrial Revolution. Most of our writers have been in reaction against the industrial scene, especially those who were born into it like Rhys Davies and Idris Davies, though a few, such as Glyn Jones, have sometimes seen the beautiful side of industrialism. There is such a thing as an industrial aesthetic, as many painters such as Joseph Herman and George Chapman have shown – except they weren't Welsh. Among the few natives who have taken the industrial scene as their main subject are Will Roberts and Ernie Zobole.

When I go home I intend using the few hundred pounds the Literature Committee gave me when I retired from the Arts Council last year to buy a picture by Zobole, whom I've never met but whose work I admire.

My sister-in-law, Margaret Bowen Rees, has a very fine sonnet, in Welsh, in which she suggests that Wordsworth, in writing his poem about Lucy Gray, may have had in mind the story of Lleucu

Llwyd. It may be he first heard of Lleucu from Robert Jones of Llangynhafal, his companion during a walking tour of Snowdonia in the 1790s. The Welshman would almost certainly have known the elegy for Lleucu written by Llywelyn Goch ap Meurig Hen, one of the finest love-poems in the Welsh language. The idea is discussed by Rendel Harris in his *Afterglow Essays* (1935).

> An englyn's just like angling – cast a line
>   For fine bits of writing;
>   Alliterate your lett'ring,
>   See that your consonants sing.

I think it was Wallis Evans who wrote that. He and I knew old Trystan Edwards, the architect and cartographer, who used to live near us in Courtland Terrace in Merthyr. He was highly eccentric, the distinguished author of books such as *The Things that are Seen* and *Towards Tomorrow's Architecture* – and the only man I've ever seen wearing a smoking-cap, a pince-nez and spats in the street. He was well-known for a projection of the world that was named after him and, as one of the Protectionists, had been prominent in the attempt to save parts of Aberdare from demolition. I used to walk behind him sometimes and listen to him talking to himself, and often he'd stop and we'd have a chat about Plaid Cymru, which he supported.

The first picture I ever bought was one of a pit-head by John Uzzell Edwards, who used to come to see us at Garth Newydd from his home in Deri, near Bargoed. I paid a fiver for it in 1962 and we still have it.

I also went to see another of Hugh Lloyd's daughters, Kathleen Tait, at her home in Oswestry, but although I was well received, she could provide me with no information about her aunt whatsoever. I had the distinct impression that this woman, who'd married a tea-planter in Tanganyika and had retired to Alicante before settling in Oswestry, didn't want to talk about her father and her upbringing in Glascwm because she was ashamed at how poor they'd been. She had trained as a nurse and, having lived abroad for most of her adult life, hadn't seen much of her father and almost nothing of her Aunt Annie. She told me her sister Dolly, who had died young, had been carried down from

Blaenbedw to Gladestry on a barn-door and that when Hugh Lloyd's horse died he had to give up farming and move to Hereford, where he'd worked in a market garden. By his second wife, Emily *née* Willoughby, he'd had a daughter named Mercia, later Davies, who was a bus-conductress in Hereford, but she'd died in 1982 before I could contact her. His third wife, Sarah Maude Owen, whom he married at the age of 61, had been the schoolmistress at Glascwm. I later contacted Donald Jones, the Builth solicitor who had been a schoolfriend of the poet T. H. Jones, and he let me have a few photographs of Hugh Lloyd and his third wife, for whose estate he'd acted. Hugh Lloyd had died in 1968.

Another of Hugh Lloyd's daughters, Maisie Harris, then living in Birmingham, refused to speak to me when I 'phoned her shortly after meeting her sister Kathleen. Both Maisie Harris and Dilys Pickersgill struck me as but poorly educated and certainly didn't know how to behave in response to my enquiries. In any case, I don't think their refusal to help me should have been quite so rough.

Tuesday, 12 November
Leslie read his poetry to my class today, very well and to great effect. Afterwards we went to his office and had a long chat about this, that and the other. He told me an anecdote about Yeats, whose doctor, Oliver St. John Gogarty, broke the news to him that he was seriously ill. 'I'm afraid, Yeats, you have arterial sclerosis,' said Gogarty. 'Say that again,' said Yeats. 'You have arterial sclerosis.' 'Ah', said the poet, 'what beautiful words!'

Leslie also told me his 'tundish' anecdote about the opposite of good. When he was a boy in Merthyr there was a lad in his class by the name of Verdun who wasn't very bright. The Headmaster was in the habit of going the rounds and springing tests on the boys. One of his favourites was Opposites. 'What's the opposite of hot?' he would ask. 'Cold, Sir.' When he came to Verdun, he asked him, 'What's the opposite of good?' The boy thought for a moment and then replied, 'Rotten, Sir.' He was caned for getting it wrong. Leslie, enraged at the injustice that had befallen his friend, put up his hand and said to the Headmaster, 'Please, Sir, Verdun's father is a grocer and they have good fruit and rotten fruit.' He was caned as well – for impertinence. Leslie concluded his tale with the observation that from then on he was aware that he knew more about the English language than his headmaster did.

I remember a visit to Cardiff by the Cultural Attaché from the Nigerian Embassy in London. Over sherry in the City Hall, we were making polite conversation with Mr Mbumba Oboke, or whatever his name was, and his son Nigel, both of them handsome men and immaculately turned out in Savile Row suits, when one of the city fathers turned to the son and asked, 'And what do you do?' 'I'm in my fifth year at Guy's,' said Nigel. 'Oh, aye,' said the Councillor, 'A medicine man, is it?'

Now that I knew my father had been searching for his mother, I felt it right I should tell him what I knew. I broke the news first to my mother and she agreed, in April 1984, that I should raise it with him. When I did, that same evening, my father was very cast down, holding his face in his hands for a long while, but then seemed to recover his composure and was ready to talk about it. He told me that, although he'd had a happy childhood in the home of the Stephenses in Heolgerrig, the knowledge of his illegitimacy and the fact that he'd been unwanted had preyed on his mind for fifty years. My mother had often wanted to tell me and my brother the truth of the matter but he'd always persuaded her to put it off, so ashamed and hurt was he. 'It's been like a cancer all these years,' he said.

He also revealed that in 1958 he'd changed his name by deed poll from Herbert Arthur Lloyd, as he legally was, to Herbert Arthur Lloyd-Stephens, the name he'd since used for all official purposes and which his wife and heirs were also entitled to use. It's strange to think I could have a double-barrelled name – just like Anglesey people – if I so wished!

My father told me about his many visits to Builth in the years after he'd bought a car and how he'd walked up and down the High Street and sat on the Gro in the forlorn hope of seeing someone who looked like him, and to Old Radnor, where he'd searched in vain for his mother's grave. I then handed him the photos of Annie Lloyd and gave him all the information I'd gathered about her. He said he was 'greatly relieved' now the matter was 'out in the open'; so was I.

A fortnight later Ruth and I took him and my mother to Michaelchurch-on-Arrow to see the graves of Hugh and Martha Lloyd, his grandparents on the distaff side, to Walton where he'd been born, and to nearby Old Radnor for lunch in a pub. He was particularly interested to learn that the Lloyds were bonesetters, especially since his great interest (after the game of bowls) had been the St. John's Ambulance Brigade; he too had the knack of healing which had come down from his Radnorshire forebears.

He had no interest whatsoever in who his father may have been and charged me not to make any further enquiries in that direction. I did his bidding while he lived but he didn't live long thereafter. He died in East Glamorgan Hospital on 22 June 1984, two days after being taken ill.

I was glad I'd told him what I knew about his mother but wished he could have had a little longer to live with the knowledge – I think it would have made us both a lot happier. I felt much closer to him in the last few weeks of his life and we talked much more than we'd used to. The burden he'd carried for so long had doubtless made him the cautious, introverted, inarticulate, emotionally reticent man he was and, at the end, with greater understanding, I felt a tremendous affection – no, love, for him.

Wednesday, 13 November
I rang Dr Bratman today in Cupertino, California, and arranged to visit him and his wife, Marilyn, who's from Aberdare. The air-fare is about $300 and I'm going on 27 November. It will be a welcome break from the rigours of Provo.

When I rang Ruth this evening she told me Pennar Davies has dedicated a new novel to me. I remember a trip to Finland during which I got to know Pennar a little better. Among the group from Wales were Sam Adams, John Rowlands, Gwyn Williams (Trefenter) and Sue Harries, the Academi's officer. On Midsummer's Night we were taken by our hosts to a small, uninhabited island in the Gulf of Bothnia to observe the sun going round in the sky without setting. We built a huge bonfire out of driftwood and cooked sausages on it. Pennar joined in the fun, even taking part in a performance of 'Oh, the hokey-pokey' which we put on to entertain our Finnish friends. It tickled him to think the dance might catch on and, in a hundred years' time, might rank with the *Kalevala* in the folkore of those parts.

A snowstorm is on its way south into Utah. I stayed up late reading Leslie's stories, which are finely done: he always manages to make something out of very little by the sheer power of his imagination and command of language. I've also been sketching out some ideas for my own stories. One of them is based on my earliest memory, an exercise I've set one of my classes.

I remember coming in from playing in the Bute woods one hot summer's day in 1944, when I was about six, to find two strangers sprawled on either side of our hearth. They had their boots off, their ties were undone and they were in conversation with my grandfather. The remains of a meal were on the kitchen table and I was astonished to see they'd each eaten two boiled eggs. In those days you had to have coupons for fresh eggs. I couldn't understand what was being said, though I gathered the men were from somewhere known as the East End. One was named Frank and the other Gerry.

Next day, the soldiers left the village. I went up to the top of Meadow Street to see them climbing into camouflaged lorries which took them to the sidings, where they clambered aboard a huge train that had been waiting there for days. Some of the soldiers were Americans and they gave us chewing-gum. One was a huge, handsome negro by the name of Homer, not unlike Paul Robeson, the first black man I'd ever seen. My father explained they were getting ready for the Big Push. I've often wondered what happened to Frank, Gerry and Homer and, in particular, whether they made it off the Normandy beaches.

In 1968 I called together a number of English-language writers who wished to create a new section of Yr Academi Gymreig, hitherto a preserve of Welsh-language writers. There was some reluctance on the part of the *Cymry Cymraeg* but not as much resistance as I'd expected. The first meeting between representatives of both camps took place in Swansea on 10 April.

Among the Anglo-Welsh writers present were Harri Webb, Roland Mathias, John Tripp, Leslie Norris, Sally Roberts and John Stuart Williams. It was on that occasion D. J. Williams, who was warmly in favour of the new initiative, uttered his famous remark: 'Please excuse my English – I learned it in Wormwood Scrubs.'

Apart from Harri Webb and A. G. Prys-Jones, there haven't been all that many Welsh poets who have written humorous verse in English. The only Welsh contributor to *The New Oxford Book of Light Verse* was Wynford Vaughan-Thomas. Shortly before he died in 1978, I heard Wynford declaiming some of his verse during a convivial gathering in the boardroom of HTV. He needed no prompting when it came to spouting his own work and, liking what I heard, I suggested he should consider publishing a selection of the more printable pieces. A few days later he sent me a sheaf of poems that is perhaps one of the few typed copies in existence, for he belonged very much to the oral tradition, preferably late at night. Much of his verse is slapdash, though no slapdasher than Harri's, but he was a dab hand at decasyllabics. I remember this couplet in which he decided to stay with chapel and not become a Catholic after all :

> My place is here so I come singing home:
> The second tenors need me more than Rome.

But the most memorable of all are these powerful lines from a poem cursing the touristification of the North Wales coast:

> Lord, let thy glaciers come again:
> Out from Snowdonia's fortress flow
> Thy rivers of avenging ice,
> Remote, remorseless, cold and slow,
> To crush in one supreme moraine
> Our godless cities of the plain.

After my father's death in 1984 I felt able to resume my search for information about the circumstances of his birth. I began by making enquiries in the vicinity of Sheep House, near The Hay, where Annie had been employed before moving to Priestweston. I found a bright, dignified old lady, Mrs Gwladys Worts, then in her nineties, living at Disserth Mill. She could remember her well and had good cause to, for she was the younger sister of Billy Davies of the Mill at Hundred House who'd been Annie's sweetheart. She told me Annie had been alone at Sheep House on the day of the Hay Fair, which was held on 17 May 1909, when a waggoner, calling at the house, had 'had his way with her – what today would be called rape'. Annie had left the farm shortly afterwards, gone home to Blaenbedw and started working at the Mill.

On realizing her condition, however, she had left Blaenbedw and gone to live with her aunt and uncle, Sarah and Arthur Powell. Arthur was a postman and they lived at The Green, Walton, where Annie was delivered of a child, my father, on 25 February 1910, her twentieth birthday. A few days later, Billy Davies came looking for her and was shocked to find her in bed with a new-born child. As he left the house he was berated by the aunt for getting Annie into trouble, which he vehemently denied. He was greatly upset by the fact that Annie had had a child and the incident put an end to the courtship. Mrs Worts was certain Billy Davies wasn't the father of Annie's child: if he had been, she told me, he would have married her, especially as his parents were fond of Annie and wanted them to marry. I was shown a photo of Billy Davies and he bore no resemblance to my father. The old lady's advice to me as I took my leave of her was, 'Let the matter rest now'.

Thursday, 14 November

There was a heavy fall of snow last night but not enough to stop me from getting about today. I had a lunch of roast beef in the Wilkinson Restaurant for $5, then 'by a commodious vicus of recirculation' came back to Wymount to catch up on my sleep after staying up late last night.

In bed with a bowl of porridge, and still wearing my shirt, I read *Spoon River* again. I wonder whether it had an influence on Dylan Thomas when he was writing *Under Milk Wood*. Be that as it may, it's time we in Wales claimed Minerva Jones, whose father, Indignation Jones, came from good Welsh stock. She was left to her fate with Dr Meyers. Will someone go to the village newspaper and gather into a book the verses she wrote? She thirsted so for love, she hungered so for life!

Homoteleuthon. Hysteron proteron. Heptateuch. Houynhnims. H'mm.

I did my best to raise money for Rhydwen Williams when he was faced with bankruptcy in 1971 and managed to collect several thousand pounds for him. But it didn't stop him being declared bankrupt. During one of his frequent court appearances there was an exchange between him and the presiding magistrate, an account of which I read in the *Pontypridd Observer* and which I found so funny that I carried the cutting around with me for years thereafter. Rhydwen was accused of not having paid his insurance stamps and had pleaded he didn't know he had to.

'Come, come, Mr Williams,' said the magistrate, 'every schoolboy knows about stamps.'

'Sir,' said the defendant, 'philately was never one of my hobbies.'

The magistrate persevered.

'Mr Williams, every builder knows about insurance stamps.'

'Sir, are you comparing the writing of Welsh literature with the mixing of cement?'

The defendant went on in this vein until the magistrate gave him a warning not to cross the Clerk of the Court, whose name was Jordan.

'Sir,' replied Rhydwen, 'I have no more intention of crossing the Clerk of this Court than I have of crossing the river that bears his name.'

The defendant was fined £200 and ordered to pay £150 costs.

I've grown very fond of Rhydwen over the years and have enjoyed many hours in his company. The great heart of Glamorgan beats in his breast. He's an excellent raconteur and the stories he tells never fail to make me laugh. One of my favourites is about the time he took his one-man Daniel Owen show to a theatre in Mold in Flintshire. On the night his parents and brother, who was by trade an electrician, were in the audience. Just as the curtain was about to go up the lighting system failed and the auditorium was plunged into darkness. The call came: 'Is there an electrician in the house?', at which Rhydwen's brother went backstage and, a few minutes later, the lights came back on. Rhydwen went on to perform his show to great applause. Afterwards, a select group of admirers congregated in his dressing room to congratulate him. During the chat, one remarked to Rhydwen's father, a former collier, of his actor son, 'I think your son's a marvel, Mr Williams, don't you?' 'Oh, aye,' said the old man, beaming with pride, 'he's always been that way inclined – anything 'lectrical.'

Another of Rhydwen's stories is about the time he won the Crown at the National Eisteddfod in 1946. His mother, who was living at the time in Chester, was so thrilled to hear the news on the wireless that she rushed out into the street and told a neighbour, 'My Rhydwen has won the Crown!' 'Oh, that's nothing, Mrs Williams,' the man replied. 'My brother-in-law won an alarm clock in a raffle the other day.'

> *'O saisons! O châteaux!*
> *Quelle âme est sans défauts?'*

I couldn't leave the matter of my father's birth rest. From further enquiries in The Hay area, I learned that Margaret, the wife of John Watkeys Jones, the owner of Sheep House, was a Merthyr woman and had been known for her kindly disposition and good works in the district. She was the daughter of the Reverend Rees Evans and a sister to J. R. Evans, who taught History at Cyfarthfa Grammar School when Glyn Jones was a pupil there; his wife kept an ironmonger's shop in Glebeland Street, for which reason he was known as Evans the Nails. That's almost certainly how my father had come to be given to PC Stephens and his wife in Heolgerrig – the Merthyr connection. The hundred gold sovereigns, a small fortune in those days when agricultural workers earned only a few shillings a week, had probably been provided by the Joneses of Sheep House, out of a sense of responsibility for her well-being. I have discounted the possibility that the father of Annie's child was John Watkeys Jones, as has been suggested to me, since in his photograph he bears no resemblance to my father. Mrs Jones had been killed in a road-accident near the farm gate in 1929 and in a report of her funeral in the *Brecon and Radnor Express* I read that among those who had sent wreaths was an Annie Lloyd.

John Watkeys Jones, who was known as Johnny-go-buy-'em, was quite well-to-do. A freemason and pioneer of the National Farmers' Union, he had two sons, Elwyn and Eustace (known as Stacey), both of whom became champion cattle-breeders. Stacey's daughter, Sue Hudson, still lives at Sheep House and she was kind enough to show me around.

Friday, 15 November
I ate half a packet of Cornflakes for breakfast this morning. I've read somewhere that the reason why there's a cockerel on packets of Kellog's Cornflakes is that someone once told the maker that his name resembled '*ceiliog*', the Welsh word for 'cockerel'. *Sans blague.*

When I was a student at Aberystwyth one of the books I found absorbing was *The Uses of Literacy* by Richard Hoggart. I suppose I was really a Hoggart boy, and although his account is of growing up in the back-streets of Leeds, I found much in his book that chimed with my own experience, which proves that class can be just as important as nationality.

I always found Hywel Evans, as Chairman of the Arts Council, a very unsympathetic man, and remember how he bristled when, after a meeting at which the lion's share of the Council's funds had gone, as usual, to Opera, I quoted Francis Bacon's remark: 'Money is like muck – not fragrant except it be spread.' As a mandarin at the Welsh Office, he wasn't used to being contradicted and never spoke to me again.

Whenever the discussion at Council meetings turned to the Welsh National Opera's urgent need for a huge injection of funds, which happened frequently, the money was always found. There were enough fat cats around the table, all cigar-smoking members of the Tory mafia from the Cardiff and County Club, to ensure that. But when the Literature Committee put in a bid for some comparatively paltry sum there would be argument lasting half an hour. 'Opera is the brandy of the damned.'

I was fortunate in having six staunch and effective Chairmen of the Literature Committee: T. J. Morgan, Glyn Tegai Hughes, Roland Mathias, Prys Morgan, Walford Davies, and Wynn Thomas; all these, with the exception of T. J. Morgan, who's dead, are still my friends.

When I retired last year, Gwyn Jones wrote me a very warm letter which I greatly appreciated. Even so, I remember that when the minutes of the first meeting of the Literature Committee were presented to Council in the autumn of 1967, Gwyn insisted on rejecting them on the grounds that we proposed awarding bursaries and prizes to writers: he was against giving writers money, he said, because he and his generation had had no such largesse. We had to wait for a new Chairman, Colonel William Crawshay, to be appointed before we could launch a scheme for direct financial support to writers.

I can't get my students to write about anything or anyone they dislike or hate. One of them explained to me the other day that they're taught not to hate anyone, but to pray for their soul. In the end they write rhymes about piffling matters like their room-mate's sniff or their brother-in-law's purple socks. This may be why there are no great Mormon writers – they can't muster enough animus.

One of the things my father told me on the night I revealed what I knew about the circumstances of his birth was that when he was in his teens he'd been taken by Elizabeth Stephens to a house in Maesycwmer, near Bedwas in Monmouthshire, where he remembered seeing a tall, fair-haired lady who'd shown a great deal of interest in him, pressing him to tell her about himself. The house was probably the home of Arthur and Sarah Powell, Annie's uncle and aunt, who had moved to Maesycwmer from Walton some years before, and the lady was almost certainly his mother.

Saturday, 16 November

I drove west through Santaquin to Eureka, a former tin-mining town, almost a ghost-town now, with a population of only 600. It was very rundown, with the window-frames of deserted houses flapping in a fierce wind laden with sand, and the desert reclaiming what man has built, just like in *The Grapes of Wrath*. A man I met on the street offered to show me around the shabby museum, which consisted mainly of old photographs and rock specimens, but I thanked him heartily. He was about the only living thing I'd seen all day. It was so quiet on the road that, every now and then, I'd drive on the left for a mile or two, for the sheer hell of it. The main silver mine in Eureka was known as Swansea Mine.

'It's my dirt – it's no good, but it's mine!'

I went on to Mammoth and Silver City, both ex-mining towns. Most of the first miners had been Cornish but there were some Welsh and Scots, and the doctor was a man named Stephens, though whether he was Cornish or Welsh no one could tell me. There was nothing to delay me here so I pushed on through Jericho Junction and Lynndale to Oak City and Leamington, which were even less interesting and the last-named was certainly no spa. The liveliest place I saw on this trip was Sand Mountain in the Little Sahara area, where lads on motor-bikes were churning up the dunes.

It has always intrigued me to think Dafydd ap Gwilym might have met Geoffrey Chaucer on the occasion of the English court's visit to Beaumaris. They would have conversed in French, I suppose, and they almost certainly talked about Welsh prosody, I like to think.

When I lived in Garth Newydd in the 'sixties, one of the things Harri Webb and I enjoyed doing was baiting the London Welsh. We only did it to annoy and it always had its desired effect. I wrote a ballad that got so far up the nose of Tudor David, editor of *The London Welshman*, that he wrote an editorial denouncing it. It went something like this:

I am a London Welshman, from Gwalia so fair,
I sing my country's praises to show that I still care;
I spend the English penny to buy the exile's bun
In all the Welsh Societies from Slough to Paddington.

I am a London Welshman, I am a Cymro Da
Like George and Iori Thomas and Dai Llewellyn are;
I'm much more Welsh in London than I have ever been –
I stand up for my country and for 'God Save the Queen'.

I am a London Welshman, to Wales I've always clung;
I have a loyal corgi who knows our ancient tongue;
But to my little children I speak it not at all –
One has to be broad-minded, the world is growing small.

I am a London Welshman, I have a lot to say
In speeches after dinner upon St. David's Day;
The daffodil and dragon, the harpist and the leek,
They fill my heart with hiraeth throughout Eisteddfod Week.

I am a London Welshman, I love my country most –
I would return tomorrow if I could find a post;
The Tourist Board might have me, or perhaps the BBC,
Such places are depending on patriots like me.

I am a London Welshman, I love my country best;
I speak of my dear homeland with hand upon my breast;
It's said to love one's country that there one must abide –
My heart's back home in Gwalia, my wallet's on this side.

I am a London Welshman, for Wales I am on fire;
When I have made my fortune to Wales I shall retire,
Or I shall give my money, like good Sir David James,
To help more London Welshmen play patriotic games.

Whenever we sang 'God Bless the Prince of Wales' at primary school, I used to wonder where the prairie was that echoed.

I spent a good deal of my time in 1987/88, and drove hundreds of miles, going up many lanes, knocking on many doors and being barked at by many a dog, in my search for information about the men who, in 1909, had been employed at Sheep House or were working for John Watkeys Jones. I called on scores of people in Radnorshire, Breconshire, Gloucestershire, Shropshire and

Herefordshire, and kept a record of my interviews in a large file that I call the Black Book of Blaenbedw. In this long search I was assisted by Sheila and David Leitch of Glasbury, leading members of the Powys Family History Society, two splendid people who have become my very good friends.

Sunday, 17 November
I drove down to Provo Park this morning. There was hardly anyone else around, but I had the only nasty experience of my stay so far. I was walking along a breakwater by the lake when a small truck (I mean lorry) caught up with me and followed me for a few hundred yards. I turned back and so did the lorry until we were both back on the main road. I set off in another direction and it followed me again, pulling up now and then right in front of me so that my path was blocked. The vehicle was driven by a young roughneck and he had with him a girl of about seventeen. Obviously, he was showing off his skills as a driver, laughing at my discomfort and the girl giggling adoringly.

'La vie n'est pas sérieuse quand on a dix-sept ans.'

Not many of my friends know I was a Boy Scout. I joined the Cubs when I was about seven and stayed with the movement until I went to University, by which time I was a Rover and a Queen's Scout. I have somewhere a certificate signed by one Elizabeth R in which she expresses the hope that Life, for me, will be a Joyous Adventure. Perhaps I'll send her a postcard to let her know how I'm getting on here. I gave my dark-blue Scout shirt, together with lariat, white neckerchief, toggle and a complete set of proficiency badges, to the Folk Museum at St. Fagans a few years ago.

I owe a lot to the Scouts. They taught me self-reliance and awoke my interest in the natural world. With Ron Giles and Pip Eyles, the Scoutmasters, I went motorcycling and camping and walking in the Brecon Beacons, Snowdonia, the Highlands of Scotland and the Lake District – a rare opportunity for a working-class lad in those days. I don't remember ever having to salute the Union Jack or anything like that, and the British Empire had nothing to do with our version of public service. The badge for all Scout troops in Glamorgan was a miner's lamp and we in the 2nd Pontypridd troop wore the Red Dragon epaulette with pride.

The Scout Hall, where I spent most of my evenings and weekends, was at the bottom of Meadow Street. It was burned down by vandals a few years ago. One of the things we did in the years after the war was collect waste paper around the shops and offices of Pontypridd. We had a huge handcart, pulled by ropes and steered by means of a huge wheel. Some of us would perch on top of this bogey while the other boys pulled it up and down the streets under the guidance of Pop Phillips, a veteran Scoutmaster, slightly eccentric but devoted to the cause. On a good day we would return to Meadow Street with the cart piled high with scrap paper and cardboard, which was then unloaded and stored in the Scout Hall, after which Pop would treat us to a supper of faggots and peas washed down with Vimto.

Lascia dir le gente.

One of the other things I did in my search for Annie Sophia Lloyd was make contact with Eddie Powell, the son of Arthur and Sarah Powell at whose home in Walton my father had been born. The Powells had later lived in Mortimer Street in Leominster and Annie had been married from their home. To my great surprise, Eddie Powell was still living there and he could remember her. But there was something lacking in Eddie which made it difficult to hold a conversation with him. He was a radio enthusiast and had a room full of sets which he insisted on demonstrating whenever I called on him. In fact, he could talk about little else. He was nevertheless hospitable and gave me a dozen postcards that Annie had written to his parents from Blaenbedw as well as a few addressed to her in Mortimer Street. He also let me have a photo which showed my father at the age of ten months and across the bottom was written: 'Herbert Arthur Lloyd, December 1910'. My father had been given a copy of the self-same photo on first discovering the truth about his birth. His mother must have had it taken just before handing him over to the Stephenses in Heolgerrig.

Among the cards Eddie Powell gave me was one that had been sent to Annie by a man named Joseph Morgan of the Meer, a district between Broxwood and Almeley in western Herefordhsire, who'd been a gamekeeper at Eywood in Titley. I'd been told by Joan Whittaker that Annie had had another sweetheart, that his name had been Joe and that he'd been killed in the first world war. Joe Morgan had died, a victim of a flu epidemic, in 1918, while serving with the Machine Gun Corps; he's buried in a military grave at Broxwood, in the Catholic cemetery on the state of the Snead-Cox family. I found an entry for him in one of the many volumes of *Soldiers who Died in the Great War*. I have been given a photo of Joe Morgan in which he wears a Glengarry cap but, more intriguingly, the postcard shows a group of soldiers who include his brother, marked in the usual way with an x. This man bears a striking resemblance to my father but, unfortunately, I've failed to find out anything about him. That Joe Morgan was not the father of Annie's child is suggested by the postcard he sent her at Blaenbedw from Kington on 7 February 1910, shortly before she gave birth, in which the message, though affectionate, makes no reference to her condition: 'Just a line, sorry I could not come up as I have been away when your letter arrived . . . were all disappointed you did not come as they all expected you. Goodbye, my dear one, Your Joe.' At the time of his death in 1918 Joe Morgan was engaged to another woman.

I also tried to enquire about an Arthur Herbert, only because he's the only man I've come across who had the same names as my father and there is, after all, a tradition of naming illegitimate children after their fathers. This man, too, was killed in the Great War. He was a native of Yarsop, near Yazor in Herefordshire, where his name appears on the war-memorial; he died of wounds in Egypt in 1915. But there was no trace of anyone called Herbert on the electoral roll for Yazor and I could find nothing in the Hereford County Records Office either. Nor was I able to contact anyone who could remember him or his family.

Monday, 18 November
I've been asked to read in public on 5 December, the first time

since I've been here, so stayed in this morning to prepare for it.

Leslie rang in high dudgeon at my casual remark last night that there are no books by Welsh (or Irish or Scots) writers in the BYU Library, and very few books by English writers. He's had a word with the Librarian who says many such books are held by the Library but there's so little call for them they're stored in the vaults and have to be specially ordered. Leslie says magazines like *Planet* and *Poetry Wales* are too 'parochial' and would not be read here and that most British poets are unknown and of no interest. I suppose the same could be said for Mormon writers in the libraries of Wales. But I happen to know that many great works of American literature are not easily found at the BYU Library, including *The Grapes of Wrath* and *The Catcher in the Rye* and *The Naked and the Dead*, because I've asked for them at the counter and looked for them in the card-index.

I think of my friend Brinley Jones, with whom I've edited the *Writers of Wales* series for nearly twenty years now. He's a keen Churchman, though I've never had a conversation with him about religion. I suppose the Church represents a middle way between the extremes of Roman Catholicism and Dissent, but it's never held any attraction for me, perhaps because it's synonymous in Wales with Toryism and landlordism and an anglicized class who pray for the Queen.

The funniest film about Wales I've ever seen is *Only Two Can Play*, based on the novel by Kingsley Amis, *That Uncertain Feeling*. Peter Sellers as the hapless librarian, John Lewis, and Kenneth Griffith as his odious rival for promotion, are performances that stay in the memory. The scene in which Lewis is waiting to go to the lavatory in the seedy digs where he lives with his young family is also memorable: as an old codger comes out of the lavatory trailing his braces and with fag in mouth, Lewis wrinkles his nose and pulls up the wick of an air-freshener.

The only time I've been stuck in a lift was in Rotterdam during the Poetry Festival in 1973. That was when I met the black American poet, Ted Joans, with whom I got talking as we waited for the lift to move again. On hearing I was from Wales, he asked me whether I knew 'a city called Baa-laa, not far from Liverpool', and when I said I did, he told me he had a child living there. He had, in fact, ten children, all by different women, he said, and it was his ambition to make enough money to pay for a grand family gathering in Timbuctoo, where he had a large house.

I watched *Casablanca* on tv last night – for the umpteenth time, but I never tire of it. Ingrid Bergman is stunningly beautiful, not unlike those other blondes I admire so much, Ruth and Liv Ullmann. I wish I had more opportunity of using some of the famous lines in the film: 'Here's looking at you, kid'; 'How's business at the Blue Parrot?'; 'Play it, Sam'; 'Of all the gin-joints in all the towns in all the earth, she has to walk into mine'; and, of course, 'Round up the usual suspects'. I often use them, anyway.

'Vat vatch, meine liebe? Such watch!'

In my search for my father's father my suspicion fell at last on another man, whose name I can't bring myself to write down, not even in the privacy of this journal, until I have more conclusive evidence. I first heard his name, as that of the man some villagers thought may have been the father of Annie Lloyd's child, from an old lady in Glascwm. I've seen photographs of this man and there's a strong resemblance between him and my father and between one of his sons and my brother. He was a waggoner who worked at Sheep House in 1909. When I go home I intend pursuing my interest in this man, who's now dead, until I have enough information to make up my mind one way or another.

It's a melancholy story and I haven't yet brought it to a satisfactory conclusion. I have to ask myself why I've gone to all this trouble, and over so many years, in pursuing the matter. I think I did so, at the outset, in the belief that my father would have liked to know something about his mother, but since his death I've decided I want to persevere with it for its own sake. I shall do so for the satisfaction of knowing who my paternal grandfather was.

'A doeth, meddir, yw'r sawl a ŵyr ei ddoe dyrys ei hun.'

Tuesday, 19 November
Today I turned down an invitation to address the Women's Relief Society, whatever that may be. Perhaps I should have accepted, in

the hope of finding out.

The shops are preparing for Christmas. There's one in the Mall that has nothing but Yuletide things in stock. I wonder how Christmas is celebrated in a society which believes Christ to be only one of the prophets on whom its faith is based. But by then I shall be eating turkey, pulling crackers and wearing silly hats at home.

I gave notice to the Wymount accommodation office that I shall be vacating my apartment (I mean flat) on 11 December.

Wednesday, 20 November

I was once in the Throne Room of the Swedish Parliament, where I'd gone to ask for advice in preparing the Academi's nomination of Saunders Lewis for the Nobel Prize. As I was chatting to the Secretary of the Committee, a large, ornate telephone on his desk started ringing loudly. He picked it up and said, 'It's for you.' The call was from Alun Creunant Davies, Director of the Welsh Books Council, who – assiduous as ever – wanted to know whether I was free to attend a meeting of one of his committees in about a fortnight's time. I spoke to him in Welsh, of course, at which the functionary was goggle-eyed, but he didn't ask who it was or why he'd rung. As soon as I told Alun I was free on the day in question, he put down the phone, as if I'd been speaking to him from Llangeitho.

It was on the same trip I danced with Liv Ullmann, the actress. I'd admitted to my hosts that I admired her, as much for her blond good looks as for her acting, whereupon they arranged to take me to a party given by her publisher for the launch of her autobiography, *Forandringen*, later published as *Changing*. I don't know whether it was a joke at my expense, but that evening, in a crowded room, I was astonished to find myself being introduced to Liv Ullmann. She was standing very near and I was struck by how she looked just as she did in *Face to Face* – hardly any make-up, a natural hair-style, those vulnerable blue eyes, and a beaming smile. I've always had a soft spot for blondes with blue eyes and good teeth – like my mother and my wife.

Anyway, I swallowed hard and, after a moment's pause, heard

her say, 'Why don't you ask me to dance?' So I did and we danced for all of ninety seconds, just long enough for me to tell her I came from Wales and that Wales . . . and then it was someone else's turn. I can't remember anything else about the party but at the time I thought it was the most wonderful I'd ever been at.

Next day, in a large bookshop in central Stockholm, I joined a long queue of people waiting to buy copies of Liv Ullmann's book. On reaching the table, I said, 'Hello again!' The actress looked up at me with those fantastic blue eyes – and asked me where I came from. I told her I was from Wales and that Wales . . . She gave me her famous smile and wrote her name in the book. And then it was someone else's turn.

Thursday, 21 November

I taught my classes today. The writing of some of the students has improved; a few have talent but some have none at all. 'You can send a boy to college but you cannot make him think.' The best are Jack Harrell, George Weatherington and Sara Cleaver, and perhaps one or two others. For the most part they are a likeable bunch of kids and I get on well with them. I think they enjoy talking to me as someone who's not part of their conservative world. Perhaps their lack of talent stems from the fact they don't know much about sin, or are not supposed to. Without sin, no literature.

Apart from my students, I haven't spoken to anyone all day today. It's much colder now, about 46 degrees, and there's snow on the ground. I cooked myself a steak for the first time and was surprised by how much I enjoyed it. '*Rhaid cofio'r bol*,' as Gwenallt once remarked to me over lunch at the Metropole Hotel in Llandrindod in 1967.

The tv informs me the Serbs and Croats are still butchering one another. I think of my trip to Yugoslavia a few years ago and the people I met there, in particular a priest of the Orthodox Church somewhere in the mountains of Macedonia. He was a young man, resplendent in his robes, with a tall black hat and a thick black beard under a heavy crucifix dangling on a golden chain. We chatted pleasantly for a while and then, on hearing I came from

Wales, he asked me a question that took me completely by surprise. 'Tell me,' he said in impeccable English, 'how many miles did Mary Jones walk to collect her Bible from Thomas Charles?' I had to admit I didn't know. But when I came to compile the *Oxford Companion*, I made sure it gave the precise distance from Llanfihangel-y-Pennant to Bala: 25 miles.

Among members of the editorial board of the *Companion* was Thomas Parry. He put in a lot of hard work reading the early drafts and saved us from several gaffes, inveighing against those who had written what were, in his view, inadequate entries, especially if they were on the staff of the Welsh Departments of the University of Wales. But he just couldn't accept that the book should include entries on people and institutions which were not strictly literary, though they figure in the English literature of Wales as allusions. Two examples were the South Wales Miners' Federation and Aneurin Bevan, though he didn't object to my including entries for the North Wales Quarrymen's Union and W. J. Parry. It was all I could do to dissuade him from resigning from the board. Anyway, I stuck to my guns and in due course the entries appeared. I was spared Tom Parry's wrath because he died in 1985, about a year before the book appeared.

Friday, 22 November
Today I set out in the Chevrolet for Las Vegas, a journey of more than 400 miles, through Cedar City on the 1-15 to St. George and then another 180 miles into Nevada. My first view of the place, at about 8pm, was stunning: it stretched like a glittering lake, much bigger than Salt Lake City, with desert all around.

I found a room at the Lady Luck Motel for $20 and then went out to see the Strip. I went into four casinos: Stardust, The Mirage, Caesar's Palace and the Excalibur. In one there were two large white tigers, behind glass, of course, but looking very fierce in their own jungle habitat. In another there were dolphins. In Caesar's Palace all the staff were dressed as Roman centurions or Vestal Virgins. Outside the Mirage I saw the artificial volcano erupting in flame and smoke. The streets are lined with magnificent palm-trees.

Inside the enormous buildings there are, besides the gambling halls, many restaurants, bars, lounges, shopping malls, cinemas, swimming pools and, of course, thousands of rooms where people stay. I saw a lot of rich people, dressed only as rich Americans dress, mostly in their sixties and seventies, but no drunks or rowdies. The quality of the goods in the gift shops was cheap and nasty, as if the vulgarity of the place were something to be celebrated.

After a blowout meal for $8.50 – shrimps, fish, chicken, vegetables, cheesecake and coffee – I wandered around the casinos again, huge halls crammed with people playing roulette, blackjack, baccarat, and gaming machines. By one in the morning I'd seen enough and went back to the Lady Luck. It's strange to think the Saints had a lot to do with the creation of Las Vegas as a gambling town and that the Mormon mafia still has a finger in the pie. The place is vulgar, garish, mindless, but it's also spectacular, a real pleasure-dome such as Kubla Khahn might have built in Xanadu if the Person from Porlock hadn't called.

'Loud, heap miseries upon us, yet entwine our arts with laughters low.'

Saturday, 23 November
I was up this morning by seven and out on the Strip by eight. The casinos were as busy as they'd been last night and all the restaurants crowded. Inside the Excalibur everything was in Arthurian and Olde English style. In the snackery there were Excaliburgers on the menu and you could order a Guinivere sandwich or a Lance-a-lotta pasta and eat it at a round table decorated with the names of Arthur's knights, all hideously mis-spelt. There was also a mock-medieval village and a life-size plastic Sherwood Forest. I saw lots of professional gamblers who are said to spend their days and nights in places like this, often gambling on behalf of other people. There were also quite a few naughty ladies and touts for the legalized brothels, even at this time of morning. I saw a huge neon-lit advertisement for a concert to be given by Tom Jones – not bad for a lad from Trefforest, said I to myself.

I'm not a gambling man, but I just had to place a bet. In one of the casinos I happened to stop at a table where, during a short lull in business, the croupier told me he came from Tredegar. 'What are Neil Kinnock's chances this time?' he asked. 'Pretty good,' I replied. He smirked and, thus emboldened, I put my $5 on a red Number 10. The wheel of fortune spun, and I lost.

I was with Neil Kinnock, and others, on the night J.F. Kennedy was assassinated in 1963. We were taking part in a debate at the Students' Union in Cardiff and the motion was: that this House believes in the principle of self-government for Wales. Emrys Roberts and I spoke in favour of the motion and Kinnock was, of course, against. The motion was lost. What Kinnock and Leo Abse did during the Devolution referendum of 1979 was disgraceful. I am sorry to think ill of Kinnock, because he and I have a lot in common and our backgrounds are quite similar.

Some of my friends in Wales were thoroughly disheartened by the result of the referendum in 1979 and have virtually given up the political struggle. But there will be another chance and we must go 'back up the line', as John Tripp used to say. If a Parliament had been set up after 1979, I, like many others, might have been tempted to join, or at least support, the Labour Party, at least for the time being. I consider myself more of a Socialist these days than a Nationalist, but a Welsh Socialist for all that, and that's why I'm sticking with Plaid Cymru – for all its shortcomings.

Next time we must make sure it's a Parliament that's on offer, not a glorified county council. I for one wouldn't be interested in an Assembly or anything less than a Parliament with legislative and tax-raising powers. It would have too small a remit to be effective and would attract the worst kind of politico, and people would soon get fed up with it because they wouldn't see what difference it made to their lives.

Cock-a-doodle-don't!

I left Las Vegas at about noon, having seen enough to last a lifetime. The place looks quite different by day, in the way a theatre does with all the lights off and the magic gone. It was now quite warm, in the 70s, and there was no sign of snow. The mountains look like tips of rubble and nothing grows on them, but

I saw my first cactus. I crossed the Virgin River at noon and went through Mesquite, cut across a corner of Arizona and then back into Utah, where I started to see snow on the mountains again. I was back in Provo, the Athens of Utah, by seven.

'If a nation that has lost its political machinery becomes content to express its nationality thenceforward only in the sphere of literature and the arts, then that literature and those arts will very quickly become provincial and unimportant, mere echoes of the ideas and artistic movements of the neighbouring and dominant nation. If the Welsh people decide that the literary revival shall not broaden out into political and economic life and the whole of Welsh life, then inevitably Welsh literature in our generation will cease to be living and viable.'

I'm able to copy out those words from Saunders Lewis's *The Banned Wireless Talk* because, every year, I write them at the beginning of my new diary.

Sunday, 24 November

This evening I had supper with the Norrises. They were perturbed to hear that I've been talking to my students about sex, war, politics, religion, famine, social deprivation, the media, and so on, all subjects in which a writer, and a student, should be interested, in my view. They stress that BYU is not a State University but a private, Church institution and that I am in danger of giving offence to young devout Mormons who aren't used to talking about such things. Young Mormons, they tell me, particularly those from rural Utah and Wyoming, have lived only in Mormon communities and have little or no experience of non-Mormons. I tried to defend myself, saying young minds need to be concerned with current affairs, that my classes were lively and no offence had been caused anyone, and that my students seemed to find my 'liberal' views stimulating. If I were a Mormon, the Norrises said, I'd have been reported and in hot water by now. I found this, if true, appalling and went on a bit about academic freedom. Kitty was particularly agitated and I had the impression Leslie was only bringing up the rear. The discussion grew a bit heated at one point but the evening ended amicably enough. It is all very unfortunate.

Leslie and Kitty are splendid people, kind and warm-hearted, and I don't like falling out with people of whom I'm fond. I see, too, that unlike me they have to go on living here.

Dilys, Waldo Williams's sister, once told me that D.J. Williams, his old friend, called to see him shortly before he died in 1970, but Waldo refused to see him. 'Tell him I'm communing with God,' he said.

I wrote my book, *Linguistic Minorities in Western Europe*, a total of 200,000 words, in the short space of eighteen months in 1975/76. The idea occurred to me as we were sitting on the beach, with the children, at Biarritz. Painted on the sea-wall behind us was the equation $3 + 4 = 1$. When I met the writer Txillardegi at his home in Hendaye later that week, he explained that it referred to the seven provinces of Euzkadi (three in Spain and four in France) making one country.

Txillardegi lived in Hendaye, on the French side of the border, because as one of the founders of ETA, he was exiled from Spain, though his engineer's office was on the Spanish side and he communicated daily with his colleagues by telephone. When I called at his house, he observed me from an upstairs window before coming down to let me in; he lived in constant fear of assassination by Franco's police.

My book sold well, some three thousand copies, I think, and the publisher, Gomer, managed to sell the rights in a German translation, *Minderheiten in Westeuropa*, which was published by a small firm in Schleswig Holstein, but I didn't receive a *pfennig* for it.

Monday, 25 November
It's a bad week for turkeys. This evening I went with Cynthia Hallen to a Thanksgiving Supper for the residents of Wymount Terrace. The meal consisted of a slice of turkey, cold mashed potatoes and some limp lettuce. The hall was full of young married couples and their kids, and it was all over within the hour. I find these young Mormons polite, friendly and utterly bland. The key to an understanding of their character, I suppose, is their religious certainty. They are absolutely sure that they're

going to live for ever in the Mormon Heaven. They see no suffering or sacrifice in the story of Jesus and His agony on the Cross has no part in their dogma; that's why they don't mark Easter or have crosses on their graves. They believe Joseph Smith was a divine prophet on a par with Christ. They consider the Bible to be 'true' only in those parts which have been 'correctly translated', whereas the *Book of Mormon* is infallible in its entirety. Cynthia Hallen told me all this over a cold supper.

I wear a *triban* in my lapel, the badge of Plaid Cymru, but no one here has yet shown the slightest curiosity as to what it is.

> *Rhyddid Cymru a'i heiddo sy'n ei llais,*
> *Ennill hyn mae'n geisio;*
> *Ei thir a'i hiaith yn ei thro*
> *A Senedd heb Sais yno.*

Glyn Jones once told me he didn't like the poetry of Vernon Watkins because 'it has no sweat under its armpits'. Lots of people think Glyn is incapable of saying anything unkind about anyone but from time to time he's delivered some crushing opinions about his fellow writers while we've been alone together.

Tuesday, 26 November

Sara Cleaver came to see me again, this time about a reference. She wants to transfer to one of the Ivy League universities. I shall write a reference for her gladly, as she's one of my best students.

I also talked to a young man named Tory Anderson who intends starting a new literary magazine and wanted me to give him some advice.

A third student came to see me: Mathew Alexander, who keeps an SF magazine shop in Provo. We discussed an excellent elegy he'd written for his grandfather who was gunned down in his shop by young hoodlums. His father is very strict and disapproving of Mathew's literary interests and he won't show any of his work to him for fear of his anger.

The fliers are up in the Department for my reading on 5 December. I am billed as a member of the Welch Academy.

I spent the evening packing for my trip to San José tomorrow. A snowstorm is expected in Utah for Thanksgiving but I hope to get away before it arrives.

'Mais où sont les neiges d'antan?'

When I lived at Garth Newydd and was contemplating bringing out a small selection of poems with Harri Webb on the Triskel Press imprint, we needed a third poet who would contribute about a dozen poems. Horace Jones turned up with his Collected Works, about 500 poems in all, and demanded we publish all of them. With him it was always the whole cauliflower or nothing. When we declined he walked out in a huff and was our sworn enemy from then on. He used to stand outside W. H. Smith's in the High Street and shout insults at anyone against whom he happened to have taken umbrage, and my name and Harri's joined the long list. He would also put the hex on people he disliked. Eventually he published his poems under the title *The Challenger* and conned Keidrych Rhys into writing a foreword. He once told me he was thinking of changing his name to Charles because Horace wasn't literary enough.

They say you haven't started to live until you've come near death. The nearest I've come was last year when, on two occasions in the same day, a dark wing passed over me. Crossing the road in Park Place, I stepped in front of a bus which was coming down its own lane. The driver managed to swerve onto the pavement and into a wall, but it was a close shave and I was very shaken. Later that day, which was very stormy, I was driving Gillian Clarke to lunch at the Winged Dragon for a discussion about funding Tŷ Newydd, when a long section of roof blew off one of the houses and came crashing down into the street. I braked sharply and it missed us by about a foot, the débris covering the windscreen and bonnet of the car.

Ah, on a vécu!

Wednesday, 27 November
I got up at 4am and drove to the airport at Salt Lake City where I

had breakfast of eggs on toast, 'sunny side up', as I've learned to say, then caught the plane to San José in California. We went over some of the most spectacular terrain I've ever seen from the air, and I've flown over the Caucasus several times. This was the Nevada desert and the Rockies, snow-covered and majestic, with no sign of roads or habitation.

Kyffin Williams has a yarn about meeting an old woman leading a sheep by a piece of rope in a lane somewhere in Anglesey. 'What's its name?' he asked her jocularly. 'Elin,' the old woman replied drily. 'Elin Jones, I expect,' said Kyffin. 'Oh, no, indeed,' said the old woman, 'Elin Lloyd Jones.' Why is it that so many Anglesey people have three names? I shall have to ask Gwerfyl Pierce Jones or Bedwyr Lewis Jones or Menna Lloyd Williams or Harri Pritchard Jones.

I was met at the airport by a woman called Roselle Civelli who's from Hirwaun: her people, the Morrises, keep the New Inn at Rhigos and she's the sister of Dai Morris, the rugby-player. Despite living in California for 27 years, she's kept her 'Rhicos' accent in pristine condition, so much so I thought at first she was putting it on for my sake. She took me to the home of Dr Robert Bratman and his wife, Marilyn, leaving me there alone until lunch-time when they came home from work. They are a most charming couple, hospitable and articulate. He's an obstetrician and she a librarian and they've been married for about four years. Marilyn (*aet.* 42) is from Aberdare, where she still has a house, and is a typical Valleys Girl, outgoing and jovial. Her first husband, the late Colin Williams, was a lecturer at the College of Knowledge in Aberdare.

This afternoon Marilyn took me to see Stanford University, a complex of elegant buildings in the Spanish style, about a hundred years old. I was struck by the bookstore, which was much bigger and better than the one at BYU; it had a good selection of books by British and European authors.

After supper, we had a long chat and during the night Robert was called out to deliver a baby at his clinic.

I was present at the birth of all four of our children. So was Ruth.

'Eheu, fugaces, postume, postume, labuntur anni.'

Thursday, 28 November

It's warm here, in the 80s, and there are palm-trees in the street. This morning I had breakfast in the garden with Marilyn. The first things that caught my attention were the humming-birds and bluejays (they look like large kingfishers), then a device for cleaning the pool which moves about as if it has a mind of its own, spouting water from time to time; it's called Humphrey after a whale that was famously stranded in San Francisco Bay a few years ago.

Cupertino is in Silicon Valley and there's an unmistakeable air of prosperity here. The streets are much greener, the vegetation lusher, the houses bigger and the architecture more opulent than anything I've ever seen, and that includes Montreal and Quebec, Rome and Florence, Paris and Brussels, Madrid and Lisbon, Berlin and Copenhagen, Oslo and Stockholm.

Today is Thanksgiving Day, when Americans celebrate the landing of the Pilgrim Fathers on their shores. Marilyn is cooking a huge turkey, though the feast is not until Sunday, when a number of people with Welsh connections will be coming here. As she works, Marilyn tells me there was an earthquake in the San Francisco area a few years ago. Everything in the house was thrown into disarray during the 45 seconds it lasted. There was no structural damage to her house but the water from the pool was lifted in a huge wave and spilt into the street.

Robert is Jewish, a New Yorker, and a distinguished member of his profession, lecturing at Stanford as well as running his own clinic in Cupertino. He also has a degree in History and is active with the Salvation Army and the Rotary Club. Among the books he's read is one by Trevor Fishlock and he quotes from it what the New York cab-driver said when told Fishlock was from Wales: 'Wales?' asked the man in the yellow cab, 'Whales? D'ya mean da fish or dem singing bastards?'

After a splendid meal we sat up until midnight.

Of all the *englynion* written for me (for and against), this by T. Arfon Williams, a neighbour of ours, about the *Companion/Cydymaith* is the one I like best :

O weld mor llawn y grawnwin, winllanwr
ein llên, buost diflin
iawn er rhoi dau fath ar win
yn hwylus wrth benelin.

Friday, 29 November
The Bratmans took me into San Francisco on a fine, warm morning. The countryside is very green and much of the architecture in the Spanish style. We drove over the Golden Bridge (actually a rusty red) and I saw Alcatraz on its island out in the bay. The skyscrapers here are real skyscrapers. We had lunch, starting with oysters, at the Alcatraz Restaurant where there's a prisoner's cell and photos of Al Capone and other notorious inmates. I bought a T-shirt for Huw with the words 'Alcatraz Swimming Team' emblazoned on it; I preferred it to one which read, 'Yeah, whatever'.

We went on to Ghiardelli Square to see the lighting of the Christmas Tree and saw the trams that go up and down the steep streets of the city, as in so many films. Robert is very knowledgeable about the history of San Francisco and is the perfect guide.

By six o'clock we were in the City Lights Bookshop in downtown Frisco, the famous shop founded by Laurence Ferlinghetti in the 'fifties. I used to read him and Allen Ginsberg and Gregory Corso when I was a student but I had no idea he was still alive. To my astonishment, I was taken to have supper with him and his companion, Nancy Peters, a very handsome, elegant woman of about 50, with an almost regal bearing, who is Chief Editor of the City Lights publishing house, which he founded.

I had a long talk with Ferlinghetti, partly about Jacques Prévert, whom he's translated, and partly about Emile Verhaeren, on whom both he and I did a thesis (he at the Sorbonne). This was the first time I'd talked to anyone other than my tutor about the Belgian poet and it was a real pleasure so to do with Ferlinghetti, a very courteous man. He has recently been in Wales and made the obligatory pilgrimage to Laugharne. A gentle, urbane, humorous man now in his seventies, he gave me a poem inspired by a statue in the National Museum, an anti-war statement as eirenic as any he wrote during the conflict in Vietnam. In return, and at his request, I recited an *englyn* in French:

> *Déjà nous sommes à Dijon – jolie ville,*
> > *Je la vois en vallon;*
> *Et viens, Bill, le vin est bon,*
> *Et la bière nous la boirons.*

This was a most memorable occasion for me, spoilt only by Colin Edwards, ex-Gorseinon and Plaid Cymru fellow-traveller, who tried to hog the conversation, insisting on telling me about all the important people he knew, including Gwynfor Evans, as if I'd never heard of them. His Chinese wife seemed baffled by his enthusiasm for Wales and smiled inscrutably throughout the meal.

The restaurant, Chez Moustache, was remarkable in that, as we sat down at table, one of the waiters came up and asked whether he could entertain us with some jokes, which he did, and the owner, a Dutchman, sang us a folksong as we drank our coffee.

I meant to ask Ferlinghetti whether he's ever tried translating Prévert's poem, '*Barbara*', whom the poet saw being kissed by her lover in a shop-doorway in the Rue de Siam, in Brest, in the days before that town was flattened by American bombs. It's a simple poem and I've tried several times to turn it into English or Welsh, but never to my satisfaction: '*Rappelle-toi, Barbara, il pleuvait sans cesse sur Brest . . . dont il ne reste rien.*' But I couldn't get a word in edgewise with the confounded Colin Edwards prattling on.

If nothing else, my search for my father's parents has given me an interest in the old county of Radnor, where I often go walking, and I am a paid-up member of the Radnorshire Society. At least I've learned a little about John Lewis of Llynwene, George Cornwall Lewis of Harpton and Jonathan Williams, the county historian, and I've read the two splendid volumes by Ffransis G. Payne, *Crwydro Sir Faesyfed*.

I've deliberately refrained from dwelling too much on why Annie Lloyd gave her baby away. After all, she could so easily have kept him; there's a tradition in the country, particularly in Radnorshire, of bringing up illegitimate children as part of the family, except she didn't have a family apart from her brother, Hugh. Nor have I allowed myself to think about her subsequent life in Priestweston and, as the wife of Alf Passant, in Great Hanwood. But did she, I can't help wondering, ever regret her decision and did she sometimes think about her child and the man he'd become? I hope so. For the grandmother I never knew I have nothing but sympathy and a forlorn sense of loss, though more for my father's sake than my own. Things could have turned out so differently for them both.

The story I like best about Radnorians concerns the new vicar of St. Harmon and Pantydwr, behind Rhaeadr. A public meeting was held to discuss whether the vicarage should be in one village or the other. Neither place has more than a few hundred inhabitants. Eventually, after much keen debate and a close vote, it was decided the vicar should live in St. Harmon, the lower of the two villages, at which an old man who had voted in favour of Pantydwr, his native place, rose to his feet and said, 'Very well, so be it. But you mark my words – once you give a man a taste of town life, he'll never be up in the hills again.'

Saturday, 30 November
I spent the day with Robert, Marilyn and their friend, Marilyn Presdee, who's from Bishopston, near Swansea, and over here on a Fulbright Scholarship, teaching at a school in San Francisco. We drove down the coast to Monterey. The first place we had to visit was the waterfront known as Cannery Row, which John Steinbeck immortalized in his novel of that name. We saw a memorial to Ed Ricketts, the real-life marine biologist who's called Doc in the novel.

There were seals, otters, pelicans and cormorants on the rocky shore, but the really astonishing sight were the sharks we saw close-up in a submarine aquarium which serves as a scientific centre as well as a tourist attraction.

I paddled in the Pacific and collected a few pebbles as souvenirs of my visit. *Thalatta! Thalatta!* I was once told by a Greek writer named, if my memory serves me right, Nasos Vayenas, that the phrase 'the wine-dark sea' doesn't occur anywhere in Homer.

We drove around the scenic route through Pebble Beach and Carmel, a very up-market resort and shopping centre.

I get on well with Marilyn and Robert. She's full of beans and we laugh a lot. She's very keen on her Welsh identity – the house is full of trinkets: Welsh Lady tea-towels, miners' lamps and table-mats with pictures of castles on them, and so on. Robert listens to our chat about South Wales with fond amusement.

Among the American Navy phrases I've picked up from Robert is the acronym MEGO – my eyes glaze over.

Sunday, 1 December

This evening Robert and Marilyn gave a Thanksgiving Supper for friends they know through the South California Welsh Society. These included Roselle Civelli and her husband, Marilyn Presdee, and a woman called Ruth whose family I recall living in John Street, Trefforest, when I was a boy; she had a sister, Judith, with whom I went to Parc Lewis School. Also invited were Gareth Williams, ex-Aberystwyth, who teaches Physics at Stanford, and his wife, Ann, both from Dowlais and very pleasant people.

Then there was David Vernon Thomas, known as Dai the Gas because he's an anaesthetist. I took one look at him and asked, 'You're not the son of E. R. Thomas, are you?' He looked exactly like Piggy, my Headmaster when I was in the lower school, and even had the conker-shaped fingertips that used to hurt so much when poked vigorously into my shoulder. 'No,' he replied, 'I'm his nephew.' He was born in Bertha Street in Trefforest. There's a detailed portrait of Piggy in Alun Richards's autobiography, *Days of Absence*, and I promised to send Dai the Gas a copy when I get home.

We had a magnificent supper at a long table, perhaps twenty of us, and it was all very pleasant, except Marilyn insisted on my reading a few things I've written, and Robert referred to me as 'Sir Meic'.

'When you call me that, Mister, smile.'

Everyone sympathizes with me when I tell them I'm spending the Fall Semester in Provo and that I'm not seeing 'the real America'. Well, yes.

Over supper I told a story about a conductress who used to work on the buses in Pontypridd. Known to us all as Olive, she was famous for her brusque manner and the spiel with which she would regale passengers. Her stock-in-trade was the cry, 'Fares, please, and mind my bloody feet!' On Saturdays, when the bus was usually overcrowded, she'd shout, 'All aboard the Lusitania!'

Late one winter's night, Olive's bus was the last to leave the Tumble for Trefforest. There was already standing room only and she had some difficulty in restraining passengers who wanted to get on. One man, more persistent than the rest, implored her to make an exception in his case. But she refused, barring his way with a brawny arm, at which the man, in desperation, informed her he was a rabbi.

'I don't care if you're Popeye,' retorted Olive, 'you're not getting on my bloody bus!'

This was the cue for Robert to tell a stream of Jewish jokes. The only one I can remember is about the widow who was asked what she wanted put on her late husband's tombstone. 'Well,' she said, 'his name and dates for a start.'

'Anything else?' said the undertaker. 'There's plenty of room and the price is the same.'

She thought for a moment and then said, 'Oh, alright. Put "Secondhand Volvo for sale." '

Marilyn shares my antipathy towards George Thomas, whom she describes as 'a horrible man'. I told her the story of his audience with the Pope, at the end of which he's reputed to have clutched the Vicar of Christ by the sleeve and said, 'Well, goodbye, Your Holiness – God bless!'

When I was teaching at Tonypandy last year it was a given among the staff that the Viscount is homosexual. It was cited as the reason why he didn't marry Annie Powell, the Communist councillor whom he courted for years.

Monday, 2 December

After getting up at 5am I was taken to the airport for the plane to Salt Lake City. Marilyn got up too and cooked me a huge breakfast. She and Robert have been very kind to me and I hope to see them again, in Wales.

I arrived in Utah in the middle of a blizzard and had some difficulty finding the Chevrolet in the parking lot. Yes, the newspapers were right, snow is general all over Utah: a hundred inches have fallen in the last hundred hours – 'upon all the living and the dead'.

The first thing I did on reaching the flat was to ring Ruth to let her know I'd come back from California. Siân Lloyd and Gwyn Williams have been staying at our house so she had good company while I was living it up among the long-distance patriots of Silicon Valley. Huw told me about his engagement as a magician at Felindre Hospital, where he was paid a fee of £25. There was a long letter from Lowri and photos of her home in Bethesda and another from Lloyd in which he quotes the verse by Longfellow about 'the bivouac of life'.

I went down to campus after lunch. It was snowing so heavily my dai-cap looked like a huge snowball on my head and the quad was deep in drifts. The pines outside my flat are heavily laden with snow.

'Ardd cŷd bych; ardd cŷd ni bych.'

When Lowri was about six, she asked Ruth, 'Mam, where do I come from?' Her mother, thinking the moment had arrived to tell her about the birds and the bees, proceeded to do so in some detail, but still she asked, 'Yes, but where do I really come from?' After several more attempts to explain 'the facts of life' to her, Lowri still persisted with her question, 'Where do I come from?' Ruth then asked her why she wanted to know. 'Well,' said Lowri, 'when I was at the Eisteddfod I was standing in a queue for icecream when I heard two little girls talking. One asked the other where she came from and she replied, "Maesteg", and when they asked me where I came from I didn't know what to say. Do I come from Whitchurch or from Cardiff?'

Tuesday, 3 December
In the post this morning came a copy of Ferlinghetti's translation of Prévert's *Paroles*, signed, and including a version of *'Barbara'*; I'm very glad to have it. He has marked the line *'Il ne faut pas laisser les intellectuels jouer avec les allumettes'*, perhaps in response to my telling him about Saunders Lewis at Penyberth.

I taught my classes today and started marking the students' folders. I found one had written:

It is better to fight for the good than to rail at the ill;
I have felt with my native land, I am one with my kind,
I embrace the purpose of God and the doom assigned.

I thought this was good and gave her a B+. But after a while it started to sound familiar, and then the penny dropped: it's from

Tennyson's 'Maud'.

The most famous case of plagiarism in recent times, as far as I know, was when Hugh MacDiarmid lifted part of a short story by Glyn Jones and used it in a poem entitled 'Perfect'. Of the poem's eight lines, seven were taken from Glyn's story, 'Porth-y-rhyd'. There was some lively correspondence in the *TLS* after the matter came to light in the 1960s, during the course of which MacDiarmid made out the borrowing had been unconscious and was therefore valid.

A few years later, Christopher Murray Grieve (Hugh MacDiarmid was his *nom de guerre*), and his wife, Valda, were staying at our home in Cardiff. One evening, after checking with our guests, I asked Glyn and Doreen to call. This was going to be the first time the two writers had met. At Glyn's arrival, Valda withdrew to another room and Doreen busied herself in the kitchen, expecting sparks to fly, but they needn't have worried. On being introduced, the two writers shook hands warmly and Chris began, 'My wife thinks a meeting between you and me might prove an embarrassment. But I'm not embarrassed, are you?'

'No,' said Glyn, with a broad grin, 'I'm not embarrassed, why should I be?'

The two Titans then sat down, the Scot with a glass of his favourite Glenfiddich and Glyn with an orange juice, and we spent the rest of the evening in most pleasant literary conversation. I remember how they both laughed when they discovered their fathers had both been employed by the Post Office – men of letters!

For years after Chris and Valda Grieve's visit, our daughters always referred to her as the lady with hair the same colour as Cardiff's buses – a bright orange.

Among the manuscripts Glyn has given me is a scrap of paper on which he's written:

> Than Vernon I'm a better novelist,
> I'm cuter at libretti than Jones, D. ;
> Gwyn Thomas as a bard is my inferior
> And at short stories so is R.S.T.

Leslie called at my office this afternoon. He told me he thought my visit has been a huge success and hoped the Semester has been as much a pleasure for me as it's been for him. He'd felt much happier while I was here, he said, though still thought of himself as much of an outsider in Utah as he did in Wales.

I had supper alone in my flat with the bottle of Californian claret given me by Dai the Gas. I've never been a great boozer but I enjoy a glass of good wine, despite my diabetes.

How does that squib entitled 'Social Mobility' by Tony Harrison go?

> Ah, the proud advantages of scholarship!
> Whereas his father took cold tea for snap,
> He works at nuances, knows at just one sip
> Château Lafitte from Châteauneuf du Pape.

I talked to my class today about coincidences and to what extent they can be used in writing short stories. They all had examples, for the most part quite banal. The most astonishing coincidence I've ever heard was told me by Winnie McQuaid, my mother's 'cousin'. She was brought up in the East End of London. Her real father, a man by the name of Wilfred Jones, abandoned his wife and child when she was only a few months old. A year or so later her mother met another man, my grandfather's brother, Walter Symes, who for many years was Chief Compositor with the *News Chronicle* in Fleet Street.

Winnie's mother and Walt Symes lived together happily as man and wife for about fifty years and Winnie looked upon him as her father. When he died, in the 1950s, her mother applied for a widow's pension, only to be told she wasn't a widow until she could prove that her husband, Wilf Jones, was dead. So Winnie and her mother set out to look for him. One day, while walking down a street in the part of the East End where they'd used to live, Winnie's mother said, 'That's him, over there!' They saw a dapper old gentleman, carrying a briefcase and with a flower in his lapel and wearing a bowler hat. They followed him down the street until he turned off and through a factory gate. The two women were so excited about finding the man on which so much depended that they went home to get over the shock. The

238

following week, they went back to the factory gate and asked whether they could speak to a Mr Wilfred Jones. The gatekeeper didn't know anyone of that name but rang the Personnel Department and was told a Mr Wilfred Jones had worked at the factory about twenty years before. They were given his address and they went there immediately.

When they knocked the door in a block of high-rise flats, it was opened by a wizened old man, filthy dirty and dressed in rags. 'A bit like Steptoe,' said Winnie, 'only not so clean.'

'Are you Wilf Jones?' asked Winnie's mother.

'Yes,' said the man.

'Well, I'm your wife and this is your daughter.'

'In that case you'd better come in.'

They'd found the man who had abandoned them all those years before. But this is the thing: he wasn't the man they'd seen in the street the previous week. How's that for coincidence?

On the whole I find comedy on S4C very unfunny. It's as if Welsh-speakers are expected to laugh only at village idiots and the humour of the *tŷ bach*. One of the few homegrown comedians who always tickles me, apart from the late Ryan Davies, is Dewi Pws Morris. I remember him in a series of sketches set in Chemical Gardens somewhere in industrial south Wales. It was a skit on *How Green Was My Valley* and featured all the worst clichés of the genre. The daughter, Elsan, played by the delectable Nia Caron, worked in a secretarial capacity for Mr Crawshay up at the Castle, and the spotty son, played by Gareth Lewis, was a Theology student who kept on seeing naked women flash past the kitchen window. Dewi Pws, the brutish father, was always going out the back to kill *'y blydi mochyn'*, and the cherubic mother, played by William Thomas in drag, would meet every crisis in the family's affairs serenely with the question, *'Beth am gael basined o de?'*

In the 1930s Winnie McQuaid worked with the publisher Allen Lane. She was present when the first box of Penguins arrived from the printer and shared her employer's apprehension that these paperbacks would never catch on. Just after the war she used to send me parcels of books published by Penguin, among which I remember *The Golden Ass* and Moravia's *The Woman of Rome*, both novels suitable for a growing lad.

The only time I've seen strippers was at the home of Tom Davies, the novelist, when he was living in Peterstone-super-Ely in about 1972. He'd hired two girls to entertain his guests at a Christmas party and they performed on a table-top in the dining-room. I've always thought that a bit odd for someone who makes a lot of being a born-again Christian.

Wednesday, 4 December

I didn't do much today, except read a fascinating book I found in the 'Recent Acquisitions' section of the Library at BYU. It's called *Ancient Powys: A Celtic Synergy* and was published by The Golden Salamander Press earlier this year. The author, J. Kurt Matonis, is Professor of Gaulish and Old Norse at Deseret College in Utah. He is particularly interested in the borderlands between what are now Wales and England, especially the old kingdom of Powys which once extended for many miles into modern Shropshire. Basing his argument on 'the evidence of the spade', he studies the character of border society during the late Romano-British period when native princes were beginning to stake out their territories in defiance of marauding Mercians and other Saxon barbarians.

Professor Matonis was alerted to the possibility of a British burial site on the Welsh side of the border by the chance discovery of a left-handed sword, richly ornamented, similar to those found near Hallstadt, one of the cradles of Celtic civilisation, in what is today Austria. The subsequent unearthing of a huge treasure hoard near Cruckmeole, a hamlet near Shrewsbury whose name is still pronounced Crugymoel by local people, proved that the district was a fortified stronghold of the Pagenses, the tribe that gave its name to Powys.

One intriguing fact to emerge from the first digs, which was sponsored by the Viroconium Trust, was that women's hair was plaited from left to right and shields constructed so that they could be held only with the right arm, thus leaving the left free to brandish a sword. Combs, brushes, and cooking utensils all showed signs of use by left-handers. The archaeologists then widened their search by examining the castles, manor houses and burial chambers along Offa's Dyke, on the lookout for other signs that the natives may have left a sinistral legacy in the area. The team found that on the English side the buildings tended to have staircases that gave advantage to right-handed defenders, while those on the Welsh side favoured left-handed swordsmen. This pattern, not fully studied up to now, confirms the age-old distinction between 'dextrous' Saxons and 'sinister' Celts. There is a high incidence of south-paws in the district of Cruckmeole and many people incline their head to the left when kissing or drinking from a tap. The epither 'cack-handed' is still a term of abuse for the village people.

The implications of these findings for the interpretation of the earliest Welsh poetry, Professor Matonis argues, especially of the Heledd cycle in which the princess laments the downfall of her brother Cynddylan and the royal house of Powys, are to be the subject of a second volume. When, for example, Heledd says, '*Dyn decheu, odditano ydd wyf, mechteryn da*', she may be using '*decheu*' to mean 'dextrous', a remnant of the Old Welsh word '*deheuig*' or 'right-handed', in fealty to her lord. The word '*decheu*' in modern Welsh, meaning 'tidy', may have entered the language when Mercian rule, after much bloodshed, was established in the borderlands.

Among other discoveries by Professor Matonis is a large boulder inscribed with the words: 'ASTO NE FORAS SESTOR UBON'. This is clearly a Romano-British inscription but its precise significance in the Powysian context has not yet been established.

I also started reading an article by F. S. Lyons, 'The Twilight of the Big House', in a back-number of the magazine *Ariel*: 'To be born in a country and to grow up to love it, but never fully to possess it, never completely to belong to it, may create not just great literature but also unhappy men and women.' Discuss, with reference to old Curtis Langdon.

Lewis Carroll. Albert Einstein. Nietzsche. Fidel Castro. Paul McCartney. Bob Dylan. H. G. Wells. Elizabeth Windsor. Fred Astaire. Marilyn Monroe. Jimi Hendrix. Jack the Ripper. Aneurin Bevan.

Thursday, 5 December

Today I cleared my office in readiness for my departure in about a week's time.

More than a hundred people turned up for my reading in the Alumni House this afternoon – about a dozen faculty and the rest students, including quite a few of my own. Leslie gave me a fulsome introduction and there was long applause at the end.

'A poet's hope: to be, like some valley cheese, local, but prized elsewhere.'

Afterwards I went alone to the Cougareat and treated myself to a beefy meal with one of two vouchers I'd been given by the Dean's office. I used the other to get a free nosh for an unknown student who was astonished by his good fortune.

The last of the American hostages were released today, after five or six years in captivity.

I once heard a woman in a Bristol café say, 'I don't know what the world's coming to what with Lumumbal in the Congol and Castrol in Cubal.'

Friday, 6 December

I went into the office again today to type up the grades I've given my students. I've given As to ten students but mostly Bs, including one to Clint Graviet because he's tried hard and written one or two good cowboy poems. I also took a large box of chocolates to Joyce Baggerley and Anne Smith in the departmental office, for being so helpful, thus encouraging them in 'the Mormon vice'.

The only person around was John Harris, with whom I had a last talk. He smiled when I said, 'John, it's time to light out for the territory.' When he asked me what my impression of BYU was, I said I thought the Saints had created a closed society and that there was a blandness, a smugness even, to the Mormon character that I didn't care for. I told John I'd found it hard but interesting to live in a place where intelligent people are expected to obey orders and to ask no questions, and he smiled enigmatically.

I went to a party at the Norrises this evening but came away at about 10pm.

Today is the fiftieth anniversary of the Japanese attack on Pearl Harbor.

Saturday, 8 December

It snowed heavily again last night and I had to clear about five inches off the car before setting out for church with the Owenses. I had asked to be taken to church, out of sheer curiosity, I suppose. At 9am there was a Sacrament Meeting, in which I didn't partake, with a family saying goodbye to a son called Heath who was going on a mission to Japan. The mother spoke under great stress and wept profusely throughout the ceremony, while the father hoped his boy would live strictly according to the *Book of Mormon*. The young man grinned as if he were enjoying the public display of emotion and was looking forward to the trip. We all remained seated while singing the hymns. The children were dressed in extravagant bows and frills, and their mothers looked like Ewings – big hair and wide shoulders.

Then there was a Sunday School at which the teacher used a map to explain the journeys of the Apostle Paul. Shades of Libanus!

During the main service I heard no reference to Joseph Smith or the *Book of Mormon*. Everything seemed pretty orthodox, except for the raw emotion of those who gave testimony of their belief in God and Jesus Christ.

'I stood among them but not of them in a shroud of thoughts which were not their thoughts.'

Afterwards I spoke to Jaynann Payne, the leader of the Mormon women's troupe coming to Wales next year, and to Gordon McClean, a chiropractor, with whom I was able to talk from my knowledge of the bonesetting Lloyds.

I quoted the words on the plaque in memory of my great-great-great-grandfather, Hugh Lloyd (1770-1856), the bonesetter, in the church at Michaelchurch-on-Arrow:

> A talent rare by him possessed
> T'adjust the bones of the distressed;
> When ever called he ne'er refused
> But cheerfully his talent used.
> But now he lies beneath this tomb
> Till Jesus comes to adjust his own.

Hugh Lloyd, who was baptized at Llanddewi Ystradenni, had a

wife whose maiden name was Ann Deakins and they had a son named Thomas, born at Cascob, who married a Sarah Sophia Lloyd (no relation) of Llansantffraid-yn-Elfael.

In the graveyard at Michaelchurch lie my great-grandparents, Hugh and Martha Lloyd of Blaenbedw, Glascwm, and later of nearby Baynham Hall, who died within a week of each other in 1890, shortly after the birth of their daughter, Annie Sophia, and during a 'flu epidemic. The inscription on their gravestone, now badly weathered and flaking away, is taken from the Psalms: 'Teach us to number our days that we may apply our hearts unto wisdom.' Martha, of whom I have a photo in which she bears a striking resemblance to Heledd, was the daughter of Margaret Powell of Upper Hengoed, Huntington, and her husband, Arthur, a cobbler, who lived at New House and Bungy's Head. It was Margaret and Arthur who brought up Annie Sophia and Hugh Lloyd after their parents died in 1890 and it was to the home of their son, also called Arthur, and his wife, Sarah, at Walton, that Annie went to have her baby in 1910.

The most eminent of the Lloyds was Evan Thomas Lloyd, born at Empton in 1885, who was a surgeon at Guy's Hospital in London and later in Cardiff. There's a chiropractor named Gareth Lloyd in Cardiff today and he's descended from the same family. The Lloyd family tradition of bonesetting has been carried on by the Baywaters at Craven Arms and the Drews of Lyonshall, some of whom I met at the family reunion in Cheltenham. There's even a Lloyd's Oil that is supposed to cure man and beast, though I haven't yet been able to buy a bottle.

Lunch at the Owenses' home with their daughters, Katie, Emily and Sarah. Then a chat with Noël about the structure of the Church. It's clear that he's of an extremely conservative mindset and against change of any kind. The Church can change, he explained, only 'by revelation' among the Twelve Apostles. Good Mormons accept the authority of these nonagenarians without question. Mormons deplore the Church of England for what they see as its failure to take a stand against the ordination of women priests. Among the Saints only men can be Elders.

The Soviet Union ceased to exist today, and in its place there's a Commonwealth of Independent States with its capital at Minsk.

The Yanks are worried about the breakup – for which they've been working for forty years -- because of the danger of nuclear proliferation.

Monday, 9 December

I was interviewed last week by a member of the English Department. He's a nice chap and I wish I'd had a chance to get to know him better, but Oh, when he sent me a transcript today, I was dismayed at how little he'd understood. The worst howler was: 'The greatest living Welsh poet is Horace Thomas, who is a priest with the Church of Wales'.

I've started a small collection of mishearings. Most are by children, including my own. The other day Huw came home from seeing the film *Chariots of Fire*. He thought it was 'wicked', his favourite word of approval, but expressed his disappointment that there was no one in it called Charlotte Sophia.

Some children were burying their dead cat in the garden. As the animal's body was committed to the earth, one of them said, 'In the name of the Father, the Son, and into the hole he goes.' And a little girl in Dowlais, during the Depression, prayed thus: 'Thy will be done, in Merthyr as it is in Devon.'

But adults are also capable of mishearing things. The County Surveyor's wife of Denbighshire went on a shopping spree in London and, in due course, a large parcel was delivered to her husband's office, addressed to the Countess of Ayr, Denbigh.

I recently heard of a boy who, after a visit to the Folk Museum at St. Fagans, asked his mother what 'merched ladies' were.

I've noticed that several faculty members who have never said as much as 'Hi' to me up to now have begun to smile and several express regret that I'm leaving and they haven't got(ten) to know me. I only smile wanly back.

Without being asked to, I wrote a report on my classes and sent it to the departmental Chairman whom I've seen only once; I don't expect a response. I also left a complete set of page-proofs of the *Oxford Guide* in the common room, to what purpose I have no idea, but they're too heavy to take home.

There were carol-singers in the quad this evening, but the carols must have been Mormon because I didn't recognize any of them.

I watched the last episode of *Brideshead Revisited* this evening, the best thing I've seen on tv here – though I've never worn a dinner-jacket in my life. Well, I did once, albeit with disastrous consequences. It was the only time I ever went on a blind date. I'd arranged to take a girl, the friend of a friend, to the Students' Union Ball in Cardiff. After a few jars in the Park Hotel, I went into the cloakroom to freshen up and as I washed my face, my collar-stud popped out and disappeared down the plug-hole. I had to borrow a paper-clip from a porter and went to the Ball without a collar in the days before that became fashionable. Yet for the life of me I can't remember the name of the girl!

Tuesday, 10 December

'Le vierge, le vivace et le bel aujourd'hui.'

I took my classes for the last time today. I read them my 'Twenty things you always wanted to know about Mormons', or Meic's Maxims, culled from my journal and a letter from John Davies (Prestatyn), and they took them in good part, *ware teg.*

Here are some of the most acerbic: BYU was nearly named Orson Pratt University after one of its first Presidents. The Mormon vice is chocolate. If Robert Redford is not a Mormon, why not? There is nothing so dead as a stuffed cougar. The *Daily Universe* lacks a certain something hard to define except in terms of readability. The Poet Laureate of BYU is Clinton Larson, believe it or not. There is no graffiti except in Creative Writing classes. The most beautiful building in the Wasatch Valley is the Geneva Steelworks. Shasta Root Beer is excellent, if you have a sore throat. Mormons are obsessed by water, perhaps because there will be none where they are going. At certain seasons of the year a lot of blood is spilt, some of it by animals. It's always Sunday morning in Provo. Those seeking excitement go to Salt Lake City to see the rows of parking meters. I believe in jackalopes. Wales is famous for its turkeys. All blackbirds are robins, except thrushes. The letter Y is seen everywhere but the question why is seldom heard. In the middle of Provo there is an Empty Sea. A skunk is a skunk is a skunk.

Both classes applauded after I made my final speech. Then we all went outside to have a group photograph taken. Many of the students were a bit emotional and shook my hand warmly, promising to contact me if ever they are in the Yookay and to let me know when they publish their first book. Yeah, yeah.

Clint Graviet said he would bring some of his ceramic work to my flat tomorrow morning as a farewell gift.

I said goodbye to Sally Taylor and tried to find the departmental head but he wasn't there again today, so I came away.

Gisrevedo!

Wednesday, 11 December

'The feast of Pope Damaseus on the 11th day of the month of December on the Day of Venus, then all Wales was cast to the ground . . . ' I've never been much of a Llywelyn man, preferring Owain Glyndŵr -- at least no one betrayed him.

> *Mae'r byd yn fwy na Chymru –*
> *'Rwyn gwybod hynny nawr,*
> *Ond diolch fod hen Gymru fach*
> *Yn rhan o fyd mor fawr.*

I spent the morning hoovering the flat and cleaning it thoroughly. Then, about noon, I left it for the last time. It's a strange feeling taking a last look at a room where one has lived for a while and then closing the door on it for ever, but I felt no pangs this time. Clint Graviet didn't turn up with his ceramics, which was a small mercy as I didn't have room in my cases, though I would have enjoyed a last chat with him. I cleared what were left of the tins in the fridge and stacked them outside Cynthia Hallen's door with a note: 'With the compliments of the Welsh fairies.'

I met Leslie, as arranged, in the parking lot (I mean carpark) on campus. He followed me in his car while I took the Chevrolet, unwashed and with empty tank, back to Freedom, and then drove me to his home. The car has done 62,000 miles in the three months I've had it and nothing went wrong with it. We went for a walk with Gwenno along the river bank where we walked during the first few days after my arrival. Supper with Leslie and Kitty at the Olive Garden restaurant. During the meal one of my students, the inestimable Charlotte Yen, came over to our table and told me again how much she'd enjoyed my classes.

After supper we went to see the houses of Orem lit up for Christmas. Some of them were so illuminated it was difficult to make them out as houses. This is a custom that hasn't arrived in the Yookay yet but it will, I have no doubt.

Over a cup of cocoa, Leslie told me a story that reflects rather badly on the Church. Just before my arrival old Taft Benson had 'a revelation' that it was okay for Mormons to drink decaffeinated Coca-Cola, hitherto prohibited. There was a scandal when a non-Mormon newspaper subsequently discovered the Church had recently invested heavily in Coca-Cola.

So ends my last day in Provo. *Teg edrych tuag adref.*

Thursday, 12 December

I got up at 8am, played one last time with Gwenno, then Leslie took me to the airport in Salt Lake City. We parted on the best of terms and I thanked him sincerely for arranging for me to spend the Fall Semester at BYU and for all the help he and Kitty have given me. I think we shall be friends for the rest of our lives.

I caught the Delta flight to Atlanta at 12.05. The plane was half-empty and there was nothing to do but snoooze as we flew at 35,000 feet and 400 miles an hour – ah, 'the keen impassioned beauty of a great machine!' We got to Atlanta at 3.15pm.

While waiting for the connection to London I sat in the lounge and observed scores of North Africans on their knees and praying to Allah. O Allah, if there is an Allah, save my soul, if I have a soul, and don't let anyone hit me across the head with the Koran.

As I boarded the plane out of Atlanta I was greeted by musak playing *'Ar hyd y nos'* and the evergreen 'Shenandoah'. The flight took seven and a half hours, which I spent reading some of Ray Bradbury's stories, devouring the papers left on the plane by previous passengers, and eating two plastic meals. I also looked through this journal/commonplace book -- I don't know what to call it -- not without a feeling I've been a bit like the spinster aunt who left, at her death, a box neatly labelled 'Pieces of string too short for any use'.

We landed at Gatwick at 8.15am, or 1.15 by my clock, just as a rosy dawn was coming up. I had the usual lug with my cases: no porters or trolleys around. On the train to Reading, England looked dirty, small, congested, a mean country full of shabby, pale, glum people and grim, grey buildings, as we passed waste land, tenements, and the backsides of factories. It's very cold and there's a severe ground frost. At Reading I had a chance to ring Ruth in her office to say I was on my way.

> *Mae'n werth troi'n alltud ambell dro,*
> *A mynd o Gymru fach ymhell,*
> *Er mwyn cael dod i Gymru'n ôl*
> *A medru caru Cymru'n well.*

On the train to Cardiff, the girl selling coffee and sandwiches had a strong Merthyr accent, and I said, 'There's nice to hear a Welsh voice', to which she replied nonchalantly, 'Aye, it's lovely, mun, innit?'

Then I was home.